Student Study Guide With IBM SPSS® Workbook for *Research Methods for the Behavioral Sciences*

D1309942

Student Study Guide With IBM SPSS® Workbook for *Research Methods for the Behavioral Sciences*

Gregory J. Privitera

St. Bonaventure University

Los Angeles | London | New Delhi
Singapore | Washington DC

Los Angeles | London | New Delhi
Singapore | Washington DC

FOR INFORMATION:

SAGE Publications, Inc.
2455 Teller Road
Thousand Oaks, California 91320
E-mail: order@sagepub.com

SAGE Publications Ltd.
1 Oliver's Yard
55 City Road
London EC1Y 1SP
United Kingdom

SAGE Publications India Pvt. Ltd.
B 1/I 1 Mohan Cooperative Industrial Area
Mathura Road, New Delhi 110 044
India

SAGE Publications Asia-Pacific Pte. Ltd.
3 Church Street
#10-04 Samsung Hub
Singapore 049483

Printed in the United States of America

This book is printed on acid-free paper.

Acquisitions Editor: Reid Hester
Associate Editor: Nathan Davidson
Editorial Assistant: Sarita Sarak
Production Editor: Olivia Weber-Stenis
Copy Editor: Melinda Masson
Typesetter: C&M Digitals (P) Ltd.
Proofreader: Lawrence W. Baker
Cover Designer: Bryan Fishman
Marketing Manager: Lisa Sheldon Brown

13 14 15 16 17 10 9 8 7 6 5 4 3 2 1

Contents

How to Use
This Workbook

As you prepare for exams and course materials, you will benefit from using this workbook. It can help you prepare for exams, test your mastery and retention of learning objectives, and assess the SPSS learning objectives. You will find many features for each chapter that meet these aims. Here, we will describe the contents of each chapter and the additional contents of this workbook.

The contents of each chapter are as follows:

- Chapter Learning Objectives
- Chapter Summary
- Chapter Summary Organized by Learning Objective
- Tips and Cautions for Students
- Practice Quiz
- Key Term Word Search and Crossword Puzzle

To give you a sense of how the chapter contents in this workbook can help you study and test your knowledge, we will briefly look at what is included for each chapter.

Chapter Learning Objectives. Chapter learning objectives are listed in the book and in this workbook. Learning objectives allow you to organize the chapter topics into manageable units. Studying one learning objective at a time is far more manageable and possibly less overwhelming than studying all chapter content at one time. In addition, the learning objectives allow professors to assign readings that are specific to content in each chapter that they will cover or test most heavily. The learning objectives are important inasmuch as they organize the content of each chapter and how you can study it.

Chapter Summary. The chapter summary is organized by the major chapter headings with a review of material covered and key terms included for each chapter. You may find it easier to organize your notes using this summary, which can give you a good sense of where in the chapters you need to study more and where you are mastering the material. Each chapter summary gives a brief description of the material covered. The summary is a good resource for reviewing chapter material and studying for exams.

Chapter Summary Organized by Learning Objective. A chapter summary is given at the end of each chapter in the book and in this workbook. The chapter summaries are organized by learning objective. This can help you quickly review learning objective material as you take the chapter quizzes. If you get a few questions wrong for a learning objective, you can then quickly refer to the chapter summary for that learning objective. Including the chapter summaries by learning objective in this workbook allows you to efficiently study chapter material.

Tips and Cautions for Students. This section in the workbook will bring your attention to topics in each chapter that tend to be the most difficult for students. Tips are provided to help you master some of the most difficult material. If you are having difficulty mastering material in the chapter, then refer to this section. It is likely that you are not alone and that this section will have useful tips to help you master the material.

Practice Quiz. It is always important to study prior to an exam. It can often be just as effective—sometimes more effective—to complete practice quizzes prior to taking an exam. At least 20 questions are given for each chapter, with over 300 quiz questions in all. These chapter quizzes help you check your mastery of the chapter content. If you get questions wrong, then you can refer to the chapter and learning objective summaries to find and review the content that you are struggling with most. The answers to all quiz questions are given in the back of this workbook to allow you to check your answers after you complete a quiz.

Key Term Word Search and Crossword Puzzle. It is important to review key terms and definitions in each chapter. In each chapter, key terms are bolded and defined. The bolded terms are then listed in the end material of each chapter. In this workbook, most key terms are included in word searches and crossword puzzles. Reviewing definitions can be boring. The crossword puzzles and word searches are aimed to make this review a little more fun and interesting. It is also a nice break from standard multiple-choice and fill-in-the-blank question formats.

The additional contents of this workbook are as follows:

- SPSS in Focus Exercises With General Instructions
- Grammar, Punctuation, and Spelling (GPS): A Brief Writing Guide
- End-of-Chapter Materials

To give you a sense of how the additional contents can benefit you, we will briefly look at those that are included.

SPSS in Focus Exercises With General Instructions. Most researchers in the behavioral sciences use the Statistical Package for the Social Sciences (SPSS) computer software to compute and analyze data. For this reason, SPSS in Focus sections are included in many chapters of the book. Included in the SPSS in Focus sections are step-by-step instructions for how to use SPSS to analyze the statistical techniques taught in the book. The student workbook supports the SPSS in Focus sections by including (1) exercises that allow you to practice using SPSS with a research example developed from studies published in the peer-reviewed literature, and (2) a General Instructions Guidebook (GIG) that provides general step-by-step instructions without the context of a specific research example. An answer key for the SPSS exercises is not included in this workbook to allow professors or instructors to use these exercises as a way of assessing your mastery of the SPSS learning objectives.

Grammar, Punctuation, and Spelling (GPS): A Brief Writing Guide. The GPS guide to grammar and writing is an essential tool for any student. It is written as a bulleted list of rules with examples for every rule. Most examples are statements similar to those you may read in professional or scientific articles. Grammar, sentence structure, spelling, and punctuation tend to be areas of weakness for many students. This brief guide addresses the most common areas of weakness in student writing and is written to be easy to follow and read. This guide alone can help you earn many more points on writing assignments and papers. Indeed, you may want to keep it with you for other courses you take in which writing assignments are due.

End-of-Chapter Materials. At the end of the student workbook, you will find answer keys to the key term word searches and crossword puzzles. Also given are answer keys to all of the chapter practice quizzes.

Keep in mind that this workbook is designed to help you study and to learn the material covered in each chapter. This student workbook supports chapter content by testing your retention and mastery of the material in each chapter and allows you to quickly review content that you are struggling with the most. The workbook provides quick references to key terms and learning objectives in each chapter, includes assessments of SPSS learning objectives, and provides an invaluable reference to support student writing using the GPS guide to grammar and writing. These contents are included with the ultimate goal of helping you achieve your personal goals for this course.

SECTION I

Scientific Inquiry

1

Introduction to Scientific Thinking

CHAPTER LEARNING OBJECTIVES

1. Define science and the scientific method.

2. Describe six steps for engaging in the scientific method.

3. Describe five nonscientific methods of acquiring knowledge.

4. Identify the four goals of science.

5. Distinguish between basic and applied research.

6. Distinguish between quantitative and qualitative research.

Chapter Summary

1.1 Science as a Method of Knowing

Science is one way of knowing about the world. The word *science* comes from the Latin *scientia*, meaning knowledge, and from a broad view, science is any systematic method of acquiring knowledge apart from ignorance. To use the scientific method we make observations that can be directly or indirectly observed.

1.2 The Scientific Method

To engage in the scientific method, the process used to acquire knowledge is organized into six steps:

- Identify a problem. Identify an area of interest to you, and then review the scientific literature, typically using online search engines, to identify what is known and what can still be learned about your area of interest. After conducting a literature review, identify new ideas in your area of interest by making a statement of prediction called a **research hypothesis.**

- Develop a research plan. Once a research hypothesis is stated, you need a plan to test that hypothesis. Identify the **variables** being tested and define them in terms of how they will be measured (i.e., state an **operational definition**). Identify a **population** of interest and determine how to select a **sample** of participants to observe from this larger population. Then, select a research strategy and a design for your study; also evaluate ethical implications of the research design and obtain institutional approval to conduct the research.

- Conduct the study. Execute the research plan by conducting the research study.

- Analyze and evaluate the data. Typically we analyze and evaluate numeric **data**. Once the data are analyzed, concisely report the data in the text of a paper, in tables, or in a figure or graph.

- Communicate the results. The most typical ways of sharing the results of a study are orally, in written form, or as a poster. Written research reports conform to the style and formatting guidelines provided in the *Publication Manual of the American Psychological Association* (APA, 2009), also called the *Publication Manual.*

- Generate more new ideas. The study you complete can be informative. If you find support for your research hypothesis, then you can use it to refine and expand on your ideas. If the results do not support your research hypothesis, then you need to propose a new idea and begin again.

1.3 Other Methods of Knowing

Five nonscientific ways of knowing are tenacity, intuition, authority, rationalism, and empiricism. **Tenacity** is a method of knowing based largely on habit or superstition. **Intuition** is an individual's subjective hunch or feeling that something is correct. **Authority** is knowledge accepted as fact because it was stated by an expert or respected source in a particular subject area. **Rationalism** is any source of knowledge that requires the use of reasoning or logic. Finally, **empiricism** is knowledge acquired through observation. The nonscientific ways of knowing may be used during the scientific process; however, they are only used in conjunction with the scientific method.

1.4 The Goals of Science

The four goals of science are to describe, to explain, to predict, and to control. To *describe* refers to understanding the behaviors and events we study. To *explain* refers to identifying the conditions within which behaviors and events operate. To *predict* refers to foretelling the occurrence of behaviors or events in the future. To *control* means that we can make a behavior occur and not occur. The four goals of science serve to direct scientists toward a comprehensive knowledge of the behaviors and events they observe.

1.5 Approaches in Acquiring Knowledge

Basic research is used to address theoretical questions regarding the mechanisms and processes of behavior; **applied research** is used to address questions that can lead to immediate solutions to practical problems.

Quantitative research restricts observations to categories and numeric measurements to obtain statistical results. **Qualitative research** does not include statistical results; instead, researchers draw conclusions that provide a series of interpretations for the observations they make. Quantitative and qualitative research can be effectively used to study the same behaviors, so both types of research have value.

Chapter Summary Organized by Learning Objective

LO 1: Define science and the scientific method.

Science is the acquisition of knowledge through observation, evaluation, interpretation, and theoretical explanation.

Science is specifically the acquisition of knowledge using the **scientific method**, which requires the use of systematic techniques, each of which comes with a specific set of assumptions and rules that make it *scientific*.

LO 2: Describe six steps for engaging in the scientific method.

The scientific process consists of six steps:

Step 1: Identify a problem: Determine an area of interest, review the literature, identify new ideas in your area of interest, and develop a research hypothesis.

Step 2: Develop a research plan: Define the variables being tested, identify participants or subjects and determine how to sample them, select a research strategy and design, and evaluate ethics and obtain institutional approval to conduct research.

Step 3: Conduct the study. Execute the research plan and measure or record the data.

Step 4: Analyze and evaluate the data. Analyze and evaluate the data as they relate to the research hypothesis, and summarize data and research results.

Step 5: Communicate the results. Results can be communicated orally, in written form, or as a poster. The styles of communication follow standards identified by the APA.

Step 6: Generate more new ideas. Refine or expand the original hypothesis, reformulate a new hypothesis, or start over.

LO 3: Describe five nonscientific methods of acquiring knowledge.

Tenacity is a method of knowing based largely on habit or superstition. A disadvantage of tenacity is that the knowledge acquired is often inaccurate.

Intuition is a method of knowing based largely on an individual's hunch or feeling that something is correct. A disadvantage of intuition is that the only way to determine the accuracy of an intuition is to act on that belief.

Authority is a method of knowing accepted as fact because it was stated by an expert or respected source in a particular subject area. A disadvantage of authority is that there is typically little effort to challenge an authority, leaving authoritative knowledge largely unchecked.

Rationalism is a method of knowing that requires the use of reasoning and logic. A disadvantage of rationalism is that it often leads to erroneous conclusions.

Empiricism is a method of knowing based on one's experiences or observations. Disadvantages of empiricism are that not everyone experiences or observes the world in the same way, perception is often illusory, and memory is inherently biased.

LO 4: Identify the four goals of science.

The four goals of science are to **describe** or define the variables we observe and measure, **explain** the causes of a behavior or event, **predict** when a behavior or event will occur in the future, and **control** or manipulate conditions in such a way as to make a behavior occur and not occur.

LO 5–6: Distinguish between basic and applied research and between quantitative and qualitative research.

Basic research uses the scientific method to answer questions that address theoretical issues about fundamental processes and underlying mechanisms related to the behaviors and events being studied. **Applied research** uses the scientific method to answer questions concerning practical problems with potential practical solutions.

Quantitative research is most commonly used in the behavioral sciences and uses the scientific method to record observations as numeric data. **Qualitative research** uses the scientific method to make nonnumeric observations, from which conclusions are drawn without the use of statistical analysis.

Tips and Cautions for Students

Identify an area of interest. Too often students tend to choose the first idea that comes to their mind when choosing a research topic. Keep in mind that research is a commitment that can take a substantial amount of time. Even for a project in class, this can mean months of commitment.

If you have an opportunity to choose an area of interest, make an effort to explore what aspects of human behavior interest you. You can explore your areas of interest by a Google search or a literature review. Type in keywords, such as *addiction*, *dieting*, or *spirituality*, and have fun searching the different types of behaviors that may interest you. Doing an initial web or literature search can help you identify areas of behavior that interest you. Once you identify an area of interest, you can follow the remaining steps of the scientific process introduced in this chapter—and throughout the book.

Data are plural for usage in APA-style writing. For example, say "The data *are* significant," not "The data *is* significant." *Datum* is singular, although this term is more typically called a *score* or *raw score*. Keep note of this distinction.

Empiricism versus the scientific method. Empiricism can often be confused with scientific observation because empiricist knowledge is acquired through *observation*. Keep in mind that empiricism is any type of observation. As an example, you may see two people walk by and "see" that they are happy. However, you do not necessarily measure your observation. Strictly speaking, simply "seeing" two people being happy is empiricism. However, in science, you will need to specifically define how "happy" is measured; for example, we can define it as the time in seconds spent laughing. Our observations will then be guided by how we define the behavior we are measuring—that is, being "happy." Hence, empiricism can be any type of observation, whereas in science observation is limited to only those phenomena that can be specifically measured.

Practice Quiz

1. Science is specifically the acquisition of knowledge using:
   a. the scientific method
   b. a random observation
   c. good study habits
   d. a multiple-choice test

2. Which of the following is *not* a step of the scientific method?
   a. identify a problem
   b. use empiricism
   c. conduct the study
   d. analyze and evaluate the data

3. A researcher defines the variables being tested, identifies participants, and determines how to sample them. She then selects a research strategy, evaluates the ethics of her design, and obtains institutional approval to conduct research. Which step of the scientific method does this describe?
   a. communicate the results
   b. conduct the study

  c. identify a problem

  d. develop a research plan

4. Which of the following is a method of communication?

  a. oral presentation

  b. written manuscript

  c. poster presentation

  d. all of the above

5. Which of the following is the initial step in the scientific process?

  a. conduct the study

  b. develop a research plan

  c. identify a problem

  d. generate more new ideas

6. Which of the following is an example of a research hypothesis?

  a. If people are nice, then are they also helpful?

  b. Nice people can be so helpful sometimes.

  c. People who are nice will also be more helpful.

  d. Being nice and being helpful: Do the two go hand in hand?

7. Which of the following is *not* an example of a variable?

  a. the value of π

  b. duration of time

  c. height in inches

  d. calories in a meal

8. A researcher explained that location was measured as the distance in feet an object was from the target location. In this example, the definition of location is an example of:

  a. a dictionary definition

  b. an operational definition

  c. a semantic definition

  d. a nondefinition

9. A professor selects 10 students to come to the front of the class out of a full class of 30 students. If the class itself is the only group of interest to the professor, then in this example how many students in this class are in the sample?

  a. 10

  b. 20

  c. 30

  d. 0

10. Which of the following is true about a population?
    a. It is a set of all individuals, items, or data of interest.
    b. It is the group about which scientists will generalize.
    c. It can constitute a large group or a small group.
    d. all of the above

11. Data are measurements or observations that are typically:
    a. vague
    b. unclear
    c. numeric
    d. not measured at all

12. To generate more new ideas we can:
    a. refine or expand the original hypothesis
    b. reformulate a new hypothesis
    c. start over
    d. all of the above

13. A method of knowing based largely on habit or superstition is called:
    a. intuition
    b. tenacity
    c. authority
    d. rationalism

14. A method of knowing based on one's experiences or observations is called:
    a. empiricism
    b. scientific
    c. authority
    d. rationalism

15. A teacher states that students do not care about being in school because they are not paying attention in class. Which of the following nonscientific ways of knowing is illustrated in this example?
    a. intuition
    b. empiricism
    c. tenacity
    d. rationalism

16. Which of the following identifies the four goals of science?
    a. describe, create, explain, control
    b. evaluate, explain, predict, control

    c. describe, explain, predict, control

    d. evaluate, create, explain, control

17. The four goals of science serve to:

    a. direct scientists toward a comprehensive knowledge of the behaviors and events they observe

    b. identify the areas in which science is flawed and needs to improve in order to become a valuable method of knowing

    c. illustrate that science has indisputably answered most questions about human behavior

    d. all of the above

18. Which of the following uses the scientific method to answer questions that address theoretical issues about fundamental processes and underlying mechanisms related to the behaviors and events being studied?

    a. basic research

    b. applied research

19. A researcher studies issues related to traffic accidents in order to create policies that can reduce traffic accidents in his city. What type of research is described in this example?

    a. basic research

    b. applied research

20. A researcher records the number of hours a sample of children spent watching television in Study 1. Another researcher records how a child describes his experiences while watching television in Study 2. _____ is an example of qualitative research; _____ is an example of quantitative research.

    a. Study 1; Study 2

    b. Study 2; Study 1

Key Term Word Search

```
Q P Z Z W E C E Y F R L G O E B U D G E N C R Q V E R
O U A V S C I E N T I F I C M E T H O D J A E Q K K I
B P A C M S J K N W M T I A A E X A B P A L K T Y C N
Q A E L K W A K E G V N H S U L F E A H U Q I X I P Y
F F S R I B Y O Q R U O O Z C B D O O Y T F P Z V K R
W L E I A T Z L L U A Q V N C I W G T P H E P M U Q V
I H Q B C T A C A Z F T X N W A E U G O O I J A N R N
Z M U S X R I T P S H B I B W K K N Q T R E P N D A G
C V A O E Y E O I O I L X O T L A X C H I M V T Z J X
J X N X Y R D S N V P N N Y N H O P N E T C T I G R Y
P M T T W G G D E A E U T H T A V T H S Y Y E A Y I N
H W I E M J A A A A L R L U N D L V X I G S F R V P S
D C T N H V D T G P R D E A I O B I Z S A P C E H B B
R S A A D D W U S E P C E S T T W O S J D N P A J S I
M Z T C X G L M O M W L H F E I I C N M H E V X W J Y
U L I I R Q E A Y C P F I S I A O O S E V M D I P V X
G J V T A S Q G Q G H I O E B N R N N V V P S K K Z Y
M K E Y X A L J N K T B R L D A I C C O K I E Y W C E
O K R I I M N R Q X W E V A C R Z T H Y S R R J V R A
V S E J S P A P C A P S C E P J E M I E H I A D C I S
U M S R Z L F A I L Y V X R E V H S H O S C G Q Q M B
F H E Z H E C N N B R C T I Q D R T E B N I H J G G U
J U A M T X C Q G W L H I N W P O H P A A S R V T H X
C X R C L U K K I B W Z P T A P U U L T R M X P K U Q
V I C I L K B M I D R D P U Y O B V A D N C O Q P G M
Q E H E P X P R P B U L W H Z P A D Q F A D H W W K A
Z Z K Q I Q R U G W V B E T H P D X J C O D Z L E O V
```

operational definition
quantitative research
qualitative research
scientific method
applied research
basic research

rationalism
empiricism
hypothesis
population
authority
intuition

tenacity
science
sample
datum
data

ACROSS

2. a description of some observable event in terms of the specific process or manner by which it was observed or measured

3. a type of scientific method used to record observations as numeric data

6. a method of knowing based largely on habit or superstition

7. the acquisition of knowledge through observation, evaluation, interpretation, and theoretical explanation

9. a type of scientific method used to answer questions concerning practical problems with potential practical solutions

12. a type of scientific method used to make nonnumeric observations, from which conclusions are drawn without the use of statistical analysis

14. a method of knowing based on one's experiences or observations

15. a set of selected individuals, items, or data taken from a population of interest

16. a method of knowing that requires the use of reasoning and logic

17. a method of knowing accepted as fact because it was stated by an expert or respected source in a particular

DOWN

1. a set of all individuals, items, or data of interest; the group about which scientists will generalize

4. a specific, testable claim or prediction about what you expect to observe given a set of circumstances

5. a set of systematic techniques used to acquire, modify, and integrate knowledge concerning observable and measurable phenomena

8. any value or characteristic that can change or vary from one person to another or from one situation to another

10. a type of scientific method used to answer questions that address theoretical issues about fundamental processes and underlying mechanisms related to the behaviors and events being studied

11. measurements or observations that are typically numeric

13. a method of knowing based largely on an individual's hunch or feeling that something is correct

Crossword Puzzle

2

Generating Testable Ideas

CHAPTER LEARNING OBJECTIVES

1. Explain what makes an idea interesting and novel.

2. Distinguish between a hypothesis and a theory.

3. Distinguish between induction and deduction.

4. Describe the process of conducting a literature review.

5. Identify four ethical concerns for giving proper credit.

6. Describe the "3 Cs" of conducting an effective literature review.

7. Distinguish between a confirmational and a disconfirmational strategy.

8. Explain the issue of publication bias.

Chapter Summary

2.1 Generating Interesting and Novel Ideas

Once a research study is complete, researchers may try to publish the results in a scientific journal called a **peer-reviewed journal**. To publish a work, you should be considerate of the aims of scientific journals and two additional criteria or questions: First, is your idea interesting (to the readership of a journal), and second, is your idea novel (i.e., does it add to an existing body of literature)? To publish your work, your answer should be yes to both questions.

2.2 Converting Ideas to Hypotheses and Theories

In science, the information obtained is of little value without organization. One way in which scientists organize information is by stating hypotheses or theories about the information that is obtained. A **hypothesis** is a specific, testable prediction or claim about what you expect to observe given a set of circumstances. A **theory** is a broad statement used to account for an existing body of knowledge and also provide unique predictions to extend that body of knowledge. The advantage of a theory is that it states unique predictions and can also be used to explain an existing body of research. A theory is often tested in one of two ways: Predictions made by a theory can be tested, or the limitations of a theory can be tested.

2.3 Developing Your Idea: Deduction and Induction

Using **deductive reasoning**, you begin with a theory and deduce a prediction that must be true if the theory is correct—the prediction you deduce is your hypothesis, which will be tested to refute or support the theory. Using deductive reasoning, then, you start with a theory or idea to generate new ideas (e.g., predictions made by a theory). Hence, the theory guides the ideas you generate and the observations you make.

Using **inductive reasoning**, you make a casual observation or collect and measure data. You then generate an idea or hypothesis to explain what you observed or measured. The idea you generate to explain the observation is your hypothesis. Using inductive reasoning, then, you start with an observation to generate new ideas; that is, you generalize beyond the limited observations you made. Hence, the data or observations guide the ideas you generate and the observations you make.

2.4 Performing a Literature Review

To develop an idea, you perform a **literature review**. The *literature* is the general body of published scientific knowledge. The *review* is the search you perform of this general body of knowledge. To get started with a literature review, first identify a research topic that interests you. To get organized, keep track of your sources and determine if each source is a **secondary source** (a source describing research or ideas that are not necessarily the author's own) or a **primary source** (a source from the original author of a work). To search the literature, use online databases that allow you to search for, save, and print thousands of primary and secondary sources in all topic areas in the behavioral sciences. Popular databases include PsycINFO, PsycARTICLES, PubMed, ERIC, and JSTOR.

2.5 Ethics in Focus: Giving Proper Credit

Four ways to avoid ethical problems are (1) always double-check your sources for accuracy, (2) obtain the primary source of an article you cite, (3) avoid "abstracting," and (4) be aware of **citation bias**. Citation bias is when an author or authors cite only evidence that supports their view and fail to cite conflicting evidence.

2.6 The "3 Cs" of an Effective Literature Review

The "3 Cs" of an effective literature review are to be comprehensive, critical, and clever. To be *comprehensive*, search for research articles by journal, search multiple databases, and search an article in the following order: title, abstract, introduction and discussion, methods and results, and references. To be *critical*, ask questions as you read an article, know your sources, and remain objective. To be *clever*, identify flaws or inaccuracies in an article, identify contradictions across many studies, identify anomalies within a study, consider subtle changes to a study that can be impactful, and think beyond the research.

2.7 Testing Your Idea: Confirmation and Disconfirmation

A **confirmational strategy** is a method of testing a theory or hypothesis in which a positive result confirms the predictions made by that theory or hypothesis. A *positive result* occurs when an effect or difference is observed. A confirmational strategy uses a logic statement called *affirming the consequent*, which can be false logic. For this reason, researchers also use a disconfirmational strategy.

A **disconfirmational strategy** is a method of testing a theory or hypothesis in which a positive result disconfirms the predictions made by that theory or hypothesis. Using this strategy, you test an outcome that is not predicted or anticipated by the theory or hypothesis being tested. One benefit of using the disconfirmational strategy is that researchers can refute a theory or hypothesis with a positive result.

2.8 Ethics in Focus: Publication Bias

Publication bias is the tendency for editors of peer-reviewed scientific journals to preferentially accept articles that show positive results and reject those that show only negative results. Because editors and peer reviewers often decide to reject a manuscript on the basis of its failure to show positive results, many researchers do not even try to publish negative findings, instead choosing to file them away, called the **file drawer problem**. While the positive results reported in the peer-reviewed literature can certainly be trusted, also take caution in knowing that many negative results may not be included in your search.

Chapter Summary Organized by Learning Objective

LO 1: Explain what makes an idea interesting and novel.

An interesting idea is any idea that appeals to the readership of **peer-reviewed journals**. A novel idea is one that is original or new.

LO 2: Distinguish between a hypothesis and a theory.

A **hypothesis** is a specific, testable claim or prediction about what you expect to observe given a set of circumstances.

A **theory** is a broad statement used to account for an existing body of knowledge and also provide unique predictions to extend that body of knowledge. A theory is not necessarily correct; instead, it is a generally accepted explanation for evidence, as it is understood.

LO 3: Distinguish between induction and deduction.

Deductive reasoning is a "top-down" type of reasoning in which a claim (hypothesis or theory) is used to generate ideas or predictions and make observations.

Inductive reasoning is a "bottom-up" type of reasoning in which a limited number of observations or measurements (i.e., data) are used to generate ideas and make observations.

LO 4: Describe the process of conducting a literature review.

Getting started: Find a research topic that interests you because it will make the scientific process more worthwhile.

Getting organized: Review **secondary sources** to identify primary sources that are most relevant to your research topic. Then follow up and read the **primary sources** to check what is reported in those sources.

Getting searching: Use online databases, such as PsycINFO, PsycARTICLES, PubMed, ERIC, and JSTOR. Each online database allows you to use keyword searches to review thousands of articles and books.

LO 5: Identify four ethical concerns for giving proper credit.

Incorrectly citing reference articles, failing to obtain or give proper credit to a primary source, citing a source after only reading the abstract for that source, and citation bias.

Citation bias occurs when citing only evidence that supports your view without also citing existing evidence that refutes your view.

LO 6: Describe the "3 Cs" of conducting an effective literature review.

Be comprehensive. Journals specialize, so search a journal name if you know it contains articles that interest you. Read sections of research articles in the following order: title, abstract, introduction and discussion, methods and results, and references. Also, be aware that one study rarely is sufficient to answer a research question or prove a hypothesis, so you should not base your entire literature review on a single article or viewpoint.

Be critical. Ask questions as you read, know the types of sources you are using, and remain as objective as possible.

Be clever. Some clever strategies are to identify flaws, identify contradictions, identify anomalies, consider subtleties, and think beyond the research.

LO 7: Distinguish between a confirmational and a disconfirmational strategy.

A **confirmational strategy** is a method of testing a theory or hypothesis in which a positive result confirms the predictions made by that theory or hypothesis.

A **disconfirmational strategy** is a method of testing a theory or hypothesis in which a positive result disconfirms the predictions made by that theory or hypothesis.

LO 8: Explain the issue of publication bias.

Publication bias is the tendency for editors of peer-reviewed journals to preferentially accept articles that show positive results and reject those that show only negative results.

The publication bias is also called the **file drawer problem** because researchers have a tendency to file away studies that show negative results, knowing that most journals will likely reject them. The publication bias means that the size of an effect could be overstated for many behavioral phenomena reported in the peer-reviewed literature.

Tips and Cautions for Students

Deductive Versus Inductive Reasoning

Here we will further distinguish deductive from inductive reasoning. Keep in mind that deductive reasoning works from more general to more specific—sometimes called a "top-down" approach. Using deductive reasoning, then, we might begin with a *theory* about our topic of interest, then narrow that down into more specific *hypotheses* that we can test and *observations* we can make to address the hypotheses. Ultimately, this process of reasoning leads us to be able to test the hypotheses with specific data to *confirm* or *disconfirm* our original theories.

Inductive reasoning works in the opposite direction, from more specific observations to broader generalizations and theories—sometimes called a "bottom-up" approach. Using inductive reasoning, then, we begin with specific or general observations and measures. If patterns or regularities are detected, then we can formulate some tentative hypotheses that can be explored and can eventually lead to some general conclusions or theories.

Confirmational Versus Disconfirmational Strategies

To simplify the distinction between a confirmational and a disconfirmational strategy for testing a hypothesis or theory, keep in mind the idea of observing a positive result. Using a confirmational strategy we look for evidence to confirm predictions from a theory; if a positive (i.e., significant) result shows evidence to support a tested prediction, then we are using a confirmational strategy. However, using a disconfirmational strategy we look for evidence to disconfirm predictions from a theory; if a positive (i.e., significant) result shows evidence to disconfirm a prediction not otherwise anticipated by a theory, then we are using a disconfirmational strategy.

To further illustrate this distinction, if a theory predicts *Y* but is contradicted by *X*, then we can use a confirmational strategy to test *Y*; if results are significant (positive), then we can confirm that the theory predicts Y. We can also use a disconfirmational strategy to test X; if results are significant (positive), then we can confirm that X is true, which provides evidence to contradict or disconfirm the theory.

Practice Quiz

1. Once a research study is complete, researchers may try to publish the results in a scientific journal called a:
   a. peer-reviewed journal
   b. nonreviewed journal
   c. partially reviewed journal
   d. none of the above

2. An idea that is tested using the scientific method should be _____; in other words, it should provide new information.
   a. questionable
   b. convoluted
   c. novel
   d. marginal

3. A _____ is a broad statement used to account for an existing body of knowledge and also provide unique predictions to extend that body of knowledge.
   a. hypothesis
   b. theory
   c. circumstance
   d. strategy

4. Which of the following is true about a hypothesis?
   a. It is a statement of prediction.
   b. It is a testable claim.
   c. It is a statement, not a question.
   d. all of the above

5. Deductive reasoning is a _____ approach, whereas inductive reasoning is a _____ approach.
   a. top-down; bottom-up
   b. top-up; bottom-down
   c. bottom-up; top-down
   d. bottom-down; top-up

6. You observe two of your friends arguing. About two minutes into the argument a comedy special airs on TV that makes both of them laugh. After that, your friends no longer argue. From this, you conclude that humor can alleviate conflict. This is an example of what type of reasoning?

   a. deductive reasoning

   b. inductive reasoning

   c. statistical reasoning

   d. evaluative reasoning

7. In a literature review, the *literature* refers to:

   a. fiction and nonfiction novels

   b. any works published on the Internet

   c. the general body of published scientific knowledge

   d. personal diaries and notes

8. Which of the following is an example of a secondary source?

   a. an author's published ideas

   b. a review article

   c. a textbook

   d. both b and c

9. Any publication in which the works, ideas, or observations are those of the author is called:

   a. a primary source

   b. a secondary source

   c. hearsay

   d. all of the above

10. PsycINFO, PsycARTICLES, PubMed, ERIC, and JSTOR are examples of:

    a. professional clubs

    b. electronic databases

    c. physical libraries

    d. famous authors

11. When searching for articles in a database, we type in _____ to find articles that are related to the topic or idea we want to search.

    a. illustrations

    b. keywords

    c. images

    d. pictures

12. The length of an abstract can vary; however, abstracts are typically how long?

    a. 250 words or fewer

    b. at least 500 words

    c. between 2 and 3 pages

    d. one or two sentences at most

13. Which of the following is a way to avoid citing sources incorrectly?

    a. always double-check your sources for accuracy

    b. obtain the primary source of an article you cite

    c. be aware of citation bias

    d. all of the above

14. Each of the following is one of the "3 Cs" of an effective literature review, *except*:

    a. be critical

    b. be clever

    c. be cooperative

    d. be comprehensive

15. Which of the following parts of an article should you read first to be comprehensive in your literature review?

    a. references

    b. discussion

    c. title and abstract

    d. results

16. Thinking beyond the research is part of which of the "3 Cs" of an effective literature review?

    a. be clever

    b. be comprehensive

    c. be charismatic

    d. be convoluted

17. Which type of strategy uses the following logic statement:

        If A is true, then B is true.

        B is true.

        Therefore, A is true.

    a. conformational strategy

    b. disconfirmational strategy

18. A disconfirmational strategy is a method of testing a theory or hypothesis in which:

    a. a negative result disconfirms the predictions made by that theory or hypothesis

    b. a positive result disconfirms the predictions made by that theory or hypothesis

    c. we use the type of logic referred to as *affirming the consequent*

    d. both b and c

19. A publication bias is the tendency for editors of peer-reviewed journals to preferentially accept articles that show _____ results and reject those that show only _____ results.

    a. negative; positive

    b. positive; negative

    c. significant; impactful

    d. impactful; significant

20. Another term for publication bias is:

    a. citation bias

    b. literature advancement

    c. primary sourcing

    d. file drawer problem

Key Term Word Search

```
U P N E T C G L Q U O A L J V F D R Q K M E B D M Q Z C O
U F M F V W A D L G L G R S E C O N D A R Y S O U R C E L
D D U G X K D U X J H A L N Y I W E I K E B G U L B O A R
E Z S H R M Z L L Z U R U O K B R E A E A R I M N S O Y N
D T V F B T G W F N A V M X N G E U P A V W P E X U G P F
U C Q E S P Q N R M L N L T B Q I A X Q B N N E E E C O I
C O N Y N L V X T B Z F O Q J T G O J B F P Y L T S J O L
T N P E E R R E V I E W E D J O U R N A L A C A T N B J E
I F W L K M Q S M B X F M M B Z G M G Y I I R U U G P U D
V I N A C H H E I K S C T T H M J C P Y T T O E B D R J R
E R N E I J P V C Z R K Q B G X H B V R S I I S U R H H A
R M W D O E R E Y C W M A C F Y Z U A L H F H N C K Q S W
E A L Y T L A H A M J G Y U F X K T A C W T J B Y L D J E
A T X P R I M A R Y S O U R C E X N A D C H Q W P A E K R
S I Q G F G P H C Q H H D T G E O B V Y E E M S B H B A P
O O F X W B A D G R Q E T U T I J E L Q E O J G S M Q Y R
N N V N A O A X M P F A S L T S Q Y D E A R J C B L R I O
I A Q C G P C C E W U I L A P E M F Q B K Y Z Z P U M J B
N L U R U E T R W C F U M W E T O O H D B V C Y W G T J L
G S J A G U L B N W F R P K W T C W P H U X H B L X L G E
M T B B R W I Y W T I H B M Z T E Y Q D A G J V S W C D M
G R J S H C D O Y F Q L I T E R A T U R E R E V I E W W Z
J A S T I A B W N P A B P U E F J I Y E Q L L I W A G W B
F T T R P U W O V O K V W R V L W C T L F B M R L U A F Z
D E H A L L C W D F H C F G L S E Z L D K J K W X L P J I
R G C C N S J U C Z I P U B L I C A T I O N B I A S C J C
C Y Q T I X S E W I C X F U L L T E X T D A T A B A S E Z
W M Q D J P F U O C I R E A P Q W N S E K H H Q L Q H X W
V I N D U C T I V E R E A S O N I N G O M D X T N D K X Q
```

confirmational strategy	literature review	inductive reasoning
secondary source	law	abstract
publication bias	disconfirmational strategy	peer-reviewed journal
primary source	full-text article	deductive reasoning
theory	file drawer problem	full-text database

ACROSS

1. another name for publication bias due to the fact that researchers have a tendency to file away studies that show negative results, knowing that most journals will likely reject them

4. a specific, testable claim or prediction about what you expect to observe given a set of circumstances

7. the tendency for editors of peer-reviewed journals to preferentially accept articles that show positive results and reject those that show only negative results

12. any source or publication in which the works, ideas, or observations are those of the author

14. a "top-down" type of reasoning in which a claim or theory is used to generate predictions and make observations

15. any source or publication that references works, ideas, or observations that are not those of the author

DOWN

2. an online full-text _____ makes full-text articles available to be downloaded electronically as a PDF or in another electronic format

3. a systematic search for and recording of information identified in the general body of published scientific knowledge

5. a "bottom-up" type of reasoning in which a limited number of observations or measurements (i.e., data) are used to generate ideas and make observations

6. a strategy or method of testing a theory or hypothesis in which a positive result disconfirms the predictions made by that theory or hypothesis

8. a misleading approach to citing sources that occurs when an author or authors cite only evidence that supports their view and fail to cite existing evidence that refutes their view

9. a type of journal publication that specifically publishes scientific articles, reviews, or commentaries only after the work has been reviewed by peers or scientific experts who determine its scientific value or worth regarding publication

10. a brief written summary of the purpose, methods, and results of an article, chapter, book, or other published document

11. any article or text that is available in its full or completed published version

13. a broad statement used to account for an existing body of knowledge and also provide unique predictions to extend that body of knowledge

Crossword Puzzle

3

Research Ethics

CHAPTER LEARNING OBJECTIVES

1. Define research ethics.

2. Trace the history leading to the Nuremberg Code and state the 10 directives listed in the code.

3. Trace the history leading to the Belmont Report and state the three ethical principles listed in the report.

4. Identify the ethical concerns for three landmark studies in psychology: the Robbers Cave experiment, Milgram's obedience experiments, and the Stanford prison study.

5. Describe the role of the IRB in regulating ethical research with human participants.

6. Describe the standards in the APA code of conduct relating to human participant research.

7. Describe the role of an IACUC in regulating ethical research with animal subjects.

8. Describe the standards in the APA code of conduct relating to animal subject research.

9. Describe the standards in the APA code of conduct relating to scientific integrity.

Chapter Summary

3.1 Ethics in Behavioral Research

Research ethics identifies the actions that a researcher must take to conduct responsible and moral research. Engaging in responsible and moral research requires a researcher to anticipate what might happen, react to what is happening, and reflect on what did happen. The best-case scenario is to avoid ethical problems altogether, and the best way to do that is to fully anticipate concerns before the study is actually conducted.

3.2 The Need for Ethics Committees in Research: A Historical Synopsis

Nazi medical experiments in concentration camps during World War II involved experiments that were unprecedented in the scope and degree of harm to unwilling participants. These crimes eventually led to trials. In August 1947 the verdict from the Doctors' Trial included a section called Permissible Medical Experiments, which has come to be known as the **Nuremberg Code**, the first international code of research ethics with 10 directives regarding the conduct of experiments.

The Tuskegee Syphilis Study is a landmark case of unethical conduct in experimentation in the United States. This study, which began in 1932 in Tuskegee, Alabama, was performed on 600 Black men, 399 who had syphilis and 201 who did not. Participants were told that they were being treated, but in fact they were not. In the 1940s penicillin became widely available as an effective treatment for syphilis. Yet, the researchers denied the participants access to penicillin, and the study continued until 1972. In response to public outrage, a national commission developed ethical guidelines for all human participant research, and in 1979 the commission drafted the **Belmont Report**, which identifies three ethical principles for human participant research: respect for persons, beneficence, and justice.

Respect for persons means that participants in a research study are treated as autonomous agents; potential participants must be capable of making informed decisions concerning whether to participate in a research study. **Beneficence** means that it is the researcher's responsibility to minimize the potential risks and maximize the potential benefits associated with a research study. **Justice** refers to the fair and equitable treatment of all individuals and groups who participate in research studies in terms of the benefits they receive and the risks they bear from their participation in research.

3.3 Ethics in Focus: Examples From Psychology

The Robbers Cave experiment was conducted with two groups of boys who were brought to Robbers Cave State Park in Oklahoma. The main aim of the study was to understand prejudice and intergroup conflict. Researchers manipulated intergroup prejudice between the two groups by creating a competitive atmosphere. To resolve ethical concerns of fostering prejudice in children, the researchers staged a situation that required the two groups to work together for a shared goal, and the prejudice between the two groups dissipated.

The Milgram obedience experiments, conducted at Yale University, were staged to make the participant think that he or she was causing harm to another participant by administering electric shocks. The participant played the role of a teacher who administered shocks to a learner (a confederate) for each wrong answer to a word pair. The experiment was set up to appear real to the participant, and participants often reported being under great stress during the experiment. To alleviate stress caused by the "shock" manipulation, participants were told the true intent of the experiment and that no shocks were ever administered, after the experiment was completed.

The Stanford prison study was conducted in the basement of the psychology building at Stanford University to better understand how social roles influence behavior. Participants were randomly assigned to be a "prisoner" or a "guard" and to play out those roles in a mock prison in the basement. In this setting, the interaction between prisoners and guards became increasingly aggressive. The study was planned to last two weeks. However, the punishments escalated so quickly that the study was terminated after only six days because the risks to participant welfare far outweighed the benefits of continuing the study as planned.

More recent examples of studies with major ethical concerns also exist. Standards of ethical responsibility are dynamic and evolving, even today, as technologies advance and research methods improve.

3.4 Human Participant Research: IRBs and the APA Code of Conduct

The American Psychological Association (APA, 2010) adopted a method of assessing risk in its publication of the *Ethical Principles of Psychologists and Code of Conduct*, which extends the ethical principles outlined in the Belmont Report to include two others: fidelity and responsibility, and integrity. The codes outlined in the APA code of conduct are summarized here.

All human participant research must receive institutional approval from an **institutional review board (IRB)**. An IRB categorizes the research as involving no risk, minimal risk, or greater-than-minimal risk, and makes the final determination pertaining to the level of risk potentially involved in the research study. Participants must give **informed consent** about whether to participate, which includes giving consent to have their voices and images recorded in research. Researchers must protect potential participants from adverse consequences associated with declining or withdrawing participation in a research study. To ensure the integrity of the data collected in a research study, it can be permissible (with IRB approval) to initially exclude information in an informed consent form. Participants can receive incentives to participate; however, researchers must ensure that the incentive is not excessive or inappropriate. **Deception** can be used in research with IRB approval when the deception is necessary and causes minimal harm to participants. At the conclusion of a study, all participants receive a **debriefing** in which the researcher discloses the true purpose of the study.

3.5 Ethics in Focus: Anonymity and Confidentiality

Confidentiality is a protection of individual identity in which the identity of a participant is not made available to anyone who is not directly involved in a study. Those involved in a study, however, are able to identify participant information. **Anonymity** is a stricter standard of protection of individual identity in which the identity of a participant remains unknown throughout a study, even to those involved in a study.

3.6 Animal Subject Research: IACUCs and the APA Code of Conduct

Protections for the use of animals in research actually have a longer history than protections afforded to humans. To protect animals in research, a research study must be reviewed and approved by an **institutional animal care and use committee (IACUC)** prior to being conducted. Many protections are put in place for use of animals in research with guidelines given in the *Guidelines for Ethical Conduct in the Care and Use of Nonhuman Animals in Research* (APA, 2012). All protections for animals extend for the full duration of time that they are under the care of a researcher: from when the animals arrive in a lab before the study, to when the animals leave the research lab at the conclusion of a study.

3.7 Additional Ethical Considerations: Scientific Integrity

Scientific integrity is the extent to which a researcher is honest and truthful in his or her actions, values, methods, measures, and dissemination of research. Displaying high scientific integrity requires the individual to truthfully report data and never **fabricate** methods or data that misrepresent aspects of a research study with the intent to deceive others. It also means avoiding plagiarism, which occurs when a researcher represents someone else's ideas or work as his or her own ideas or work.

All individuals who "have substantially contributed" (APA, 2010) to a work should be recognized as authors. **Duplication,** or the republication of original data that were previously published, should be avoided. Researchers are expected to share their data upon request from others for the purposes of inspection, reanalysis, and **replication**. Also, peer reviewers sometimes have access to information that should be protected and so are required to respect the confidentiality and propriety rights of those who submit their work for review.

Chapter Summary Organized by Learning Objective

LO 1: Define research ethics.

- **Research ethics** identifies the actions that researchers must take to conduct responsible and moral research. In science, researchers must *anticipate* ethical considerations in a research plan, *react* to ethical concerns during a study, and *reflect* on what did happen in their study after the plan is executed.

LO 2: Trace the history leading to the Nuremberg Code and state the 10 directives listed in the code.

- The individuals and physicians responsible for the conduct of harmful experiments on concentration camp prisoners were put on trial between 1945 and 1947. Many trials were held during this time. The Doctors' Trial was prosecuted between December 1946 and July 1947. In August 1947 the verdict from this trial included a section that has come to be known as the **Nuremberg Code,** the first international code of research ethics.

LO 3: Trace the history leading to the Belmont Report and state the three ethical principles listed in the report.

- In 1932, the Tuskegee Syphilis Study began in which 600 Black men—399 with syphilis and 201 who did not have the disease—were studied to determine the course of the disease through death. The true purpose of the study was not revealed to the men. In the 1940s penicillin became widely available as an effective treatment for syphilis; however, participants in the study were denied treatment, and the study continued for another quarter-century. In response to public outrage, the study ended in 1972; in 1974 Congress established the national commission that drafted the **Belmont Report** in 1979, which states three ethical principles: respect for persons, beneficence, and justice.
- **Respect for persons:** Participants in a research study must be autonomous agents capable of making informed decisions concerning whether to participate in research.
- **Beneficence:** It is the researcher's responsibility to minimize the potential risks and maximize the potential benefits associated with conducting a research study.
- **Justice:** All participants should be treated fairly and equitably in terms of receiving the benefits and bearing the risks in a research study.

LO 4: Identify the ethical concerns for three landmark studies in psychology: the Robbers Cave experiment, Milgram's obedience experiments, and the Stanford prison study.

- Muzafer Sherif conducted the Robbers Cave experiment in 1954. Two groups of boys were brought to Robbers Cave State Park in Oklahoma. The aim of the study was to understand prejudice and intergroup conflict. However, the two groups of boys were aggressive toward each other because of prejudice that the researchers manipulated. To resolve the ethical concerns of fostering prejudice in children, the researchers staged a situation that required the two groups to work together for a shared goal. Although the two groups resisted working together at first, they ultimately worked together, and the prejudice between them dissipated.
- Stanley Milgram at Yale University studied obedience using a manipulation in which participants thought they were administering significant levels of shock to another participant. One participant was told by Milgram (the authority figure) to administer shocks in increments of 15 volts to another participant (the confederate) for each incorrect response to a series of word pairs. The experiment was set up to appear real to the participant. However, in truth, no shocks were ever administered. The key ethical concern of this study involved the significant stress placed on the participant. To alleviate the stress caused by his manipulation, Milgram disclosed to participants that no shocks were ever administered, after the experiment was completed.
- Philip Zimbardo conducted the Stanford prison study in 1971. The aim of this study was to understand how social roles influence behavior. Participants were randomly assigned to be a prisoner or a guard. However, the guards began to use excessive force once the study began; the guards became aggressive whenever a prisoner was disobedient in any way, and the prisoners began to show signs of significant stress. The prisoners faced increased psychological and physical harm as the guards' actions progressed. The main ethical concern

was for the welfare of the participants, and the prisoners in particular. Because the potential for serious harm to participants escalated in only a few days, the study was terminated after only six days.

LO 5: Describe the role of the IRB in regulating ethical research with human participants.

An **institutional review board (IRB)** is a review board with at least five members, one of whom comes from outside the institution. These members review for approval research protocols submitted by researchers prior to the conduct of any research. Every institution that receives federal funding must have an IRB.

LO 6: Describe the standards in the APA code of conduct relating to human participant research.

- All research requiring institutional approval is bound by the information in a research protocol, and the research can only be conducted after receiving approval.
- **Informed consent** is obtained prior to the conduct of research, and it must provide full information regarding all aspects of a research study.
- In most cases, informed consent must be obtained prior to the recording of voices or images obtained during research.
- Client/patient, student, and subordinate research participants must be protected from adverse consequences associated with declining or withdrawing from participation.
- In some situations, it is permissible to initially exclude information from an informed consent form so long as the potential harm to participants is minimal.
- Researchers should avoid offering excessive or inappropriate incentives that are likely to coerce participants.
- The use of **deception** is allowable in research in certain circumstances outlined by the APA aimed to protect human participants from harm.
- Researchers must disclose to participants the true purpose or intent of a study in a **debriefing**.

LO 7: Describe the role of an IACUC in regulating ethical research with animal subjects.

- An **institutional animal care and use committee (IACUC)** is a review board that consists of at least one veterinarian, one scientist with experience using animals, and one public member from the community. These members review animal research protocols submitted by researchers prior to the conduct of any research. Every institution that receives federal funding must have an IACUC.

LO 8: Describe the standards in the APA code of conduct relating to animal subject research.

- Researchers are responsible for the welfare of animal subjects for the duration of time that they are under the researchers' care. This includes all aspects of care before, during, and after the completion of a study.

LO 9: Describe the standards in the APA code of conduct relating to scientific integrity.

- Researchers must not **fabricate** research data and methods.
- Researchers must not **plagiarize**.
- All individuals making substantial contributions to a work must be recognized as authors; those making minor contributions must also be recognized.
- Researchers must not **duplicate** work published by them or another author.
- Researchers must store and maintain their data for the purposes of **replication**.
- Peer reviewers must respect the confidentiality and propriety rights of those who submit their work for **peer review**.

Tips and Cautions for Students

IRBs and IACUCs. Keep in mind that human participant research and animal subject research are overseen by different committees. Human participant research is overseen by an institutional review board. An IRB has at least five members, one of whom comes from outside the research institution or university. Animal subject research is overseen by an institutional animal care and use committee. An IACUC consists of at least one veterinarian, one scientist with experience using animals, and one public member from the community.

Each research institution or university has its own IRB and its own IACUC. It is the researcher's job to submit a research protocol to the IRB when human participants are used and to submit a research protocol to the IACUC when animal subjects are used. A research protocol fully discloses the details of the study conducted and provides specific considerations for the ethical implications in all aspects of the proposed study. Only upon approval by an IRB or an IACUC is a researcher allowed to conduct his or her study, and all researchers are bound to follow the research protocol once it is approved.

Practice Quiz

1. What term is used to identify the actions that a researcher must take to conduct responsible and moral research?
   a. policy
   b. ethics
   c. options
   d. choices

2. At what point in the research process is research ethics important?
   a. before the study begins
   b. during the study

    c. after the study

    d. all of the above

3. Who were used as participants in the Nazi medical experiments during World War II?

    a. persons in concentration camps

    b. only willing participants

    c. only persons who gave full consent to participate

    d. all of the above

4. In what year was the Nuremberg Code published as the first international code for ethical conduct?

    a. 1939

    b. 1945

    c. 1947

    d. 1952

5. What was the key ethical concern in the Tuskegee Syphilis Study?

    a. Researchers denied study participants penicillin in the 1940s.

    b. Researchers began the study before penicillin was made available to treat syphilis.

    c. Penicillin was immediately made available to study participants as soon as it was approved as an effective treatment for syphilis.

    d. No ethical concerns were evident for this study.

6. The Tuskegee Syphilis Study led to which landmark report?

    a. the Board Report

    b. the Belmont Report

    c. the Research Report

    d. the Press Report

7. A risk-benefit analysis is most closely associated with which principle in the Belmont Report?

    a. respect for persons

    b. beneficence

    c. justice

    d. integrity

8. Which famous study in psychology required the researchers to reduce intergroup conflict and prejudice between two groups of boys at a camp?

    a. Robbers Cave experiment

    b. Milgram's obedience experiments

    c. the Stanford prison study

    d. none of the above

9. An institutional review board:

   a. has at least five members, one of whom comes from outside the institution

   b. reviews for approval research protocols for human participant research

   c. categorizes research as involving no risk, minimal risk, or greater-than-minimal risk

   d. all of the above

10. The *Ethical Principles of Psychologists and Code of Conduct* (APA, 2010) extends the ethical principles outlined in the Belmont Report to include which additional principle?

    a. fidelity and responsibility

    b. integrity

    c. philanthropy

    d. both a and b

11. All participants give _____ *prior* to participating in research.

    a. money

    b. their rights

    c. informed consent

    d. allowances

12. Which of the following is *not* a guideline for preparing and writing an informed consent form?

    a. use exculpatory language

    b. use numeric values

    c. write as if you are speaking to the participant

    d. avoid technical jargon

13. Researchers must protect potential participants from _____ consequences associated with declining or withdrawing participation in a research study.

    a. positive

    b. beneficial

    c. adverse

    d. fair

14. Why is it important for researchers to avoid offering excessive or inappropriate incentives to get people to participate in a research study?

    a. because it may make participants grateful

    b. because participants may participate for the "payoff" even if their actual intention would be to decline participation

    c. because monetary incentives of any kind are unethical

    d. all of the above

15. Deception used in a researcher study:

    a. can be active or deliberate

    b. is permissible, if it results in minimal or no harm to participants

c. can include giving misleading information to participants

d. all of the above

16. Which protection of individual identity is stricter?

    a. anonymity

    b. confidentiality

17. Which committee reviews for approval animal research protocols submitted by researchers prior to the conduct of any research?

    a. IRB

    b. HHS

    c. IACUC

    d. APA

18. Protections for animals:

    a. extend for the full duration of time that they are under the care of a researcher

    b. are limited only during the time of a study

    c. are limited only during daytime hours

    d. extend from the beginning to the end of a research study, regardless of how long the animals are under the care of a researcher

19. Concocting methods or data that misrepresent aspects of a research study with the intent to deceive others is called:

    a. fabrication

    b. plagiarism

    c. duplication

    d. replication

20. All individuals who make substantial contributions to a work must:

    a. be available to make additional contributions when asked to do so

    b. also contribute financially to a work

    c. be recognized as authors of that work

    d. all of the above

Key Term Word Search

```
R  H  M  C  A  F  A  N  Q  E  T  S  Y  H  P  I  W  Q  W  E  Q  A  R  O  E  G  A  F
F  M  V  Q  R  F  J  T  R  W  M  I  B  E  H  V  E  U  K  S  F  R  Z  C  W  K  N  J
B  P  K  P  I  I  Q  E  Y  E  V  C  R  D  R  F  L  N  J  Z  U  X  N  M  X  R  I  B
C  R  L  H  J  N  S  Y  J  S  S  K  O  L  D  O  A  T  D  N  P  E  J  R  X  N  N  R
N  V  V  A  K  G  M  K  N  W  Z  E  B  N  C  F  R  B  O  X  C  B  B  K  C  C  F  Z
D  Y  W  M  G  Q  E  O  B  G  Q  V  A  O  F  O  Z  I  R  I  O  W  R  C  H  H  O  P
Z  E  I  D  U  I  I  Z  C  E  Y  D  T  R  P  E  T  M  F  I  W  Z  M  K  F  Q  R  J
R  Z  B  G  J  T  A  G  N  D  N  O  D  E  C  A  D  E  E  S  C  I  O  C  O  D  M  S
F  H  J  R  P  K  T  R  L  U  R  E  R  X  C  H  N  E  E  M  L  A  C  J  M  G  E  F
F  T  S  E  I  J  N  I  I  P  R  T  F  I  N  E  E  A  R  E  A  T  T  A  Z  N  D  J
F  A  C  Q  N  E  X  S  H  S  N  E  L  I  B  S  S  T  N  A  K  U  T  I  E  O  C  V
U  E  S  I  L  I  F  C  Q  O  M  P  M  X  T  I  L  K  H  K  T  M  T  V  O  G  O  D
D  C  Z  S  T  S  R  I  M  P  E  S  V  B  I  A  A  F  D  I  K  E  A  P  R  N  N  U
N  T  R  D  E  A  E  L  N  R  J  W  G  U  E  C  N  C  E  X  C  Z  Y  Z  P  K  S  X
Z  Z  Y  V  E  N  E  G  B  G  I  F  E  W  S  R  B  A  U  Q  E  S  P  T  K  D  E  M
O  W  K  S  I  B  T  B  W  B  E  T  H  R  J  R  G  D  L  C  P  K  E  D  S  N  N  V
E  V  E  K  X  A  R  E  M  G  V  T  L  F  W  Q  X  C  C  Y  A  M  L  N  W  O  T  P
W  R  T  Y  E  N  L  T  W  W  T  L  Q  N  C  Y  C  Y  O  H  S  K  U  B  O  Y  U  E
F  P  C  J  E  Z  D  U  P  L  I  C  A  T  I  O  N  E  D  D  F  I  F  L  H  X  C  E
A  N  O  N  Y  M  I  T  Y  C  O  V  E  R  S  T  O  R  Y  E  E  F  S  Q  W  M  U  R
Q  X  M  M  F  J  J  M  G  R  E  S  P  E  C  T  F  O  R  P  E  R  S  O  N  S  Y  R
F  Q  T  R  J  U  S  T  I  C  E  I  Q  J  T  Z  R  P  B  E  A  B  W  I  P  U  R  E
Q  T  X  N  M  I  T  O  I  R  B  G  W  F  P  F  M  J  F  Z  Z  V  T  N  D  I  Q  V
K  Q  M  W  G  D  M  V  W  E  X  E  M  U  I  D  J  H  C  W  A  Q  V  E  Y  G  Q  I
V  E  P  S  C  I  E  N  T  I  F  I  C  I  N  T  E  G  R  I  T  Y  W  F  L  Y  X  E
Z  Y  R  Y  X  L  T  W  H  M  Z  U  P  M  O  L  R  R  K  R  V  C  Y  N  X  F  C  W
D  B  X  S  E  W  I  D  A  C  O  N  F  I  D  E  N  T  I  A  L  I  T  Y  K  V  R  U
V  N  R  H  X  Y  E  I  Y  I  A  M  E  P  X  X  V  M  O  A  F  D  M  C  X  N  Q  F
```

scientific integrity	beneficence	confederate
respect for persons	research ethics	cover story
justice	deception	risk-benefit analysis
informed consent	IACUC	research protocol
anonymity	replication	Nuremberg Code
plagiarism	peer review	debriefing
Belmont Report	duplication	IRB
fabrication	assent	confidentiality

ACROSS

1. a false explanation or story intended to prevent research participants from discovering the true purpose of a research study

4. identifies the actions that researchers must take to conduct responsible and moral research

7. to concoct methods or data that misrepresent aspects of a research study with the intent to deceive others

8. a type of analysis in which the researcher anticipates or weighs the risks and benefits in a study

15. the reproduction of research procedures under identical conditions for the purposes of observing the same phenomenon

17. the institutional ethics review board for human participant research

19. a procedure used by scientific journals in which a manuscript or work is sent to peers or experts in that area to review the work and determine its scientific value or worth regarding publication

20. the consent of a minor or other legally incapable person to agree to participate in research only after receiving an appropriate explanation in reasonably understandable language

21. the extent to which a researcher is honest and truthful in his or her actions, values, methods, measures, and dissemination of research

DOWN

2. an ethical principle that participants in a research study must be autonomous agents capable of making informed decisions concerning whether to participate in research

3. a strategy used by researchers in which participants are deliberately misled concerning the true purpose and nature of the research being conducted

5. a protection of individual identity in which the identity of a participant is not made available to anyone who is not directly involved in a study

6. the full disclosure to participants of the true purpose of a study; typically given at the end of a study

9. the first international code for ethical conduct in research

10. an ethical principle that it is the researcher's responsibility to minimize the potential risks and maximize the potential benefits associated with conducting a research study

11. the institutional ethics review board for animal subject research

12. an ethical principle that all participants should be treated fairly and equitably in terms of receiving the benefits and bearing the risks in research

13. the republication of original data that were previously published

14. a coresearcher or actor who pretends to be a participant in a research study for the purposes of scientific investigation

16. a protection of individual identity in which the identity of a participant remains unknown throughout a study, even to those involved in a study

18. an individual's use of someone else's ideas or work that is represented as his or her own ideas or work

Crossword Puzzle

Defining and Measuring Variables, Selecting Samples, and Choosing An Appropriate Research Design

4

Identifying Scientific Variables

CHAPTER LEARNING OBJECTIVES

1. Describe two criteria that make variables suitable for scientific investigation.

2. Delineate the need for constructs and operational definitions in research.

3. Distinguish between continuous and discrete variables and between quantitative and qualitative variables.

4. State the four scales of measurement, and provide an example for each.

5. Describe the following types of reliability: test-retest reliability, internal consistency, and interrater reliability.

6. Describe the following types of validity: face validity, construct validity, criterion-related validity, and content validity.

7. Identify the concerns of participant reactivity, experimenter bias, and sensitivity and range effects for selecting a measurement procedure.

8. Explain why the failure to replicate a result is not sufficient evidence for fraud.

9. Enter data into SPSS by placing each group in a separate column and each group in a single row (coding is required).

Chapter Summary

4.1 Criteria for Defining and Measuring Variables

To test a hypothesis using the scientific method, you must first ask the following questions: How will you observe or measure the variable? Can other people observe the variable in the same way you did? A variable that is observable is one that can be directly or indirectly measured. A variable that is replicable is one that can be observed more than once. For any variable that you measure, it should be observable and replicable.

4.2 Constructs and Operational Definitions

An operational definition defines a variable in terms of how it is measured. The reason we use operational definitions is because it minimizes ambiguity caused by observing otherwise arbitrary phenomena. Many of the behaviors and events researchers observe are actually not observed at all—not directly anyway; these types of variables are called constructs. To identify or observe a construct, we identify the observable components or **external factors** of the construct. The operational definition of a construct is the external factor of that construct that we will observe.

4.3 Types of Variables

Variables can be continuous or discrete. A **continuous variable** is measured along a continuum, meaning that continuous variables can be measured at any place beyond the decimal point. A **discrete variable**, on the other hand, is measured in whole units or categories, meaning that discrete variables are not measured along a continuum.

Variables can also be quantitative or qualitative. A **quantitative variable** varies by amount and is measured in numeric units; both continuous and discrete variables can be quantitative. A **qualitative variable** varies by class and is typically a whole number or category; only discrete variables can be qualitative.

4.4 Scales of Measurement

Four **scales of measurement** are *nominal*, *ordinal*, *interval*, and *ratio*. Numbers on a **nominal scale** identify something or someone; they provide no additional information. An **ordinal scale** is one that conveys order alone, such as rank. An **interval scale** is equidistant but has no **true zero** (0 does not mean the absence of the phenomena being measured). **Ratio scales** are similar to interval scales in that scores are distributed in equal units (i.e., equidistant). Yet, unlike interval scales, a distribution of scores on a ratio scale has a true zero. In science, researchers often go out of their way to measure variables on a ratio scale because ratio scales are the most informative scales of measurement.

4.5 Reliability of a Measurement

Reliability is the consistency, stability, or repeatability of one or more measures or observations. Three types of reliability are the following:

Test-retest reliability is the extent to which a measure or observation is consistent or stable at two points in time. To demonstrate test-retest reliability we can give participants the same measure at two times. The more consistent each participant's score from Time 1 to Time 2, the higher the test-retest reliability.

Internal consistency is a measure of reliability used to determine the extent to which multiple items used to measure the same variable or construct are related. To demonstrate internal consistency we must show that scores or items for a single test or measure are related using a statistic called *Cronbach's alpha* (see Chapter 13).

Interrater reliability (IRR) is a measure for the extent to which two or more raters of the same behavior or event are in agreement with what they observed. To demonstrate IRR we must show that scores or ratings are similar across raters using a statistic called *Cohen's kappa* (see Chapter 13).

4.6 Validity of a Measurement

Validity is the extent to which a measurement for a variable or construct measures what it is purported or intended to measure. Four types of validity are the following:

Face validity is the extent to which a measure for a variable or construct appears to measure what it is purported to measure. This type of validity is a quick judgment of what we think the measure is measuring at "face value."

Construct validity is the extent to which an operational definition for a variable or construct is actually measuring that variable or construct.

Criterion-related validity is the extent to which scores obtained on some measure can be used to infer or predict a criterion or expected outcome. Four types of criterion-related validity are predictive validity, concurrent validity, convergent validity, and discriminant validity.

Content validity is the extent to which the items or contents of a measure adequately represent all the features of the construct being measured. To demonstrate content validity we must show that the items we use to measure a construct are representative of the construct as a whole.

4.7 Selecting a Measurement Procedure

Four potential concerns that researchers should be aware of and control are the following:

Participant reactivity is the reaction or response participants have when they know they are being observed or measured. To avoid participant reactivity, reassure confidentiality, use deception when ethical, measure less obvious variables, and minimize **demand characteristics**.

Experimenter bias is the extent to which the behavior of a researcher or experimenter intentionally or unintentionally influences the results of a study. To minimize the problem of experimenter bias get a second opinion, standardize the research procedures, or conduct a **double-blind study**.

Sensitivity is the extent to which a measure can change or be different in the presence of a manipulation. A range effect can limit the sensitivity of a measure.

Range effects are limitations in the range of data measured in which scores are clustered to one extreme. To minimize range effects, perform a thorough literature review, conduct a pilot study, include manipulation checks, or use multiple measures.

4.8 Ethics in Focus: Replication as a Gauge for Fraud?

Any measure consists of a true score and a possible error that causes variability in that measure: Behavioral Measure = True Score + Error. An *error* is any influence in the response of a participant that can cause variability in his or her response. The potential errors of a measure are often not well understood and therefore difficult to anticipate. For this reason, when a result is not replicated, always consider first potential sources of error in measurement that can likely explain why a result was not replicated.

4.9 SPSS in Focus: Entering and Coding Data

Using SPSS, all variables are defined in the **Variable View** tab. Values recorded for each variable are listed in the **Data View** tab. Data can be entered by column or by row in the Data View tab. Listing data by row requires coding the variable in the Variable View tab in the **Values column**.

Chapter Summary Organized by Learning Objective

LO 1: Describe two criteria that make variables suitable for scientific investigation.

- A variable that is observable is one that can be directly or indirectly measured. A variable that is replicable is one that can be observed more than once. To meet both criteria, you must explain how the variable was measured (observable) and under what conditions the variable was observed so that other researchers can re-create the same conditions to measure the same variable you did (replicable).

LO 2: Delineate the need for constructs and operational definitions in research.

- **Constructs** are conceptual variables that are known to exist but cannot be directly observed. To observe a construct, we identify the observable components or **external factors** of the construct. The operational definition of a construct is the external factor or how we will observe the construct.

LO 3: Distinguish between continuous and discrete variables and between quantitative and qualitative variables.

- A **continuous variable** is measured along a continuum, whereas a **discrete variable** is measured in whole units or categories. Continuous but not discrete variables are measured at any place beyond the decimal point.
- A **quantitative variable** varies by amount, whereas a **qualitative variable** varies by class. Continuous and discrete variables can be quantitative, whereas qualitative variables can only be discrete.

LO 4: State the four scales of measurement, and provide an example for each.

- The **scales of measurement** refer to how the properties of numbers can change with different uses. They are characterized by three properties: order, differences, and ratios. There are four scales of measurement: **nominal, ordinal, interval,** and **ratio.** Nominal values are typically coded (e.g., seasons, gender); ordinal values indicate order alone (e.g., rankings, grade level); interval values have equidistant scales and no true zero (e.g., rating scale values, temperature); and ratio values are equidistant and have a true zero (e.g., weight, height).

LO 5: Describe the following types of reliability: test-retest reliability, internal consistency, and interrater reliability.

- **Reliability** is the consistency, stability, or repeatability of one or more measures or observations. Three types of reliability are test-retest reliability, internal consistency, and interrater reliability.
- **Test-retest reliability** is the extent to which a measure or observation is consistent or stable at two points in time. **Internal consistency** is a measure of reliability used to determine the extent to which multiple items used to measure the same variable are related. **Interrater reliability** is a measure for the extent to which two or more raters of the same behavior or event are in agreement with what they observed.

LO 6: Describe the following types of validity: face validity, construct validity, criterion-related validity, and content validity.

- The **validity** of a measurement is the extent to which a measurement for a variable or construct measures what it is purported or intended to measure. Four types of validity are face validity, construct validity, criterion-related validity, and content validity.
- **Face validity** is the extent to which a measure for a variable or construct appears to measure what it is intended to measure. **Construct validity** is the extent to which an operational definition for a variable or construct is actually measuring that variable or construct. **Criterion-related validity** is the extent to which scores obtained on some measure can be used to infer or predict a criterion or expected outcome. Four types of criterion-related validity are predictive validity, concurrent validity, convergent validity, and discriminant validity. **Content validity** is the extent to which the items or contents of a measure adequately represent all the features of the construct being measured.

LO 7: Identify the concerns of participant reactivity, experimenter bias, and sensitivity and range effects for selecting a measurement procedure.

- **Participant reactivity** is the reaction participants have when they know they are being observed or measured. To minimize participant reactivity, you can reassure confidentiality, use deception when ethical, measure less obvious variables, and minimize **demand characteristics.**
- **Experimenter bias** is the extent to which the behavior of a researcher influences the results of a study. To minimize experimenter bias, you can get a second opinion, standardize the research procedures, and conduct a **double-blind study.**

- The **sensitivity** of a measure is the extent to which it changes in the presence of a manipulation. A **range effect** is when scores on a measure all fall extremely high (**ceiling effect**) or low (**floor effect**) on the scale. To maximize the sensitivity of a measure and minimize possible range effects, you can perform a thorough literature review, conduct a **pilot study**, include **manipulation checks**, and use multiple measures.

<u>LO 8</u>: Explain why the failure to replicate a result is not sufficient evidence for fraud.

- Researchers can be subjected to criticism and even accused of fraud if other researchers reconduct their research procedures from an original study and do not obtain the same results as they did. However, a failure to replicate a result could be due to statistical error and not fraud. Any measure consists of a true score and a possible error that causes variability in that measure. An *error* is any influence in the response of a participant that can cause variability in his or her response. The error that causes variability, and not fraud, therefore could explain why a result was not replicated.

<u>LO 9</u>: Enter data into SPSS by placing each group in a separate column and each group in a single row (coding is required).

- SPSS can be used to enter and define variables. All variables are defined in the **Variable View** tab. The values recorded for each variable are listed in the **Data View** tab. Data can be entered by column or by row in the Data View tab. Listing data by row requires coding the variable. Variables are coded in the Variable View tab in the **Values column** (for more details, see Section 4.9 in the book).

Tips and Cautions for Students

Operational definitions. To identify the operational definition of a variable, ask the question "How is it being measured?" If the definition has the answer, then it is an operational definition; if not, then it is not an operational definition. For example, we can define hunger as a state or feeling of physiological need. How is hunger being measured? This definition does not answer that question, so it is not an operational definition. As an alternative, we could define hunger as the duration of time in minutes between meals. How is hunger being measured? It is measured as a length of time in minutes. Hence, this is an operational definition for hunger. Use this strategy when trying to correctly develop and identify operational definitions.

Scales of measurement. When determining the scale of measurement a variable is measured on, first assess whether the variable is categorical. If it is categorical, then it is likely on a nominal scale. If it is a ranked value or a value that indicates only that one value is larger than another, then it is likely on an ordinal scale. Interval scale measures are typically rating scales in which participants indicate their level of agreement or opinion regarding items in a survey. To distinguish an interval scale from a ratio scale, assess whether the scale has a true zero. If 0 indicates the absence of the variable you are measuring, then it has a true zero and is on a ratio scale; if not, then it does not have a true zero and is on an interval scale.

Validity versus reliability. Keep in mind that reliability indicates consistency (typically over time); it does not indicate the accuracy of a measure. For example, a clock that is 10 minutes off will consistently be 10 minutes off. In this case, the clock is reliably inaccurate. Instead, validity indicates accuracy. In this example, a valid measure of time gives the correct time. Hence, a valid and reliable clock gives the correct time (valid) over time (reliable). You can apply this reasoning to distinguish between reliability and validity for any type of variable that is measured in the behavioral sciences.

Practice Quiz

1. For a variable to be suitable for scientific study, it must be:
   a. inadequate
   b. observable and measurable
   c. important
   d. observable from space

2. A researcher stages a traffic signal to turn green and have a confederate not move. The researcher measures patience as the duration of time it takes the driver behind the confederate to honk his or her horn after a light turns green. What construct was measured in this example?
   a. traffic
   b. driving accuracy
   c. patience
   d. duration of time

3. For Question 2, what is the external factor for the variable that was measured?
   a. the duration of time it takes the driver to honk his or her horn
   b. patience while driving
   c. the traffic signal
   d. the make and model of the car

4. An external factor is:
   a. a factor that is outside
   b. an operational definition for a construct
   c. used only with factorial research designs
   d. not associated with the measurement of constructs

5. A researcher states the following hypothesis: The aroma of coffee can wake someone from sleep in the morning. The mechanism in this hypothesis is _____, and the outcome is _____.
   a. coffee; morning time
   b. aroma of coffee; morning time
   c. waking from sleep; coffee
   d. aroma from coffee; waking from sleep

6. The time in seconds it takes a participant to complete a cognitive task is recorded. In this example, the measurement is for a:

   a. continuous variable

   b. discrete variable

   c. qualitative variable

   d. both b and c

7. The number of students enrolled in a research methods class is recorded. In this example, the measurement is for a:

   a. continuous variable

   b. discrete variable

   c. qualitative variable

   d. both b and c

8. A researcher measures the income in dollars of athletes for five years following their retirements. In this example, the measurement is for a:

   a. discrete variable

   b. continuous variable

   c. quantitative variable

   d. both b and c

9. Numbers can have the following properties:

   a. order

   b. differences

   c. ratio

   d. all of the above

10. Nominal data are often converted to numeric values using what procedure?

    a. randomization

    b. coding

    c. manipulation

    d. numbering

11. Ordinal data convey what information?

    a. order and rank only

    b. values with a true zero

    c. information about someone or something, nothing more

    d. none of the above

12. Measures of temperature, latitude, longitude, and Likert scale ratings are all examples of what type of scale of measurement?

    a. nominal

    b. ordinal

   c. interval

   d. ratio

13. Researchers often go out of their way to measure variables on which scale of measurement?

   a. nominal

   b. ordinal

   c. interval

   d. ratio

14. A researcher measures the extent to which 10 survey items all consistently measure the same construct within the same survey. Which type of reliability was this researcher measuring?

   a. test-retest reliability

   b. internal consistency

   c. interrater reliability

15. Two friends watch a sporting event in which a penalty is called on the home team. One friend agrees with the penalty call; the other friend disagrees that the call was good. What type of reliability can we say is low among these friends?

   a. test-retest reliability

   b. internal consistency

   c. interrater reliability

16. A health psychologist asks a sample of participants who are obese to rank their favorite foods before and after a buffet-style meal and measures the extent to which participant rankings are consistent at both times. Which type of reliability was this researcher measuring?

   a. test-retest reliability

   b. internal consistency

   c. interrater reliability

17. If a measure for a variable or construct "looks like" it will measure what it is intended to measure, then the construct has high:

   a. construct validity

   b. criterion-related validity

   c. content validity

   d. face validity

18. Predictive validity, concurrent validity, convergent validity, and discriminant validity are all different types of:

   a. construct validity

   b. criterion-related validity

   c. content validity

   d. face validity

19. A researcher measures depression using a multidimensional assessment that encompasses all symptoms of the disorder. For this reason, the researcher likely has high _____ validity.

    a. face

    b. content

    c. construct

    d. criterion-related

20. Participant expectancy, evaluation apprehension, and participant reluctance are all types of:

    a. participant reactivity

    b. experimenter bias

    c. reliability

    d. sampling

21. During a study, a researcher notices that a participant is being shy and is not forthcoming in her responses. In this example, the researcher is concerned the participant is displaying which type of participant reactivity?

    a. participant expectancy

    b. evaluation apprehension

    c. participant reluctance

22. Which of the following can often lead to experimenter bias?

    a. random sampling

    b. participant consent

    c. expectancy effects

    d. none of the above

23. Which of the following strategies can help minimize the problem of experimenter bias?

    a. get a second opinion about a research plan

    b. standardize the research procedures

    c. conduct a double-blind study

    d. all of the above

24. A measure that can change quite readily in the presence of a manipulation is called:

    a. a weak measure

    b. a significant measure

    c. a sensitive measure

    d. a cooperative measure

25. Which of the following is *not* an example of a range effect?

    a. floor effect

    b. ceiling effect

    c. expectancy effect

26. An *error* is any influence in the response of a participant that:

    a. can cause variability in the participant's response

    b. reflects the true score of the participant

    c. is a deliberate attempt to mislead a researcher

    d. is coerced by a researcher

Key Term Word Search

```
N U C W I F H M C O I W L C R L G F U B I W C G G X C B C D S I X K Z F X L R
U B Z O G N F X K V N S B Y P N F W S I U X Y X K K E V G K M A C U F H C W W
Z O O K N L T B R P N X O C I D S T X F J T J T V A I Z G B B L T Q K T G E I
Y W O B W S A E M I P R S D M R C H E U I C U X M S L F W S F F Q G Y X L F G
Q G R A G S T P R H O O O J S E J E R V W Q H D I Y I V L P D T X Q L B O L Y
E N F V T R Z R N R W C N T F A L M I Q Z F Z V U Y N M N A I T O J A K C R A
G R R C G C A T U V A J I F E B V T A E U Y J Z K W G E J N K M Y I E V L B K
J P P F F Q D T H C F T E N A S C H O U Q A M I U O E Q J W S D R V Y N O S A
I J E Y X U R M I C T Y E I T A T X Y U Z M L Z U W F V W V O A X W Q Y D F G
B E G O D Q E C S O C V R R E E N R H N B L W I P P F N Z Z V C H C Q X T C Z
C Y O G P K W I O N S A A R R B R P E W V T Z X T G E D B E O F G K L S E Z I
T H E S M U J W A S V C T L P E X N M T D I R K Z A C V V N P W C X I J T R X
A T K E Z J P T L S C N A E I I L O A R E N V R O C T I A U K E N Y D V L E G
G S C A Q B C S U M A A B L C D Z I F L I S Z S T E T I L L H P T F Z C X L J
C C V F H E H O O P R A P L E I I J A X C O T P H A V N V C I I S X A X L I K
Z M A A P X U U I X K D P R K C L T V B J O T R T E Z K N E D D E H W Z V A O
F I H X G N X C E V C I Q H F H O G Y I I T N I E G J O B I V D I M F M I B R
X F E G I A I D V V I S S S I L Y N N S I L T S L L I S L M E A P T Q J C I D
A H X T X T E E A D N C E E H T F S S O T N I Q I T I A R L E J R U Y Q I L I
E K N M R N B M L V T R T N K O L L F T A L B T A S V A B A V Z V I H J Y I N
R O Q A F H C A U S E E S S K C O Y B U R P E L Y E T A B Y K J J T A R Y T A
C O P B M W Q N A D R T C I I F O V Q Z A U U I C T I E D I Z A P A H B I Y L
S D D J O Z S D T O V E I T Y S R N V W G P C A X R V U N P L G L Z Y D L O S
D W D V G G R C I U A V H I M U E M V I I U F T A U T H A C J I T P Y S R E C
U N W X X Q W H O B L A U V P Z F B K N E J I V A S D A H M Y Q T C U Q L J A
G U M S E H S A N L S R B I R M F S A R U I W O T D Y H V T Y B V Y G L X U L
O B R G J J Q R A E C I Y T N W E M P E W L L O G V C K W X K M N U F M N X E
B A E V R Z L A P B A A L Y B R C K Z L N F L Y C C M M J C X Z O W I X I W A
P X S A T H R C P L L B M D N F T S G X B I I T Q K N J Q W J X M Z K V J F N
M K I P C K K T R I E L P Q O I Z L S W P A C O N T E N T V A L I D I T Y H L
D R R X I A Y E E N E E E J R E X P E R I M E N T E R B I A S P N X C E O O F
H Z C E R X M R H D A Z W G J X A X C M U L Q C H D E S I B W L A K O T V K C
J E T Y O Y Z I E S G P A R T I C I P A N T R E L U C T A N C E L H B I G E I
P H Y A J T V S N T I V W K R R R V P F B F W Y U Y K A V K K V S O R P M G C
I W O B F K L T S U C I N R O M J Q B B F F B G Q W B Q E Q T L C K H O A H D
F Z E L Q V R I I D G R A N G E E F F E C T H S G S Z B C W D U A N L W B J Y
M M U U H S F C O Y B V R B P S P F G W T D X O Z M T H X S F H L G W Z V Y C
W F X J H J V S N V A N K X J O Q Z K X B T L F C S N Y V G C X E B L E Y K Z
A E D Z E P D J B C R I T E R I O N R E L A T E D V A L I D I T Y C H P J C M
```

coding	sensitivity	double-blind study	quantitative variable
validity	face validity	experimenter bias	demand characteristics
variable	nominal scale	construct validity	interrater reliability
construct	ordinal scale	expectancy effects	participant reactivity
pilot study	ceiling effect	manipulation check	participant reluctance
ratio scale	interval scale	continuous variable	test-retest reliability
floor effect	content validity	internal consistency	evaluation apprehension
range effect	discrete variable	qualitative variable	criterion-related validity
reliability			

ACROSS

2. a scale of measurement that conveys order or rank only

3. a conceptual variable that is known to exist but cannot be directly observed

5. an observable behavior or event of a construct that is presumed to reflect the construct itself

7. a limitation in the range of data measured in which scores are clustered to one extreme

8. the extent to which a measure can change or be different in the presence of a manipulation

9. a small preliminary study used to determine the extent to which a manipulation or measure will show an effect of interest

10. any value or characteristic that can change or vary from one person to another or from one situation to another

13. preconceived ideas or expectations regarding how participants should behave or what participants are capable of doing

15. a validity measurement for the extent to which scores obtained on some measure can be used to infer or predict a criterion or expected outcome

16. the procedure of converting a categorical variable to numeric values

17. a scale of measurement that has a true zero and is equidistant

19. a scale of measurement in which a number is assigned to represent something or someone

20. a type of variable that varies by value or amount

22. a type of variable that varies by class or category

23. a scale of measurement in which the value 0 truly indicates nothing

24. a measure of reliability that indicates the extent to which two or more raters of the same behavior or event are in agreement with what they observed

DOWN

1. a validity measurement for the extent to which the items or contents of a measure adequately represent all the features of the construct being measured

4. the consistency, stability, or repeatability of one or more measures or observations

6. a measure of reliability that indicates the extent to which a measure or observation is consistent or stable at two points in time

11. a scale of measurement that has no true zero and is distributed in equal units

12. a validity measurement for the extent to which a measure for a variable or construct appears to measure what it is purported to measure

14. a type of variable that is measured in whole units or categories that are not distributed along a continuum

16. a validity measurement for the extent to which an operational definition for a variable or construct is actually measuring that variable or construct

18. a type of variable that is measured along a continuum at any place beyond the decimal point

21. the extent to which a measurement for a variable or construct measures what it is purported or intended to measure

Crossword Puzzle

5

Sampling From Populations

CHAPTER LEARNING OBJECTIVES

1. Explain why researchers select samples that are representative of a population of interest.

2. Distinguish between *subjects* and *participants* as terms used to describe those who are subjected to procedures in a research study.

3. Distinguish between probability sampling methods and nonprobability sampling methods.

4. Delineate two nonprobability sampling methods: convenience sampling and quota sampling.

5. Delineate four probability sampling methods: simple random sampling, stratified random sampling, systematic sampling, and cluster sampling.

6. Define and explain sampling error and the standard error of the mean.

7. Define and explain sampling bias and nonresponse bias.

8. Identify potential ethical concerns related to sampling from subject pools in human participant research.

9. Compute an estimate for the standard error of the mean, and compute the one-sample *t* test using SPSS.

Chapter Summary

5.1 Why Do Researchers Select Samples?

Researchers select samples mostly because they do not have access to all individuals in a population. So researchers use data gathered from samples (a portion of individuals from the population) to make inferences concerning a population. Hence, researchers select samples to learn more about populations of interest to them.

5.2 Subjects, Participants, and Sampling Methods

Using the APA guidelines provided in the code of conduct, we refer to humans as **participants** and nonhuman groups as **subjects**. The term *subject* is also used to identify the names of research designs.

The **target population** is all members of a group of interest to a researcher. The target population of interest to a researcher is typically very large—so large that we can rarely select samples directly from a population. For this reason, most often researchers select samples from an **accessible population**, which is a portion of the target population that can be clearly identified and directly sampled from. If researchers want to generalize the results they observe in a sample to those in the target population, then they need to make certain that the sample is representative of the target population—that is, that the sample has characteristics that resemble those in the target population.

The methods that researchers use to select samples from one or more populations can be categorized as **probability sampling** (when the probability of selecting each participant is known) and **nonprobability sampling** (when the probability of selecting each participant is unknown). Because it is often the case that we do not know the probability of selecting each participant, nonprobability sampling methods are most often used in the behavioral sciences.

5.3 Methods of Sampling: Nonprobability Sampling

Two types of nonprobability sampling methods are convenience sampling and quota sampling.

Convenience sampling is a method of sampling in which subjects or participants are selected for a research study based on how easy or convenient it is to reach or access them and based on their availability to participate. A drawback of convenience sampling is that it does not ensure that a sample will be representative of the target population because the sample was selected on a "first come, first served" kind of approach.

Quota sampling is a method of sampling in which subjects or participants are selected based on known or unknown criteria or characteristics in the target population. Using *simple quota sampling*, an equal number of subjects or participants are selected based on a characteristic or demographic that they share. Using *proportionate quota sampling*, subjects or participants are selected such that known characteristics or demographics are proportionately represented in the sample.

5.4 Methods of Sampling: Probability Sampling

Four probability sampling methods are simple random sampling, systematic sampling, simple and proportionate stratified sampling, and cluster sampling.

Simple random sampling is a method of sampling subjects and participants such that all individuals in a population have an equal chance of being selected and are selected using sampling with replacement. Although simple random sampling leads to a random sample, when the selection of participants is left completely to chance, this can also lead to the selection of a sample that is not representative of the population.

Stratified random sampling is a method of sampling in which a population is divided into subgroups or strata; participants are then selected from each subgroup using simple random sampling, and combined into one overall sample. Stratified random sampling can involve selecting an equal number of participants in each subgroup, called **simple stratified random sampling**, or selecting a different proportion of participants in each subgroup, called **proportionate stratified random sampling**. Stratified random sampling is similar to quota sampling.

Using **systematic sampling**, a researcher randomly selects the first participant and then selects every nth person until all persons have been selected. Hence, the researcher uses simple random sampling to select the first participant, then uses a systematic sampling procedure to select all remaining participants by selecting every nth person.

Cluster sampling is a method of sampling in which subgroups or clusters of individuals are identified in a population, and then a portion of clusters that are representative of the population are selected such that all individuals in the selected clusters are included in the sample. All clusters that are not selected are omitted from the sample. Cluster sampling is different from stratified random sampling in that some subgroups are omitted from a sample using cluster sampling, whereas a random sample of individuals in each subgroup is included in a sample using stratified random sampling.

5.5 Sampling Error and Standard Error of the Mean

Sampling error is the extent to which sample means selected from the same population differ from one another. This difference, which occurs by chance, is measured by the **standard error of the mean**. An implication of sampling error is that two random samples selected by chance from the same population can produce very different scores or outcomes.

5.6 SPSS in Focus: Estimating the Standard Error of the Mean

SPSS can be used to compute an estimate of the standard error of the mean using the **Analyze, Descriptive Statistics,** and **Descriptives** options in the menu bar.

5.7 Potential Biases in Sampling

Selecting a sample can be prone to bias either due to the fault of the researcher, *sampling bias*, or due to the fault of the participants, *nonresponse bias*.

Sampling bias occurs when sampling procedures employed in a study favor certain individuals or groups over others. The implication of sampling bias is that the sample is not representative of the entire population, but instead representative of only the groups that are overrepresented in the sample.

Nonresponse bias occurs when participants choose not to respond to a survey or request to participate in a study. Individuals in a population who respond to surveys or postings asking for participants are likely systematically different from those who do not. Hence, nonresponse bias could result in a sample that is representative of only the portion of the population that is willing to respond to a survey or request to participate in a study.

5.8 Ethics in Focus: Subject Pools

Subject pools are policies established by a college or research institution that requires students to participate in academic research. To address possible ethical concerns, these institutions also ensure that subject pools are filled only with students willing to volunteer as participants in research by following two rules: Class grades are never contingent on actual participation in a research study, and students are given alternative options to receive a grade.

5.9 SPSS in Focus: Identifying New Populations Using the One-Sample *t* Test

The one-sample *t* test is computed using the **Analyze, Compare Means,** and **One-Sample T Test** options in the menu bar.

Chapter Summary Organized by Learning Objective

<u>LO 1</u>: Explain why researchers select samples that are representative of a population of interest.

- Researchers select samples from a population to learn more about the population from which the samples were selected. If researchers want to generalize the results they observe in a sample to those in the target population, then they need to make certain that the sample is representative of the target population. A **representative sample** is a sample that has characteristics that resemble those in the target population.

<u>LO 2</u>: Distinguish between *subjects* and *participants* as terms used to describe those who are subjected to procedures in a research study.

- The term **participant** is used to describe a human who volunteers to be subjected to the procedures in a research study. The term **subject** is used to describe a nonhuman that is subjected to procedures in a research study and is used to identify the names of research designs.

<u>LO 3</u>: Distinguish between probability sampling methods and nonprobability sampling methods.

- **Probability sampling** is a category of sampling in which a sample is selected directly from the target population; **nonprobability sampling** is a category of sampling in which a sample is selected from the accessible population. Sampling directly from the target population using probability sampling is possible in situations in which the exact probability of selecting each individual in a target population is known. However, it is rare that researchers know the exact probability of selecting each individual in a target population, so nonprobability sampling methods are most commonly used to select samples in behavioral research.

LO 4: Delineate two nonprobability sampling methods: convenience sampling and quota sampling.

- A **convenience sample**, as indicated in the name, is selected out of convenience or ease, meaning that participants are selected based on their availability to participate. A drawback of convenience sampling is that it does not ensure that a sample will be representative of the target population. To make a convenience sample representative of a target population of interest, researchers can use quota sampling, or they can use a combined sampling method.
- **Quota sampling** is a method of sampling in which subjects or participants are selected based on the characteristics they share in order to ensure that these characteristics are represented in a sample.
  - o For situations in which little is known about the characteristics of a target population, researchers use **simple quota sampling**.
  - o For situations in which certain characteristics are known in the population, researchers use **proportionate quota sampling**.

LO 5: Delineate four probability sampling methods: simple random sampling, stratified random sampling, systematic sampling, and cluster sampling.

- **Simple random sampling** is a method of sampling subjects and participants such that all individuals in a population have an equal chance of being selected and are selected using sampling with replacement.
- **Stratified random sampling** is a method of sampling in which a population is divided into subgroups or strata; participants are selected from each subgroup using simple random sampling and combined into one overall sample. We can select an equal number of participants from each subgroup (**simple stratified random sampling**) or a number of participants from each subgroup that is proportionate with those in the population (**proportionate stratified random sampling**).
- **Systematic sampling** is a method of sampling in which the first participant is randomly selected, and then every nth person is systematically selected until all participants have been selected.
- **Cluster sampling** is a method of sampling in which subgroups or clusters of individuals are identified in a population, and then a portion of clusters that are representative of the population are selected such that all individuals in the selected clusters are included in the sample. All clusters that are not selected are omitted from the sample.

LO 6: Define and explain sampling error and the standard error of the mean.

- The extent to which sample means selected from the same population differ from one another is called **sampling error**. This difference, which occurs by chance, is measured by the **standard error of the mean**, which is the standard error or distance that sample mean values can deviate from the value of the population mean.

LO 7: Define and explain sampling bias and nonresponse bias.

- **Sampling bias** is a bias in sampling in which the sampling procedures employed in a study favor certain individuals or groups over others, whereas **nonresponse bias** is a bias in sampling in which a number of participants in one or more groups choose not to respond to a survey or request to participate in a study. Both biases can result in the selection of samples that are not representative of the population.

LO 8: Identify potential ethical concerns related to sampling from "subject pools" in human participant research.

- The creation of subject pools could place the burden of participation too heavily on the population of college students. Two reasons why this is not the case is because class grades are never contingent on actual participation in a research study, and students are given alternative options to receive a grade.

LO 9: Compute an estimate for the standard error of the mean and compute the one-sample t test using SPSS.

- An estimate for the standard error is computed in SPSS using the **Analyze, Descriptive Statistics,** and **Descriptives** options in the menu bar. These actions will bring up a dialog box that will allow you to identify your variable, select **Options,** and choose the **S.E. mean** option to compute an estimate of the standard error (for more details, see Section 5.6 in the book).
- The one-sample t test is computed in SPSS using the **Analyze, Compare Means,** and **One-Sample T Test** options in the menu bar. These actions will display a dialog box that allows you to identify the variable, enter the comparison value for the test, and run the test (for more details, see Section 5.9 in the book).

Tips and Cautions for Students

Samples versus target and accessible populations. Sampling is the process of selecting participants for a study in such a way that the participants selected have characteristics that represent those in the target population. In much of the chapter we discussed selecting from accessible populations, meaning a portion of the target population that can be clearly identified and directly sampled from. However, when we do know about characteristics in the target population, and/or select samples from an accessible population, we can use probability sampling methods to ensure that characteristics identified in the target population will also be represented or included in the sample that is selected from a given population. In this way, we can draw conclusions about a target population even when we select a sample from an accessible population, if a probability sampling method is used to select participants to the sample.

Standard error. Standard error is really a statistical concept used as a measure of error or variability not explained by a treatment or manipulation. In terms of sampling, note that two random samples selected from the same population can produce very different scores or outcomes. Hence, standard error indicates that characteristics in a sample can vary from those in the population—the more variability that is measured in a sample, the larger the standard error tends to be.

Practice Quiz

1. Which of the following correctly distinguishes a sample from a population?

   a. A population of 20 participants was selected from a sample of 40 people.

   b. A sample of 40 participants was selected from a population of 20 people.

   c. A sample of 20 participants was selected from a population of 40 people.

   d. both b and c

2. Participant is to subject as:

   a. human is to animal

   b. animal is to human

   c. science is to welfare

   d. welfare is to science

3. Most target populations that researchers want to sample from are:

   a. small

   b. large

   c. not interesting

   d. easily accessible

4. Which of the following describes an accessible population?

   a. a smaller group that is part of the target population

   b. the portion of the target population that can be clearly identified

   c. the portion of the target population that can be directly sampled from

   d. all of the above

5. A sample that has characteristics that resemble those in the target population is called a:

   a. biased sample

   b. random sample

   c. representative sample

   d. sampling frame

6. Why are nonprobability sampling methods more common than probability sampling methods?

    a. because it is rare that researchers know the exact probability of selecting each individual in a target population

    b. because probabilities are easy to compute and apply to issues related to sampling

    c. because the probability of selecting samples from populations is not of interest to researchers

    d. because probability sampling methods are not valuable

7. Participants selected based on their availability to participate were likely selected using which sampling method?

    a. simple random sampling

    b. convenience sampling

    c. stratified random sampling

    d. cluster sampling

8. To make a convenience sample representative of a larger target population of interest, researchers can use:

    a. quota sampling

    b. simple quota sampling

    c. proportionate quota sampling

    d. all of the above

9. Using simple random sampling:

    a. participants are selected out of convenience

    b. a systematic procedure is used to select participants

    c. all individuals in a population have an equal chance of being selected

    d. participants are selected using sampling without replacement

10. A researcher finds that the probability of selecting each participant is always the same, no matter how many participants were selected to a sample. Which type of sampling must have been used to select participants?

    a. sampling with replacement

    b. sampling without replacement

11. Stratified random sampling is most similar to what other method of sampling?

    a. systematic sampling

    b. quota sampling

    c. cluster sampling

    d. sampling error

12. A researcher has students select a mock jury of 12 students from the class of 100 students using systematic sampling. Which of the following is an example of how the jury could be selected using systematic sampling?

    a. Each juror is selected at random by placing all student names in a hat and selecting all 12 names at random using sampling with replacement.

    b. All students are listed in a master file that is organized in a random order. The first juror is selected at random from that list, and then every other student on the list is selected until 12 total jurors have been selected

    c. Each juror is selected at random by placing all student names in a hat and selecting all 12 names at random using sampling without replacement.

    d. Students are asked to volunteer, and the first 12 students to raise their hand are selected to be jurors.

13. Cluster sampling involves sampling all individuals in a selected portion of subgroups or clusters in the population. Any subgroups or clusters not selected are:

    a. included in the sample at a later stage

    b. not important subgroups in the population

    c. eventually excluded from the population

    d. simply left out of the sample

14. Which of the following is a measure of sampling error?

    a. nonresponse bias

    b. sampling bias

    c. standard error of the mean

    d. the population mean

15. One way to reduce standard error is to:

    a. decrease sample size

    b. increase sample size

16. What type of bias specifically results from sampling procedures employed in a study favoring certain individuals or groups over others?

    a. sampling bias

    b. citation bias

    c. standard error

    d. publication bias

17. Which of the following can result in a sample that is not representative of the population from which it was selected?

    a. selection bias

    b. sampling bias

   c. nonresponse bias

   d. all of the above

18. Selecting a sample can be prone to bias either due to the fault of the researcher or due to the fault of the participants. Which of the following is associated with bias due to the fault of the participants?

   a. selection bias

   b. sampling bias

   c. nonresponse bias

   d. publication bias

19. To ensure that the creation of subject pools for research is ethical, which policy is included to ensure that only students who are willing to volunteer for research are selected from these subject pools?

   a. Class grades are never contingent on actual participation in a research study.

   b. Students are given alternative options to receive a grade.

   c. both a and b

   d. None of the above; no policies have ever been established.

20. A common parametric test statistic used in research aimed at identifying new populations is called the:

   a. one-sample t test

   b. two-sample t test

   c. standard error test

   d. group identity test

Key Term Word Search

```
F P E F L I R E L E U W F W U C M X S H G P G B B C J B A S E B F O P H
O T H C N X E D Q T A P N B L E T S S N Q T C G W G Y P A E S C W Y Q D
S U Q A E D Q W K V C B O Q Z X S B I R Z L S N O X I I F H P U Y S D Z
A I X P K S U B J E C T N Q D A G L E J T B O K A X B R C W A Y C A H V
M P O Q N O A B N J W J P A I N P B E D N I W N F G T M D M K I F M M B
P X H V P D K U G A F C X B I M D A H C T Z T F N B K P F E I A Y P Y R
L H F M G L J B M N X D E L A H U L G A X F P I Y U G R T R X S X L L P
I S D O A Z V Y K Z P S P S V G K E L W H I L W Y N Y I O N T Y K I R O
N C S W H E W H J C N M E X R Q H U I C M P C F I Q T R O T Z C C N V P
G K Q L I C D D F O A C P C V E P F I N M A Z L R X R G W Q J B L G W U
W F C W D A Z M P S N G W E H O P Z D A H F P T V E F G L O O W U W Y B
I T Y G O A V S A E X Z U C P X J R S J Q M U N D R A T B Q U S S I N S
T A B M T N E T I N E V X E F V U O E L A U K R X M U J Y R W E T T A T
H R T B G R O N L S T A L J I J Q G P S H A A X L D X G K E X L E H H R
O G C S N U E I H J A B H U B H Q J Y C E D N J A J F C Y O I E R R K A
U E Y O Q V G J K K I M S K H K I T H B N N P H G L B Q V T F C S E Q T
T T N W N P M W X S Q Q P I Q H I F V A U Z T O L A F L M F V T A P O I
R P A O S B Y G S L Z J J L M L H O T H D C E A M B Y F H T Q I M L S F
E O C J F Q F E G F J I X E I P H S N A X M T R T V F E Y P J O P A M I
P P Z H C V C E S I O O U B C N L S V E M N H G P I X H D K K N L C K E
L U K F L C F X B A H E A M X S G E Z Z S Z U G Q E V W N J K B I E D D
A L O B A H U T I T M B L M N A Y F R S T A T O P R R E J R B I N M M R
C A H P D P C V B C O P G K K B K Z R A Q P M O A M Y V S O T A G E G A
E T T G Y U N B E R S Z L V O T F H N A N A I P K A C Q R A Q S Y N J N
M I Y V E Z S K P E M K M I Q M W O G E M D L J L M V B I Y M C X T N D
E O L U K I B N K G K I X D N J K N U C K E O I T E X M G B O P K O O O
N N S R Q A O L T R E N A U G G K I Y E Q K I M D B T N F L B Y L T Y M
T A G D S N D Y B C N Q U H B L E C D B O U O S S M H T F A S I J E K S
M O J V O N D T E Q R D M T Y S Z R L I N Y A N O A Q F E P A R W Z B A
L D V I Y E E Q O D V J H N G I U F R Q K Q F V V Z M N R S Z F N N A M
M C J B M C C G X V E Q I W H Q G J T O H B C N A J M P F G T S D J U P
W P A R T I C I P A N T I G F B J F T S R V Y W P T J Z L S N E N G P L
K I C K C H D V M M Z F M V L L J B P B P B Z Q A I Z N M I I V L G J I
L H Z U Z A N W T J C Q H J L U K Q G B Q O K S D E J H V X N Y S X O N
R C P R O B A B I L I T Y S A M P L I N G Z A P J S O Y C C V G O J Y G
I X W L T U U U B B D C S Y S T E M A T I C S A M P L I N G A F W U G C
```

sampling without replacement
accessible population
convenience sampling
probability sampling
simple random sampling
nonresponse bias
cluster sampling
sampling frame

sampling error
representative sample
sampling with replacement
one-sample *t* test
selection bias
sampling bias
target population

quota sampling
subject
participant
stratified random sampling
systematic sampling
standard error
nonprobability sampling

ACROSS

2. a bias in sampling in which a number of participants in one or more groups choose not to respond to a survey or request to participate in a study

4. a category of sampling in which a sample is selected directly from the target population

7. a type of sampling in which subjects or participants are selected for a research study based on how easy or convenient it is to reach or access them

9. a group of accessible and available participants for a research study often created using policies that require college students to participate in academic research, typically as a condition for receiving grades or credits in introductory-level classes

10. a statistical procedure used to test hypotheses concerning the mean of interval or ratio data in a single population with an unknown variance

12. the portion of the target population that can be clearly identified and directly sampled from

14. a bias in sampling in which the sampling procedures employed in a study favor certain individuals or groups over others

15. a type of sample in which the characteristics of individuals or items in the sample resemble those in a target population of interest

16. a method of sampling in which the first participant is selected using simple random sampling, and then every *n*th person is selected until all participants have been selected

17. a term used to describe any human who volunteers to be subjected to the procedures in a research study

18. a method of sampling in which a population is divided into subgroups, then participants are selected from each subgroup using simple random sampling and combined into one overall sample

19. sampling _____ replacement, or a nonrandom sampling strategy in which each individual selected is not replaced before the next selection

20. a method of sampling in which subgroups or clusters of individuals are identified in a population, and then a portion of clusters that are representative of the population are selected such that all individuals in the selected clusters are included in the sample

DOWN

1. the extent to which sample means selected from the same population differ from one another

3. a term used to describe any non-human that is subjected to procedures in a research study and to identify the names of research designs

5. the type of population that constitutes all members of a group of interest to a researcher

6. sampling _____ replacement, or a strategy used to ensure that the probability of selecting each individual is always the same

8. a type of sampling in which subjects or participants are selected based on known or unknown criteria or characteristics in the target population

11. a method of sampling subjects and participants such that all individuals in a population have an equal chance of being selected and are selected using sampling with replacement

13. the distance that sample mean values can deviate from the value of the population mean

Crossword Puzzle

6

Choosing a
Research Design

CHAPTER LEARNING OBJECTIVES

1. Identify three categories of research design: nonexperimental, quasi-experimental, and experimental.

2. Explain how a gradient of control can be used to understand research design.

3. Define and explain internal and external validity.

4. Describe three elements of control required in an experiment.

5. Distinguish between a laboratory experiment and a field experiment.

6. Describe factors that threaten the internal validity of a research study.

7. Describe factors that threaten the external validity of a research study.

8. Define and explain mundane and experimental realism.

Chapter Summary

6.1 Designing a Study to Answer a Question

Conducting a study is important because it allows you to make observations using the scientific process to answer your research question. The type of study you conduct depends largely on the type of question you are asking. A research study applies a **research design,** which is the specific methods and procedures you use to answer a research question. The types of research questions that you can ask are generally categorized as *exploratory*, *descriptive*, or *relational* questions.

6.2 Categories of Research Design

Research design generally falls into one of three categories: nonexperimental, experimental, and quasi-experimental. The level of control that is established in the design distinguishes each type of research design. The term **control** is used in research design to describe (a) the manipulation of a variable and (b) holding all other variables constant. When control is high, both criteria (a and b) are met.

The **nonexperimental research design** is the use of methods and procedures to make observations in which the conditions or experiences of participants are not manipulated. Instead of a manipulation, the behavior or event is observed "as is" or without intervention from the researcher using a nonexperimental research design. One strength of this design is that it can be used to make observations in settings where the behaviors and events being observed naturally operate; a limitation is that it lacks the control needed to demonstrate cause and effect.

The **experimental research design** is the use of methods and procedures to make observations in which the researcher fully controls the conditions and experiences of participants by applying three required elements of control: randomization, manipulation, and comparison/control. One strength of this design is that it is the only research design capable of demonstrating cause and effect; a limitation is that a behavior that occurs under controlled conditions may not be the same as a behavior that occurs in a natural environment.

A **quasi-experimental research design** is the use of methods and procedures to make observations in a study that is structured similar to an experiment, but the conditions and experiences of participants lack some control because the study lacks random assignment, includes a preexisting factor (i.e., a variable that is not manipulated: a quasi-independent variable), or does not include a comparison/control group. One strength of this design is that it allows researchers to study factors related to the unique characteristics of participants; a limitation is that researchers do not manipulate the characteristics of the participants and so cannot demonstrate cause and effect.

6.3 Internal and External Validity

Internal validity is the extent to which a research design includes enough control of the conditions and experiences of participants that it can demonstrate a single unambiguous explanation for a manipulation—that is, cause and effect. The more control in a research design, the higher the internal validity of a study.

External validity is the extent to which observations made in a study generalize beyond the specific manipulations or constraints in the study. A *constraint* is any aspect of the research design that can limit observations to the specific conditions or manipulations in a study. The fewer constraints or the more natural the settings within which observations are made, the higher the external validity of a study.

6.4 Demonstrating Cause in an Experiment

Three elements of control in an **experiment** are randomization, manipulation, and comparison/control. Researchers use randomization to ensure that individuals are selected to participate at random (**random sampling**) and are assigned to groups at random (**random assignment**). The levels of an **independent variable** are manipulated, meaning that the researcher creates the groups or conditions in which participants are observed at each level of the manipulated variable. Participants are then assigned at random to each level of the independent variable. Random assignment is important because the procedure controls for individual differences in participant characteristics by ensuring that the characteristics of participants in each group of an experiment vary entirely by chance. A **dependent variable** is then measured in each group, and differences between groups can be compared.

A **laboratory experiment** is an experiment that takes place in a laboratory setting. Although a laboratory setting can be made to appear as if it is a natural environment, this setting often does not resemble the environment within which the behavior or event being observed would naturally operate. A **field experiment** is an experiment conducted in the natural setting within which the behavior of interest naturally operates and is associated typically with higher external validity than a laboratory experiment.

6.5 Ethics in Focus: Beneficence and Random Assignment

Some situations may produce large differences in how participants are treated in each group. In these situations, there can be an ethical concern that relates to *beneficence*, which is the equal distribution of potential costs and benefits of participation. When one group has greater benefits or risks than another group, researchers will often compensate the group that had fewer benefits or greater risks, called *compensatory equalization of treatments*.

6.6 Threats to the Internal Validity of a Research Study

The following are common threats to the internal validity of a research study: history effects and maturation, regression toward the mean and testing effects, instrumentation, heterogeneous attrition, and environmental factors.

A **history effect** is an unanticipated event that co-occurs with a treatment or manipulation in a study—for example, candy versus vegetable intake during Halloween. **Maturation** occurs when a participant's physiological or psychological state changes over time during a study—for example, changes in food likes over the life span.

Regression toward the mean is a change or shift in a participant's performance toward a level or score that is more typical or closer to the mean of an individual's true ability at a second time. A **testing effect** is the improved performance on a test or measure the second time it is taken due to the experience of taking the test. Remember that regression toward the mean can be attributed to an increase or a decrease in performance from one time to another, whereas testing effects are associated with an increase in performance from one time to another.

Instrumentation can be a threat to internal validity when the measurement of the dependent variable changes due to an error during the course of a research study. Instrumentation is particularly problematic for internal validity when the error in measurement varies systematically with the levels of the factor.

Attrition occurs when a participant does not show up for a study at a scheduled time or fails to complete the study. **Heterogeneous attrition** is a possible threat to internal validity in which rates of attrition vary systematically with the levels of the factor or between groups in a study.

Environmental factors are characteristics or dynamics of the study itself and the actions of the researchers that can threaten the internal validity of a study. Environmental factors include the time of day that a study is conducted, how researchers treat participants, and the location of the study.

6.7 Threats to the External Validity of a Research Study

Common threats to the external validity of a research study are population validity, ecological validity, temporal validity, and outcome validity.

Population validity is the extent to which results observed in a study will generalize to the population from which a sample was selected. A threat to population validity in which rates of attrition are about the same in each group is called **homogeneous attrition**.

Ecological validity is the extent to which results observed in a study will generalize across settings or environments. In general, ecological validity is high so long as observations in a study are not dependent on, or limited to, specific features of the research setting itself.

Temporal validity is the extent to which results observed in a study will generalize across time and at different points in time. **Outcome validity** is the extent to which the results or outcomes observed in a study will generalize across different but related dependent variables. Population, ecological, temporal, and outcome validity are all subcategories of external validity.

6.8 External Validity, Experimentation, and Realism

Mundane realism is the extent to which a research setting physically resembles or *looks* like the natural or real-world environment being simulated. **Experimental realism** is the extent to which the psychological aspects of a research setting are meaningful or *feel* real to participants. Increasing the mundane and experimental realism of a study will increase the external validity of the study.

6.9 A Final Thought on Validity and Choosing a Research Design

Having high internal and external validity is not a prerequisite for good research designs. Instead, all research designs have limitations, and it is important that researchers recognize them. In this way, being aware of the limitations in research design can be as important as understanding its strengths to advance scientific knowledge.

Chapter Summary Organized by Learning Objective

LO 1: Identify three categories of research design: nonexperimental, quasi-experimental, and experimental.

- A **research design** is the specific methods and procedures used to answer research questions. The types of research questions that researchers ask are generally categorized as exploratory, descriptive, or relational questions.
- A **nonexperimental research design** is the use of methods and procedures to make observations in which the behavior or event being observed is observed "as is" or without any intervention from the researcher.
- An **experimental research design** is the use of methods and procedures to make observations in which the researcher fully controls the conditions and experiences of participants by applying three required elements of control: randomization, manipulation, and comparison/control.
- A **quasi-experimental research design** is the use of methods and procedures to make observations in a study that is structured similar to an experiment, but the conditions and experiences of participants are not under the full control of the researcher. Specifically, the study includes a preexisting factor (i.e., a variable that is not manipulated: a **quasi-independent variable**) or lacks a comparison/control group.

LO 2: Explain how a gradient of control can be used to understand research design.

- Categorizing research can oversimplify the complexity of research design. Another way to approach research design is to think of it along a gradient of control. The more control present in a study, the more suited the design will be to demonstrate that one variable causes a change in a dependent variable. Studies with high control will be experimental; the less control in a study, the more quasi-experimental or nonexperimental the research design.

LO 3: Define and explain internal and external validity.

- **Internal validity** is the extent to which a research design includes enough control of the conditions and experiences of participants that it can demonstrate cause and effect.
- **External validity** is the extent to which observations made in a study generalize beyond the specific manipulations or constraints in the study.

LO 4: Describe three elements of control required in an experiment.

- An **experiment** has the following three elements of control that allow researchers to draw cause-and-effect conclusions:
  - Randomization (random sampling and random assignment).
  - Manipulation (of variables that operate in an experiment).
  - Comparison/control (a control group).

- Randomization is used to ensure that individuals are selected to participate and assigned to groups in a study using a random procedure. Manipulation means that a researcher created the levels of the **independent variable**, thereby allowing the researcher to randomly assign participants to groups in the study. A comparison or control group is used to allow researchers to compare changes in a **dependent variable** in the presence and in the absence of a manipulation.

LO 5: Distinguish between a laboratory experiment and a field experiment.

- A **laboratory experiment** is conducted in a setting that does not resemble the environment within which the behavior or event being observed would naturally operate; a **field experiment** is conducted in an environment within which the behavior or event being observed would naturally operate.

LO 6: Describe factors that threaten the internal validity of a research study.

- Factors that threaten the internal validity of a research study will vary systematically with the levels of an independent variable. These factors include **history effects, maturation, regression toward the mean, testing effects, instrumentation, heterogeneous attrition,** and environmental factors that can vary between groups in a study.

LO 7: Describe factors that threaten the external validity of a research study.

- Factors that threaten the external validity of a research study are those that are held constant across groups in a study. These factors include four subcategories of external validity:
  - **Population validity,** or the extent to which observations generalize beyond a sample to the population.
  - **Ecological validity,** or the extent to which observations generalize across settings.
  - **Temporal validity,** or the extent to which observations generalize across time or at different points in time.
  - **Outcome validity,** or the extent to which observations generalize across different but related dependent variables.

LO 8: Define and explain mundane and experimental realism.

- **Mundane realism** is the extent to which a research setting physically resembles or *looks* like the natural environment being simulated. **Experimental realism** is the extent to which the psychological aspects of a research setting are meaningful or *feel* real to participants. A study with high mundane and experimental realism will have high external validity.

Tips and Cautions for Students

Demonstrating cause using a manipulation. Each type of research design is distinguished by the level of control that is established in a design. The term *control* is used in research design to describe (a) the manipulation of a variable and (b) holding all other variables constant. A *manipulation* means that the researcher controls when and how the variable is observed. To illustrate, a researcher can pour tap water in one glass and bottled water in another identical glass. In this case, the researcher manipulates the type of water in the glass (tap vs. bottled)—because the researcher controls what is poured in the glass and when it is poured. We can then, for example, give each glass to a participant and ask him or her which glass of water tastes better (a classic taste test study). In this way, a manipulation allows for a higher level of control for the variables observed in a study.

Research design and internal versus external validity. Keep in mind that internal validity is related to the level of control in a study. High control in a research design is associated with high internal validity, which is why experiments, which have the highest level of control, are also associated with the highest internal validity. External validity, however, is something very different. External validity relates to our ability to generalize the results of a study to a natural situation. The fewer constraints or the more natural the settings within which observations are made, the higher the external validity of the study, which is why nonexperiments, which typically have the fewest constraints, are also associated with the highest external validity.

Practice Quiz

1. The types of questions that researchers ask are:
   a. exploratory
   b. descriptive
   c. relational
   d. all of the above

2. Which of the following research designs are associated with the greatest control?
   a. experimental
   b. nonexperimental
   c. quasi-experimental

3. Which of the following is *not* a requirement for establishing control in a research design?
   a. manipulate the levels of a variable
   b. observe preexisting variables
   c. hold all other variables constant
   d. control for confound variables

4. When the behavior or event being observed is observed "as is" or without any intervention from the researcher, the research design is:
   a. experimental
   b. nonexperimental
   c. quasi-experimental

5. The gender of a participant is an example of:

   a. an independent variable

   b. a quasi-independent variable

6. A study that is structured similar to an experiment, but the conditions and experiences of participants lack some control because the study lacks random assignment, includes a preexisting factor (i.e., a variable that is not manipulated), or does not include a comparison/control group is:

   a. experimental

   b. nonexperimental

   c. quasi-experimental

7. The extent to which a study demonstrates cause is identified by:

   a. internal validity

   b. external validity

   c. population validity

   d. quasi-validity

8. If a researcher determines that the results in her sample generalize beyond the constraints of her study, then she has established which type of validity?

   a. external validity

   b. internal validity

   c. quasi-independent validity

   d. nonvalidity

9. A key element of control that allows researchers to draw cause-and-effect conclusions in an experiment is:

   a. randomization

   b. manipulation of variables that operate in an experiment

   c. comparison or a control group

   d. all of the above

10. The use of a random procedure to assign participants to groups is called:

    a. random selection

    b. random sampling

    c. random assignment

    d. both a and b

11. Random assignment controls for:

    a. all possible confounds in a study

    b. individual differences between groups

    c. how participants will be selected from the population

    d. none of the above

12. A researcher records the time in seconds spent attending to an isolated versus an engaging task. The dependent variable in this example is:

    a. the type of task

    b. the sampling method used to select participants

    c. being engaged during a task

    d. the time in seconds spent attending to a task

13. Which type of experiment is typically associated with higher external validity?

    a. field experiment

    b. laboratory experiment

14. Which of the following is *not* a common threat to internal validity?

    a. testing effects

    b. regression toward the mean

    c. random assignment

    d. history effects

15. A basketball player who typically makes about 50% of his shots has an "off" night and makes only 40% of his shots. The next night he has a great shooting night and makes almost 60% of his shots. Which principle explains his change in performance?

    a. history effect

    b. regression toward the mean

    c. heterogeneous attrition

    d. instrumentation

16. In a weight training study, almost twice as many participants quit in the heavy lifting compared to the light lifting group before the study was complete. What threat to internal validity is associated with this study?

    a. testing effect

    b. regression toward the mean

    c. history effect

    d. heterogeneous attrition

17. Which of the following is an example of an environmental factor that can threaten the internal validity of a research study?

    a. time of day that a study is conducted

    b. the location of a study

    c. the physical appearance of a laboratory

    d. all of the above

18. Which of the following is *not* a subcategory of external validity?

    a. population validity

    b. temporal validity

    c. internal validity

    d. ecological validity

19. Heterogeneous attrition is specifically a threat to which type of external validity?

    a. population validity

    b. outcome validity

    c. temporal validity

    d. ecological validity

20. A researcher conditions animal subjects to swim to a platform located at a fixed point. Subjects show strong conditioning for weeks after the conditioning. This study has high _____ validity.

    a. outcome

    b. temporal

    c. ecological

    d. population

21. An experimental situation that "looks" and "feels" real has high:

    a. mundane realism

    b. experimental realism

    c. both a and b

22. Which of the following statements about validity is true?

    a. Having high internal and external validity is not a prerequisite for good research designs.

    b. Factors that threaten the internal validity of a research study are those factors that vary systematically with an independent variable.

    c. Factors that threaten the external validity of a study limit the extent to which observations made by a researcher generalize beyond the constraints of a study.

    d. all of the above

Key Term Word Search

```
T I K D M A R U R A B S J E E D D W A I S P P P C Z C T X D K C X N W Y Z Y U J C Q J U
D S V G H H S P Z C V P W C K E B B C J A Y B S V Z A F R Y I L O F O X A N V N Q X J Y
U F N P D Y R H H Z D G X R P V C I Y L J Q K N X Y J J J Q D I F Y X P Y C H N G M T H
W R O F R Q O F Q J T W A J M R P Q X F M D R K N Y C H T X T V K F Y B K U G Z S I R P
F D Q U F H O U E M J M Z G L H F Q H M N G T A C G Q A Q I P U A Y T Y T I Q I D R H Q
S I X G F I E L D E X P E R I M E N T U E U E E G X X R R Q X Q Z V A F S X L I L A I C
Q O N J Y L X Q Z Q E O J B F M N J O U R M M N M X F T Q N A K D W F E J A L F J N I O
U U F D H F G T E G C B S Q J H N F K S E N O J A P T U G G S E H B D G E A L J N D C D
A T K S E C O T C B Z I H H T T N Q D H O I B R V A O P N E A D I H M R V S L Z B O F E
S C Z G C P R L P U F U K P W O L K T I T Y S K S M B R C C K F C O L N Z D J F M M M P
I O H J R X E W W M W D V P C T C D T A R F C U B E P N A N F R D A O A T Z M O O S H E
I M S N J G N N Y N K K H Q H C R I T N S C O M A I E E G L A E T I P P N D J Q T E T N
N E K S W E D Y D G Z M H Z A A R N S A B E O D V R F I O E V N T W L I N C R R A L O D
D V Q F H N K S T E J R Z Y W T E N F C N B W U E L S L S Q E A X E F J I A M N C E K E
E A E M Y S N L T K N L Y O T M M T Q E H H K F B E X E G M L E L G X C Q S R I M C V N
P L P C K U U Y E D V T T A U D J W G Y V H F R D Z R Y I U E D S I Q R E N V D D T G T
E I Q O O I R L L L H N V R D S O O O R W I Q H Z L U R P H L K O L D Z F W S S H I X V
N D W E G L P S L T O H T A D U R L C N D Z C L A W E O Q L U B O X P I H E D A R O G A
D I P P V V O G N I O S R R R E G U S L V R U T U P P Y K H S E J T H I T G X Q O N C R
E T B M Q A H G S I N M F T T I J X A V A W N P X B I H U U L B H U O L V Y Q N V B K I
N Y Z C S E G S I I Y R V E R L A U K E V E O E S V J S W L A T Z C W Z C U V T C F W A
T Y P Y W M E J X C V Q H O O R D B S U M E Q V D X E N W M L D B N A P J D H M E V D B
V E G G O R A N G F A I A S C I R E L I J K A H T K X F Z Z K V H U Y U B R W F X Y N L
A E B R G F Z T J K T L T E V Q R A R E R E H O M O G E N E O U S A T T R I T I O N E E
R F Y E L A R M U G Y C V I F L A E X X A K T Q M B E E Q Q L V I R N E B L T U B S W C
I R R N C A V B C R E J D A A N P R E X P E R I M E N T I P G K Z U O J F L Z L F A N Z
A R A D D Q B M D F A N W T L X N F Q N I S L N Q V V B R U W V S J Q X R Y R K J W F W
B T X N P H W O F E I T N N E I K P E V A W W Q F C K L P K H F V L D V V Z Y B E R Z Q
L R W F D V I E R N E E I I Y B D I N T E R N A L V A L I D I T Y I H I Q F O U Q F C E
E O O S P O G S W A M P S O T G C I H S L X A H U E X P E R I M E N T A L M O R T A L I
O C K Y W N M E T I T A R Q N T X A T F R T K K G I G Y O H X L C N W D Y E O W M G T W
B V U N I X H S R O U O R V P T Y M E Y N P N X H Z S G F S L L H O Y Z H X P S F A M Z
U T D T U K Y E A Q R D R H M T I U V E B T J G M F G O Q N I Z Q L G H E U I T Z Z K Z
O Q S X Z J P M E M X Y E Y I B X I M Q P O I Z M X N I M U N D V S O R J L G I A B S L
P E P B O X Z H R N P X E D E I N N D V H L L Q Q F D G W O I D G P R N A D M B Q W I L
T T J J E N H U J A T L I F R X G P F A G D Z A E U Q W D M J N G G N E J O G A Z H H K
Y E H N S X T L K P A L I M F I P E J D G C Q W Q U E X C E T D C Q R B D D U G F S K H
K L B I Q W Y G C N A U D N S E R E S E A R C H D E S I G N O A A E Z N H H T Y E P W F
K H C I W N B E K V I J W S G Y C T R D R M X Z Y L W F I K C T N O A U O L B P V F X Y
Z J B B I I I S L J B Y A Y W R R T A I X E J X E J N P F H Y A G R V D J J U P O H A W
H E F C R E P A D O E M U J Q H G E S L M W D H P D H U P Q D S N Q C C J P G Q X S F C
V Z K E H V N L N M O G G C O N T R O L H E K E T I A U E N K F P N I S L L J Z L M A S
R V L K I R N X L D J O O T Q U H F B U X G N K R E Q C U W K N W A W D W H F J C E W B
S D F F E N C T N F P V J B C I H Z Q H N Z L T O B W M Z I S F B L V E H L K W S X B B
S A C T F I Y A S B O J M S G H J J Y H V A Y I H G L V T W Y M F I S X Z D M O K D S D R
C L X F E B R S X M U R G Y K Z D R S P A L G G K W X O C V W F T L Z I F K H T P A Y H
R E I Y N O N E X P E R I M E N T A L R E S E A R C H D E S I G N U M E H P P G G S F J
R X O C R E Z F G P C J F E J W I C B C I Z Y G L F X I S E T N D Q Y A C F L W U Z H M
```

factor	random assignment	maturation	independent variable
control	reverse causality	randomization	homogeneous attrition
confound	temporal validity	history effects	quasi-independent variable
attrition	dependent variable	mundane realism	experimental research
experiment	ecological validity	outcome validity	design
random sampling	laboratory experiment	random selection	nonexperimental research
research design	experimental mortality	external validity	design
testing effects	individual differences	internal validity	quasi-experimental
field experiment	heterogeneous attrition	population validity	research design
instrumentation	regression toward the mean	experimental realism	

ACROSS

1. the extent to which the psychological aspects of a research setting are meaningful or feel real to participants

4. a preexisting variable that differentiates the groups or conditions being compared in a research study

5. the extent to which a research setting physically resembles or looks like the natural environment being simulated

6. an unanticipated variable not accounted for in a research study that could be causing or associated with observed changes in one or more measured variables

7. a research design that uses methods and procedures to make observations in which the behavior or event being observed is observed "as is" or without any intervention from the researcher

10. an experiment that takes place in an environment within which the behavior or event being observed would naturally operate

11. a type of validity that indicates the extent to which results observed in a study will generalize across time and at different points in time

12. a type of validity that indicates the extent to which results observed in a study will generalize across settings or environments

16. the methods and procedures used to specifically control the conditions under which observations are made in order to isolate cause-and-effect relationships between variables

17. used in research design that requires the manipulation of a variable and holding all other variables constant

18. a possible threat to internal validity in which a participant's physiological or psychological state changes over time during a study

19. the use of methods for selecting individuals to participate in a study and assigning them to groups such that each individual has an equal chance of being selected to participate and assigned to groups

20. a possible threat to internal validity in which an unanticipated event also occurs with a treatment or manipulation in a study

21. the variable that is believed to change in the presence of the independent variable

22. the assignment of participants to groups using random procedure

DOWN

2. a type of validity that indicates the extent to which results observed in a study will generalize to the population from which a sample was selected

3. the variable that is manipulated in an experiment

8. the only research design that applies to all three required elements of control

9. the _____ of a factor are the specific conditions or groups created by manipulating that factor

13. a type of validity that indicates the extent to which the results or outcomes observed in a study will generalize across different but related dependent variables

14. the specific methods and procedures used to answer a research question

15. the improved performance on a test or measure the second time it is taken due to the experience of taking the test

Crossword Puzzle

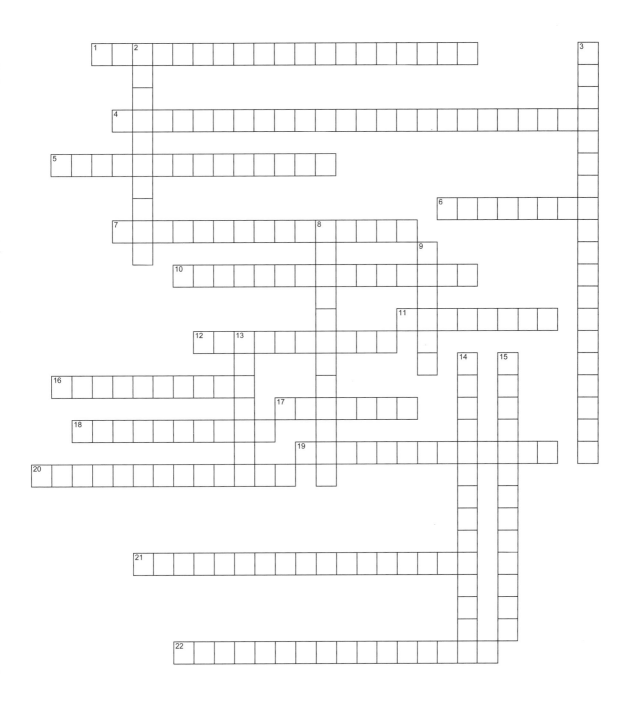

SECTION III

Nonexperimental Research Designs

7

Naturalistic, Qualitative, and Existing Data Research Designs

CHAPTER LEARNING OBJECTIVES

1. Identify and define the naturalistic research design.

2. Distinguish between natural and contrived research settings.

3. Identify and describe how researchers make unobtrusive observations.

4. Describe how researchers operationalize, quantify, and manage observation periods in a naturalistic or contrived setting.

5. Describe the philosophy of qualitative research, and explain how trustworthiness relates to validity and reliability.

6. Identify and describe three qualitative research designs: phenomenology, ethnography, and case study.

7. Identify and describe three existing data research designs: archival research, content analysis, and meta-analysis.

Chapter Summary

NATURALISTIC OBSERVATION

7.1 An Overview of Naturalistic Observation

One nonexperimental research design used to make observations in natural settings, or in places where the behaviors being observed naturally operate, is called **naturalistic observation**. The naturalistic research design is associated with high external validity. While external validity is generally high using the naturalistic research design, this design is also associated with low internal validity because we do not substantially manipulate conditions in a natural environment and therefore typically have limited control using a naturalistic observation.

7.2 The Research Setting: Natural and Contrived Settings

A **natural setting** is a location that is, or appears to be, the environment where the behavior or event being observed typically occurs. An alternative to making observations in a natural setting is to observe behavior in an arranged or **contrived setting**. Making naturalistic observations in a contrived setting has two important advantages: We can control many factors that are otherwise impossible to control in a natural setting, and we can structure the setting to facilitate the occurrence of a behavior.

7.3 Techniques for Conducting Naturalistic Observation

An **unobtrusive observation** is a technique used by an observer to record or observe behavior in a way that does not interfere with or change a participant's behavior in that observed research setting. Four strategies used to make unobtrusive observations are to remain hidden, habituate participants to the researcher, use a confederate, and use indirect measures.

To operationalize observations, we define **behavior categories** to identify the specific types of behaviors we intend to measure in the research setting. To list behavior categories we first identify all the categories of the construct we are measuring, then list or anticipate examples that will "count" in each category. We can then make observations of those behavior categories in a natural setting.

To record or quantify observations in terms of how they are measured, we can use the **interval method** (dividing an observational period into equal intervals of time), the **frequency method** (counting the number of times a behavior occurs during a fixed or predetermined period of time), the **duration method** (recording the amount of time or duration that participants engage in a certain behavior during a fixed period of time), or the **latency method** (recording the time or duration between the occurrences of behaviors during a fixed period of time).

Three strategies used to manage an observation period are **time sampling** (splitting a fixed period of time into smaller intervals of time, then making observations during alternating intervals), **event sampling** (splitting a fixed period of time into smaller intervals of time, then recording a different behavior in each time interval), and **individual sampling** (splitting a fixed period of time into smaller intervals of time, then recording the behaviors of a different participant in each time interval).

7.4 Ethics in Focus: Influencing Participant Behavior

Making naturalistic observations can be an ethical alternative to experiments because it can allow researchers to observe behavior without directly influencing the occurrence of that behavior.

QUALITATIVE DESIGNS

7.5 An Overview of Qualitative Designs

The **qualitative research design** is the use of the scientific method to make nonnumeric observations, from which conclusions are drawn without the use of statistical analysis. Qualitative research adopts the assumption of **determinism**; however, it does not assume that behavior itself is universal. Instead, qualitative research is based on a holistic, or "complete picture," view that emphasizes the following two principles: There is no single reality in nature, and behavior does not occur independent of context.

As an alternative to using validity and reliability, many qualitative researchers use four criteria of **trustworthiness**, which are the *credibility, transferability, dependability*, and *confirmability* of a qualitative analysis. Although these criteria parallel concepts of validity, reliability, and objectivity, these criteria do not conform well to quantitative research. Still, qualitative research does provide a unique understanding of behavior from the perspective of the individual and continues to develop and gain recognition in the scientific community.

7.6 Qualitative Research Designs

Phenomenology is the qualitative analysis of the conscious experiences of phenomena from the first-person point of view of the participant. A *conscious experience* is any experience that a person has lived through or performed and can bring to memory in such a way as to recall that experience. To use this research design, the researcher interviews a participant who gives a first-person account of his or her conscious experiences. The researcher then constructs a narrative to describe or summarize the experiences described in the interview. In writing narratives, the author makes additional considerations that increase the trustworthiness of the research by accounting for the context within which a participant self-describes his or her experiences.

Ethnography is the qualitative analysis of the behavior and identity of a group or culture as it is described and characterized by the members of that group or culture. It is used to study macro-level and micro-level groups and cultures. Macro-level groups are those with large membership, such as all members of a country, government, or continent. Micro-level groups are those with small membership, such as members of a college fraternity, a first-grade classroom, or a sports team. To observe a group or culture it is often necessary to use **participant observation,** which can then lead to *participant reactivity*. To reduce the likelihood of participant reactivity researchers can enter a group secretly or can announce or request entry into a group.

A **case study** is the qualitative analysis of an individual, group, organization, or event used to illustrate a phenomenon, explore new hypotheses, or compare the observations of many cases. Three types of case studies are the **illustrative case study** (used to investigate rare or unknown phenomena), the **exploratory case study** (used to explore or generate hypotheses for later investigation), and the **collective case study** (used to compare observations of many cases). Two common applications of a case study are for purposes of general inquiry and theory development.

7.7 Ethics in Focus: Anonymity in Qualitative Research

A unique characteristic of qualitative research is that the identity of participants is not entirely concealed. Revealing the identity of participants can show high regard for the Belmont principle of *respect for persons* in that doing so makes the researcher more accountable for his or her part in a research study.

EXISTING DATA DESIGNS

7.8 An Overview of Existing Data Designs

Existing data designs are the collection, review, and analysis of any type of existing documents or records, including those that are written or recorded as video, as audio, or in other electronic form. When the data already exist, the researcher does not need to spend his or her time and money selecting a sample and observing participants in the sample because the data that will be analyzed already exist.

7.9 Existing Data Designs

Two cautions should be made anytime you select data from existing records: Existing records provide a selective record of behaviors observed, called **selective deposit**, and only certain types of records may survive over time, called **selective survival**. Each caution can limit the generalizability of your results inasmuch as the selective records of behavior and the selective survival of existing records can bias the remaining records that are available for analysis.

Archival research is a type of existing data design in which events or behaviors are described based on a review and analysis of relevant historical or archival records. Archival research is used to characterize or describe existing archives or historical documents.

Content analysis is a type of existing data design in which the content of written or spoken records of the occurrence of specific events or behaviors is described and interpreted. To use a content analysis, we must identify the unit of analysis in the document or existing record, and the operational definition for the content analyzed.

A **meta-analysis** is a type of existing data design in which findings for a group of related research studies are combined, analyzed, and summarized, often in terms of effect size. **Effect size** is an estimate of the size of an observed effect or change in a population and can be interpreted in terms of differences (Cohen's *d*), proportions (*eta* squared), or degree of association (correlation). An advantage of meta-analysis is that it increases **statistical power**, or the likelihood of detecting an effect or mean difference in one or more populations, by combining the sample size of many research studies. A disadvantage of meta-analysis is that it is prone to *publication bias*, in that many studies that fail to show an effect are omitted from the published literature and are therefore not included in calculations of effect size in a meta-analysis.

7.10 Ethics in Focus: Existing Data and Experimenter Bias

To avoid an experimenter bias, you should have multiple researchers search existing data records during the initial review process. By doing so, you can reduce bias in that a consensus can be reached by many researchers prior to selecting which existing data records are included or omitted from a research study.

Chapter Summary Organized by Learning Objective

LO 1: Identify and define the naturalistic research design.

- The naturalistic research design applies a naturalistic observation strategy to make observations in natural settings. **Naturalistic observation** is the observation of behavior in the natural setting where it is expected to occur, with limited or no attempt to overtly manipulate the conditions of the environment where the observations are made.

LO 2: Distinguish between natural and contrived research settings.

- A **natural setting** is a location or site where a behavior of interest normally occurs. A **contrived setting** is a location or site arranged to mimic the natural setting within which a behavior of interest normally occurs, in order to facilitate the occurrence of that behavior.

LO 3: Identify and describe how researchers make unobtrusive observations.

- An **unobtrusive observation** is a technique used by an observer to record or observe behavior in a way that does not interfere with or change a participant's behavior in that observed research setting.
- To make unobtrusive observations, researchers can remain hidden, habituate participants to their presence, use a confederate, or use indirect measures.

LO 4: Describe how researchers operationalize, quantify, and manage observation periods in a naturalistic or contrived setting.

- Researchers operationalize observations by identifying behavior categories of interest. **Behavior categories** are the specific types of behaviors that researchers want to measure in the research setting, and are typically organized as a list of examples that "count" in each category or for each type of behavior.
- To quantify observations, researchers can use the following methods:
  - o **Interval method** (record whether or not certain behaviors occur in a given interval).
  - o **Frequency method** (record the number of times a behavior occurs during a fixed period of time).
  - o **Duration method** (record the amount of time that a participant engages in a certain behavior during a fixed period of time).

- o **Latency method** (record the time or duration between the occurrences of behaviors during a fixed period of time).
- To manage observation periods researchers can use the following methods:
  - o **Time sampling** (making observations in alternating intervals of an observation period).
  - o **Event sampling** (recording different events or behaviors in each interval of an observation period).
  - o **Individual sampling** (recording the behavior of different individuals in each interval of an observation period).

LO 5: Describe the philosophy of qualitative research, and explain how trustworthiness relates to validity and reliability.

- The philosophy of qualitative research is based on the holistic view that *reality changes* (each person experiences a unique reality or views the world from a different perspective) and *behavior is dynamic* (behavior can only be understood in the context within which it occurs).
- We cannot establish the validity and reliability of an outcome without the aid of statistics. For this reason, qualitative research uses different criteria that parallel validity and reliability. An alternative to validity and reliability is criteria of **trustworthiness** in qualitative research. The four criteria of trustworthiness are the *credibility, transferability, dependability,* and *confirmability* of a qualitative analysis. Credibility and transferability are similar to internal and external validity, respectively; dependability is similar to reliability; transferability is similar to objectivity.

LO 6: Identify and describe three qualitative research designs: phenomenology, ethnography, and case study.

- **Phenomenology** is the qualitative analysis of the conscious experiences of phenomena from the first-person point of view.
- **Ethnography** is the qualitative analysis of the behavior and identity of a group or culture as it is described and characterized by the members of that group or culture.
- **Case study** is the qualitative analysis of a single individual, group, organization, or event used to illustrate a phenomenon, explore new hypotheses, or compare the observations of many cases. Three types of case studies are illustrative, exploratory, and collective. A case study is unique in that it is often applied as a qualitative and a quantitative analysis.

LO 7: Identify and describe three existing data research designs: archival research, content analysis, and meta-analysis.

- **Archival research** is a type of existing data design in which events or behaviors are described based on a review and analysis of relevant historical or archival records.
- **Content analysis** is a type of existing data design in which the content of written or spoken records of the occurrence of specific events or behaviors is described and interpreted.

- A **meta-analysis** is a type of existing data design in which findings for a group of related research studies are combined, analyzed, and summarized, often in terms of **effect size**. A meta-analysis increases **statistical power** by combining the sample sizes from many studies, but is also prone to a publication bias because negative results, or those that do not show an effect, tend to be omitted from the peer-reviewed literature.

Tips and Cautions for Students

Natural versus contrived settings. Conducting the study in a natural setting essentially means that you are observing participants in their "real life" environments. In this way, the data that are collected in a natural setting can accurately reflect the "real life" behavior of participants. A contrived setting, on the other hand, is one in which a specific situation being studied is created by the researcher to appear as if it were natural. A contrived setting offers greater control to make observations; however, it can be more difficult to show that the observations made in a contrived setting truly reflect a "real life" situation.

Trustworthiness in qualitative research. Keep in mind that the aim of trustworthiness in a qualitative study is simply to support the argument that a study's findings are "worth paying attention to" in the similar way that we use criteria of validity and reliability to support the argument that a quantitative study's findings are worth paying attention to. Four criteria of trustworthiness require attention in qualitative research: credibility, transferability, dependability, and confirmability. Remember that qualitative research does not include the measurement and statistical analysis of numeric data. Hence, these alternative criteria of trustworthiness are needed to assess the value and importance of qualitative research in which statistical analysis is absent.

Practice Quiz

1. A _____ is an observation of behavior that is made in the natural setting within which we would expect to observe that behavior.

   a. manipulation

   b. naturalistic observation

   c. constraint

   d. hypothesis

2. A location or site arranged to mimic the natural setting within which a behavior of interest normally occurs is called:

   a. a natural setting

   b. an altered setting

    c. a contrived setting

    d. a quasi-independent setting

3. A study on the quality of child care conducted at three local preschools is an example of:

    a. a natural setting

    b. an arranged setting

    c. a contrived setting

    d. a quasi-independent setting

4. Which of the following is a strategy for making unobtrusive observations?

    a. remain hidden during the observation

    b. use indirect or less obvious measures

    c. habituate participants to the researcher before a study begins

    d. all of the above

5. Behavior categories are primarily created to:

    a. operationalize behaviors

    b. quantify behaviors

    c. manage the observational period

    d. minimize bias

6. A researcher records the amount of time people spend at an art exhibit to determine which exhibit is most preferred; the more time they spend at an exhibit, the more they prefer the exhibit. Which method of quantifying observations was used in this example?

    a. interval method

    b. frequency method

    c. duration method

    d. latency method

7. Which method of quantifying observations involves recording the time or duration between the occurrences of behaviors during a fixed period of time?

    a. latency method

    b. frequency method

    c. duration method

    d. interval method

8. Which of the following is a strategy used to manage the observation period in naturalistic observation research?

    a. time sampling

    b. individual sampling

    c. event sampling

    d. all of the above

9. Making naturalistic observations can be an ethical alternative to experiments because it can allow researchers to observe behavior:

   a. in a way that coerces participants to behave against their will

   b. without directly influencing the occurrence of that behavior

   c. in settings that are intentionally manipulated to be dangerous or risky

   d. without ever disclosing the intent of the study to participants

10. Which of the following research designs uses the criteria of trustworthiness?

    a. naturalistic research design

    b. existing data designs

    c. qualitative research design

    d. experimental research design

11. The idea that reality changes and behavior is dynamic is part of which type of view?

    a. a holistic view

    b. a universal view

    c. a deranged view

    d. all of the above

12. Which of the following is *not* a criterion of trustworthiness?

    a. credibility

    b. feasibility

    c. transferability

    d. dependability

13. Which type of qualitative research design explores an analysis of the conscious experiences of phenomena from the first-person point of view of the participant?

    a. phenomenology

    b. ethnography

    c. case study

14. Ethnography explores an analysis of:

    a. individual behavior from the first-person point of view of the participant

    b. the behavior and identity of a group or culture as characterized by the members of that group or culture

    c. behavior that is quantified based on behavior categories identified for the behavior of interest

    d. laboratory-based research in contrived settings created to mimic natural environments within which a behavior of interest naturally operates

15. In which of the following is an analysis of multiple cases compared?

    a. illustrative case study

    b. descriptive case study

    c. collective case study

16. Existing data designs are used to analyze data that:

    a. are fabricated

    b. are observed at random

    c. cannot be statistically analyzed

    d. already exist

17. Which of the following is *not* a caution you should make anytime you select data from existing records?

    a. selective deposit

    b. selective survival

    c. the selective recording of behaviors in existing records

    d. natural selection

18. Unlike archival research, content analysis is used:

    a. mostly to describe existing data as summary statistics

    b. to analyze or interpret the detailed content in the records

    c. to observe behavior in the natural setting where it is expected to occur

    d. to arrange or mimic the natural setting within which a behavior of interest normally occurs

19. A meta-analysis combines, analyzes, and summarizes many research studies, often in terms of what type of measure?

    a. effect size

    b. reliability

    c. validity

    d. an external factor

20. Which of the following is a key advantage of a meta-analysis?

    a. It is prone to publication bias.

    b. It tends to overestimate the size of an observed effect.

    c. It increases statistical power.

    d. It allows for behavior to be observed in a natural setting.

Key Term Word Search

```
Z Q T Z J S P K U L E H N G D C Y L V E I R B T X W H N J C Q B K J T C W Z V V T T Z
Y A D N Q Q T L V B R H X K Y D U E A D C A S E S T U D Y N O M J L F G W V J N F K F
T U V S O C F C B R Q K I N D I V I D U A L S A M P L I N G Y Q E E W G D G Z D H C G
E C J D L T S N A T U R A L S E T T I N G P H E N O M E N O L O G Y W J M F S M W X U
E I E G W S Y D H M S B I E K N U A R C H I V A L R E S E A R C H X F T P I U N X F W
L S Z U E C I T N K Q Q K V K Z M Y T G J A F J G F W V M W F C O L A U S G Y F I B V
Q F J L Y X E I B A T L Q R Q S F F J B Y E A N P F O E G P T W H R U Y R C C L W B U
U O I T T P A M M B S H J G A U A Z F S I Q I R O A O R T D C P H G L T T N J U L D D
A T X M S I C E P E C I N T E R V A L M E T H O D Q O I F X M E U A U G R Y S I S K O
Y B Q A B Y G S N M O U A Z X L C H Y V T F D D Z M S G L S V Q N C C S U D D C E F H
H Z U X O Z D A W Y J I F E R B C H R E W N Q M W O X V B B I A N V I Q S Z R O T W U
Q E B G A L G M W W K A B F B M P G S X L J I I P P E H J W T X I N G P T I G O V N V
N L C V P G S P J N M H B V A A R D K Y H M O E G A P W W N H Z N G T F W U M L K A N
M E T A A N A L Y S I S Y Q R F E B H G F P D Q M K P R E Y E D K Q B N O I B P P V J
K M V L S J I I B B X P O G U V R Q Y S F E T V H R Z T J Z D U Q C A V R A S K Z J I
Q S L B T U G N O P K X O P I J M E Q I V F I S Q Z N B I G V R K E E K T J G Z S R V
X T J W H K G G G N I N L R Q L R A Q I K Z X F Q O V S C R F A L I C B H U B N X T I
U R I A R R W B C E H T T G M C W N T U C B Z X C G T O B A G T R E D A I B S E H M W
N U L U O I P Q Q T G N T F N H P C N T E X E M G C M W F J P I K R U Z N U E L S F W
W C I N A G C T E O O B E N S A E P O D X N G H E S Z V A J S O M C M F E Q L Q G J S
U T W O L E L F Q C Y B T D C L T L Z P W D C F A P B V X S N N O G Z Z S J E X K I R
W U A B T J A E Q H A B F Z E J H U Y W S Y F Y C V V Q M F Z M B M T K S O C H W N U
B R Z T A M T O Z J D Z T S W D I K R U J E J Y M S I C W H F E D H C S C H T H P P Q
V E Z R V H H P R L K F N C U Z U W W A O O V T B E M O F N T T E M B N B B I N W S H
V D J U Z G W A G E P E V E N T S A M P L I N G H M T R R K X H M M E Y Q Z V Y L H H
K O Y S D W F R M B D V G G S M Q V E M H I I K M J E H M C H O Y U U H C V E I I R H
V B C I M J I T L Y O Q L P K P L S T O Z K S U G W N G O W A D K C J V J H S R X E M
H S K V L A R I E B L R O J W X V F K F D J W T O R Z Q P D Y T Q Y D V P M U A Q M Q
X E D E F Q W C A O T I Y Y B V E A W Y K Z R P I O L O B E W J E Q Z D Y A R G W R R
C R W O Q T A I G B K P F J A F G P H D S M T I L C Y N Y I K D S G R R M N V Z M M N
R V Z B O B Y P K T K D I U I M Q G M J D T J E I A O L M G D P F X O L R G I M P C B
J A M S Z M W A Z N E O T M S K F U C H N D S T C X T B G H H E Z C P R U Y V O K U K
W T B E U D N N Z K F F K Z K E Z L A S A N M B T K S E S T O A T B S X I G A Y Z Q Z
C I D R C E B T Q V X E A N O V R P S R K R I H E V P U N E P X N E P F V E L U T P M
I O J V S H F S A Y U W G T I L M S E M Q G X B P Q P J B C R R M X R L N L S Z R E S
Y N S A B J K A A W J B M W G M A A H P J B I B K U E R Y F Y V H Z S M S X I A B L Y
H O V T W F Z M A L N J A K G C X G I A K Z A L B X M P E X J M A H W N I V G C Y U I
D Z S I V Z G P R Z I L L T D V Z W S G G F O I N G F J Z P X E E T J J Y N X M G G D
V Q Z O S Y P L Q I U P Y R O W J L T A U N E P R Y V S B N H E W T I I V C I Q Q E J
H G Q N C U K I O K I N U L Q E P B O B F C M H R X O L X C L B P K H O F G O S N I Z
P I W F G B U N U I G F G C N M K F R H C E D A L S M Z M T B Z U U Y O N G B X M B N
P H L D H D W G Q H C U W G W T W R Y F Q L C X D D I N B B L Y L B M U D W H H O U F
N M T S C G B B Q M Y C G I K E C J G U U R Y C A M Q E U X O A K J T D Z K F U P A Y
```

power

case study

effect size

case history

determinism

ethnography

meta-analysis

time sampling

event sampling

latency method

phenomenology

duration method

interval method

natural setting

content analysis

frequency method

trustworthiness

archival research

contrived setting

selective deposit

selective survival

behavior categories

individual sampling

participant sampling

structured observation

unobtrusive observation

naturalistic observation

ACROSS

2. the observation of behavior in the natural setting where it is expected to occur, with limited or no attempt to overtly manipulate the conditions of the environment where the observations are made

5. the qualitative analysis of the behavior and identity of a group or culture as it is described and characterized by the members of that group or culture

7. a type of existing data design in which findings for a group of related research studies are combined, analyzed, and summarized, often in terms of effect size

10. the likelihood that data in a sample can detect or discover an effect in a population, assuming that the effect does exist in the population of interest

11. a type of observation or technique used by an observer to record or observe behavior in a way that does not interfere with or change a participant's behavior in that observed research setting

15. a statistical measure of the size or magnitude of an observed effect in a population

16. the sampling strategy used to manage an observation period by splitting a fixed period of time into smaller intervals of time, then making observations during alternating intervals until the full observation period has ended

17. the sampling strategy used to manage an observation period by splitting a fixed period of time into smaller intervals of time, then recording a different behavior in each time interval

19. the sampling strategy used to manage an observation period by splitting a fixed period of time into smaller intervals of time, then recording the behaviors of a different participant in each time interval

20. the name of the research design that uses the scientific method to make nonnumeric observations, from which conclusions are drawn without the use of statistical analysis

21. the method used to quantify observations made in a study by recording the time or duration between the occurrences of behaviors during a fixed period of time

22. a type of existing data design in which the content of written or spoken records of the occurrence of specific events or behaviors is described and interpreted

DOWN

1. a method of observation in which a researcher participates in or joins the group or culture that he or she is observing

3. a type of case study used to investigate rare or unknown phenomena

4. the location or site where a behavior of interest normally occurs

6. the qualitative analysis of the conscious experiences of phenomena from the first-person point of view of the participant

8. an assumption in science that all actions in the universe have a cause

9. the process by which existing records survive or are excluded/decay over time

12. the credibility, transferability, dependability, and confirmability of a qualitative analysis

13. the method used to quantify observations made in a study by dividing an observational period into equal intervals of time, then recording whether or not certain behaviors occur in each interval

14. a type of case study used to explore or generate hypotheses for later investigation

18. the method used to quantify observations made in a study by recording the amount of time or duration that participants engage in a certain behavior during a fixed period of time

Crossword Puzzle

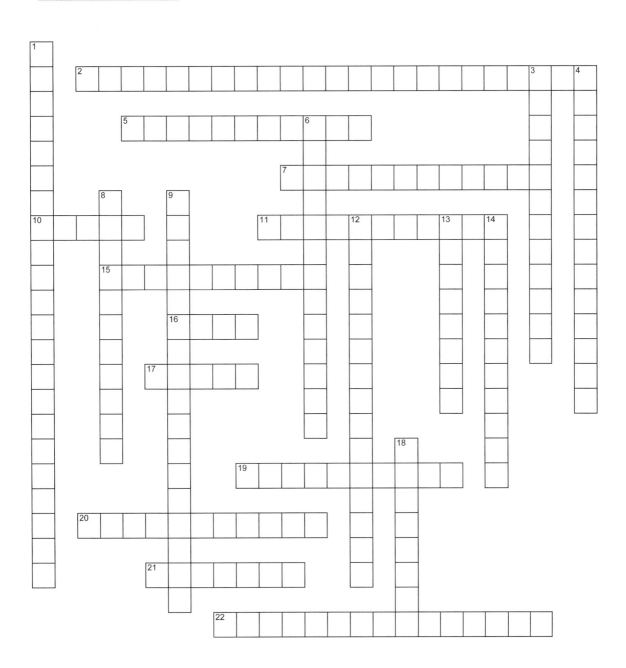

8

Survey and Correlational Research Designs

CHAPTER LEARNING OBJECTIVES

1. Identify and construct open-ended, partially open-ended, and restricted survey items.

2. Identify nine rules for writing valid and reliable survey items.

3. Describe methods of administering written surveys and interview surveys.

4. Explain how response rates to surveys can limit the interpretation of survey results.

5. Identify how to appropriately handle and administer surveys.

6. Identify and describe the direction and strength of a correlation.

7. Explain how causality, outliers, and restriction of range can limit the interpretation of a correlation coefficient.

8. Explain how linear regression can be used to predict outcomes.

9. Compute the Pearson correlation coefficient and linear regression using SPSS.

Chapter Summary

SURVEY DESIGNS

8.1 An Overview of Survey Designs

The **survey research design** is the use of a survey, administered either in written form or orally, to quantify, describe, or characterize an individual or a group. A **survey** is a series of questions or statements, called items, used in a questionnaire or interview to measure the self-reports or responses of respondents.

8.2 Types of Survey Items

Three types of questions or statements can be included in a survey: open-ended items, partially open-ended items, and restricted items. An **open-ended item** is a question or statement that is left completely "open" for response. A **partially open-ended item** gives participants a few restricted answer options and then a last option that allows participants to respond in their own words in case the few restricted options do not fit with the answer they want to give. A **restricted item** is one that includes only a restricted number of answer options. A **Likert scale** is an example of a restricted item.

8.3 Rules for Writing Survey Items

There are many rules for writing valid and reliable survey items. Nine rules described in Section 8.3 of the book are:

1. Keep it simple (use less than a high school–level vocabulary).

2. Avoid **double-barreled items** (ask one question in each item).

3. Use neutral or unbiased language (do not use offensive language).

4. Minimize the use of negative wording (to avoid confusion).

5. Avoid the **response set** pitfall (to avoid bias).

6. Use rating scales consistently (to avoid confusion).

7. Limit the points on a rating scale (keep a scale between 3 and 10 points).

8. Label or **anchor** the rating scale points (to avoid confusion).

9. Minimize survey length (to avoid participant fatigue).

8.4 Administering Surveys

A written survey can be administered in person, by mail, or using the Internet. An *in-person survey* has the highest response rates but is time consuming because it requires the researcher to be present while each and every participant completes the survey. *Mail surveys* are less time consuming than in-person surveys but are associated with low response rates and are more expensive in terms of the costs associated with sending mail. *Internet surveys* are the most convenient survey administration method but may limit the generalizability of the results to only those people who are computer-literate.

An interview survey can be administered face-to-face, by telephone, or in focus groups. *Face-to-face interviews* have the advantage of being more interpersonal but the drawback of requiring the interviewer to be present for each survey and can be prone to an **interviewer bias**. *Telephone interviews* can be interpersonal (e.g., the researcher asks the questions) or automated (e.g., computer-assisted technology asks the questions); however, they can be associated with few people willingly agreeing to complete the survey. *Focus group interviews* can allow for more dialogue or conversation on a topic; however, they can be associated with the same drawbacks as face-to-face interviews.

8.5 Surveys, Sampling, and Nonresponse Bias

The goal of administering a survey is to gain a high survey **response rate**, which is the portion of participants who agree to complete a survey among all individuals who were asked to complete the survey. Issues of response rate are associated with *nonresponse bias*, which occurs when participants choose not to complete a survey or choose not to respond to specific items in a survey. Although at least a 75% response rate should be obtained to minimize bias, the typical response rate to surveys in published research is less than 50%.

While the low response rates in published articles can be problematic, the goal is not always to generalize to a population in survey research. Instead, the results in survey research are often generalized to a theory (**theoretical generalization**) or generalized to other observations (**empirical generalization**).

8.6 Ethics in Focus: Handling and Administering Surveys

Four responsible and appropriate ways to handle and administer surveys are as follows: Make sure that the survey itself is not offensive or stressful to the respondent; do not coerce respondents into answering questions or completing a survey; do not harass respondents in any way for recruitment purposes; and protect the confidentiality or anonymity of respondents.

CORRELATIONAL DESIGNS

8.7 The Structure of Correlational Designs

A **correlational research design** is the measurement of two or more factors to determine or estimate the extent to which the factors are related or change in an identifiable pattern. To set up a correlational research design, we make two or more measurements for each individual observed. Once we measure two variables, we compute a **correlation coefficient** to identify the extent to which the values of the two variables or factors are related or change in an identifiable pattern. A correlation coefficient ranges from –1.0 to +1.0 and is used to identify a pattern in terms of the *direction* and *strength* of a relationship between two factors.

8.8 Describing the Relationship Between Variables

The extent to which two factors are related is determined by how far they fall from a **regression line** when data points are plotted in a **scatterplot**. The regression line is the best-fitting or closest-fitting straight line to a set of data points. The best-fitting straight line is the one that minimizes the distance of all data points that fall from it.

Direction of a correlation: In a scatterplot, a **positive correlation**, $r > 0$, means that as values of one factor increase, values of a second factor also increase; as values of one factor decrease, values of a second factor also decrease. A **negative correlation**, $r < 0$, means that as values of one factor increase, values of the second factor decrease. A zero correlation ($r = 0$) means that there is no linear pattern or relationship between two factors.

Strength of a correlation: The strength of a correlation reflects how consistently scores for each factor change. When plotted in a graph, scores are more consistent—meaning that their values change in a related pattern—the closer they fall to a regression line, or the straight line that best fits a set of data points.

The **Pearson correlation coefficient** is used to determine the strength and direction of the relationship between two factors on an interval or ratio scale of measurement. The formula for the Pearson correlation coefficient is a measure of the variance of data points from a regression line that is shared by the values of two factors (X and Y), divided by the total variance measured.

8.9 Limitations in Interpretation

Three considerations for interpreting a significant correlation are **causality** (a correlation does not demonstrate cause), **outliers** (which can change both the direction and the strength of the correlation), and **restriction of range** (which is a problem that arises when the range of data for one or both correlated factors in a sample is limited or restricted, compared to the range of data in the population from which the sample was selected).

8.10   Correlation, Regression, and Prediction

We can use the information provided by r to predict values of one factor, given known values of a second factor. We can use the value of r to compute the equation of a regression line and then use this equation to predict values of one factor, given known values of a second factor in a population; this procedure is called **linear regression**. To make use of the regression equation, we identify the following equation of a straight line:

$$Y = bX + a$$

In this equation, Y is a value we plot for the criterion variable, X is a value we plot for the predictor variable, b is the slope of a straight line, and a is the y-intercept (where the line crosses the y-axis). Given a set of data, we can find the values of a and b, then use the equation we found to predict future outcomes of Y.

8.11 SPSS in Focus: Correlation and Linear Regression

SPSS can be used to compute the Pearson correlation coefficient using the **Analyze, Correlate,** and **Bivariate** options in the menu bar. SPSS can also be used to compute linear regression using the **Analyze, Regression,** and **Linear. . .** options in the menu bar.

Chapter Summary Organized by Learning Objective

<u>LO 1</u>: Identify and construct open-ended, partially open-ended, and restricted survey items.

- An *open-ended item* is a question or statement in a survey that allows the respondent to give any response in his or her own words, without restriction. This type of question is most often used in qualitative research.
- A *partially open-ended item* is a question or statement in a survey that includes a few restricted answer options and then a last option that allows participants to respond in their own words in case the few restricted options do not fit with the answer they want to give.
- A *restricted item* is a question or statement in a survey that includes a restricted number of answer options to which participants must respond. This type of question is most often used in quantitative research.

<u>LO 2</u>: Identify nine rules for writing valid and reliable survey items.

- Nine rules for writing valid and reliable survey items are as follows:
  - Keep it simple.
  - Avoid double-barreled items.
  - Use neutral or unbiased language.
  - Minimize the use of negative wording.
  - Avoid the response set pitfall.
  - Use rating scales consistently.
  - Limit the points on a rating scale.
  - Label or anchor the rating scale points.
  - Minimize survey length.

<u>LO 3</u>: Describe methods of administering written surveys and interview surveys.

- A survey can be written (in print or electronically) or spoken (such as in an interview). A written survey can be administered in person, by mail, or using the Internet. An interview survey can be administered face-to-face, by telephone, or in focus groups. In-person and face-to-face surveys have the best response rates. Also, written surveys are preferred to interview surveys in quantitative research partly because interviews are prone to a possible interviewer bias.

<u>LO 4</u>: Explain how response rates to surveys can limit the interpretation of survey results.

- The problem of low response rates is that people who respond to surveys are probably different from those who do not respond. Because we cannot collect data from people who fail to respond, it is difficult to know the exact characteristics of this group of nonresponders. For this reason, we cannot know for sure whether survey results of those who do respond are representative of the larger population of interest, which includes those who do not respond to surveys.

<u>LO 5</u>: Identify how to appropriately handle and administer surveys.

- To appropriately handle and administer surveys, make sure that the survey itself is not offensive or stressful to the respondent; do not coerce respondents into answering questions or completing a survey; do not harass respondents in any way for recruitment purposes; protect the confidentiality or anonymity of respondents.

<u>LO 6</u>: Identify and describe the direction and strength of a correlation.

- The **correlation coefficient**, r, is used to measure the extent to which two factors (X and Y) are related. The value of r indicates the direction and strength of a correlation. When r is negative, the values for two factors change in opposite directions; when r is positive, the values for two factors change in the same direction. The closer r is to ± 1.0, the stronger the correlation, and the more closely two factors are related.
- When plotted in a graph, the strength of a correlation is reflected by the distance that data points fall from the **regression line**. The closer that data points fall to a regression line, or the straight line that best fits a set of data points, the stronger the correlation or relationship between two factors.

<u>LO 7</u>: Explain how causality, outliers, and restriction of range can limit the interpretation of a correlation coefficient.

- Three considerations that must be made to accurately interpret a correlation coefficient are: (1) correlations do not demonstrate causality, (2) outliers can change the direction and the strength of a correlation, and (3) never generalize the direction and the strength of a correlation beyond the range of data measured in a sample (restriction of range).

<u>LO 8</u>: Explain how linear regression can be used to predict outcomes.

- We can use the information provided by r to predict values of one factor, given known values of a second factor using a procedure called **linear regression**. Specifically, we can use the value of r to compute the equation of a regression line and then use this equation to predict values of one factor, given known values of a second factor in a population. Using the following equation of the regression line, $Y = bX + a$, we can predict values of the criterion variable, Y, so long as we know values of the predictor variable, X.

LO 9: Compute the Pearson correlation coefficient and linear regression using SPSS.

- SPSS can be used to compute the Pearson correlation coefficient using the **Analyze, Correlate,** and **Bivariate** options in the menu bar. These actions will display a dialog box that allows you to identify the variables and to run the correlation (for more details, see Section 8.11 in the book).
- SPSS can be used to compute linear regression using the **Analyze, Regression,** and **Linear . . .** options in the menu bar. These actions will display a dialog box that allows you to identify the variables and to run the linear regression (for more details, see Section 8.11 in the book).

Tips and Cautions for Students

Survey length. A survey can be too short, and a survey can be too long. It can often be difficult to identify the appropriate length of a survey. One simple strategy is to review the items in a survey and for each item ask: If this is deleted, will the survey still address the hypothesis or research question being tested? If *yes*, then delete the item; if *no*, then keep the item in the survey. This strategy should help you identify items that should remain and items that should be removed in a survey.

Direction of a correlation. Keep in mind that a negative correlation indicates direction only. A negative correlation does not mean all the scores are negative or that two factors are not related. Instead, a negative correlation refers to the relationship between two factors such that as values for one factor increase, values for a second factor decrease. The closer a negative correlation is to −1.0, the stronger this relationship is between the two factors.

Correlation is not causality. Causality cannot be inferred with correlational data. A correlation never demonstrates that changes in one factor cause changes in a second factor. Instead, always think of two factors as changing together but not necessarily due to one another—their relationship is associative, not causal. Hence, to interpret a correlation, we can conclude that changes in one factor are associated with or correspond to changes in a second factor; changes in one factor do not *cause* changes in a second factor.

Practice Quiz

1. A series of questions or items used in a questionnaire or interview to measure the self-reports or responses of respondents is called a:

   a. survey

   b. questionnaire

   c. self-report measure

   d. all of the above

2. What is the following item called? "What are your views on the obesity being a global epidemic?"

   a. open-ended item

   b. partially open-ended item

   c. restricted item

   d. Likert scale item

3. Which of the following types of items are most commonly used in quantitative research?

   a. open-ended items

   b. partially open-ended items

   c. restricted items

   d. both a and b

4. Which of the following is *not* a rule for writing valid and reliable survey items?

   a. limit the points on a rating scale

   b. use at least a college-level vocabulary

   c. avoid double-barreled items

   d. use rating scales consistently

5. If the following item were rated on a 5-point scale from 1 (*never*) to 5 (*often*), then what would be wrong with it? "I wake up before sunrise and feel good most mornings."

   a. The item has too many points on the scale.

   b. The item includes biased language.

   c. The item is double-barreled.

   d. The anchors on the scale are not labeled.

6. Suppose 20 "attitudes" survey items are all anchored from 1 (*strongly disagree*) to 5 (*strongly agree*). If all items were written such that higher ratings indicated more positive attitudes, then what problem might occur?

   a. double-barreled

   b. response set

   c. anchoring

   d. bipolar scale

7. Points on a scale should generally be limited to:

   a. 3 to 10

   b. at least 4

   c. no more than 9

   d. Scales can have any number of points without limitation.

8. What is the characteristic of a bipolar scale?

   a. The scale includes negative values.

   b. The scale typically has a midpoint.

    c. Values are centered around 0.

    d. all of the above

9. When conducting a face-to-face interview, the demeanor, words, or expressions of a researcher can influence the responses of a participant. This concern is called:

    a. face time

    b. face-to-face bias

    c. anchoring bias

    d. interviewer bias

10. The goal for administering a survey is to gain a high _____.

    a. response set

    b. response rate

    c. total score

    d. nonresponse bias

11. Which of the following is a measure for the strength and direction of the relationship between two factors?

    a. correlation coefficient

    b. standardized exam scores

    c. data point aggregate

    d. scatterplot

12. The graphical display for correlated data is called a:

    a. bar graph

    b. line graph

    c. scatterplot

    d. all of the above

13. The strength of the direction between two factors is identified by:

    a. the distance of data points from the regression line

    b. the value of the correlation coefficient

    c. the sign of the correlation coefficient as positive or negative

    d. both a and b

14. Which of the following indicates the *weakest* correlation?

    a. $r = +0.77$

    b. $r = +0.10$

    c. $r = -0.50$

    d. $r = -0.80$

15. Which graph indicates a negative correlation?

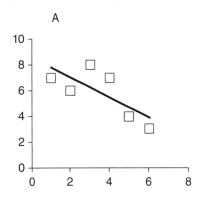 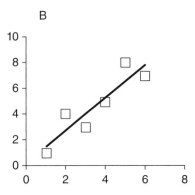

    a. Graph A

    b. Graph B

16. A significant correlation shows that two factors are:

    a. causal

    b. coincidental

    c. related

    d. all of the above

17. Outliers can change:

    a. the strength of a correlation only

    b. the direction of a correlation only

    c. the strength and direction of a correlation

    d. the sign of a correlation, but not the value of a correlation

18. A researcher should never describe a correlation beyond the range of data observed in a sample to avoid what problem?

    a. file drawer problem

    b. restriction of range

    c. reverse causality

    d. covariance

19. We can use the value of *r* to compute the equation of a regression line and then use this equation to predict values of one factor, given known values of a second factor in a population, using a procedure called:

    a. linear regression

    b. survey monkey

    c. predictor enhancement

    d. advanced equation modeling

20. Which of the following is an equation of a straight line?

    a. $E = mc^2$

    b. $Y = abX$

    c. $Y = X + ba$

    d. $Y = bX + a$

Key Term Word Search

```
J D L D H B M G U N T C U Z D B R E S P O N S E R A T E V X D V Y Z Q L V S D G A R J S
Y Y A P O I F P O T A E U G J I L I R G S D P S P E Z A K T R R N R I V O V I O C V I G
V E T E V N T G U P P O S I T I V E C O R R E L A T I O N E Q O Z Q I W F E S U Y B P B
U V O J Y T P T T E Y J N G R J M Q A Q U U N T Q C M E T P I S V G G L J W Q S P W V F
N V L M L E K F L A K T F U M X T G J D Q R Y Q X N A H B T V R N J I V C S E D T B W V
G G K R E R G T I R Z T A K C W J C R O J N N C Z O F M A R E P V V T L U E C S A Z M T
W X T B A V V J E E C U Q I X F C H I L H N R Z R T I Z W F Y F N T A Y T W I E T O A C
X S I I V I R F R S E L I R Y O J M U L U T Q D Y I I T A Z Z R X P G A D Q F R B K H L
E Q D N M E O P V P L G G N H G I P F P X Y E T X L T L X T J W Q B X C E P Q M Z T V P
N W V A I W B W L O N H S O B L D E M P I R I C A L G E N E R A L I Z A T I O N O H J M
F X X F P E Q M A N C N P S B M Y X W I V L U R S S Y N R M D N I Y Y V W Z Q T V S I T
A X G E F R H Q I S R R Q V S T V N T R A K E P N P F D Z I C G N P I L V W N S T L D G
Q N H W G B Z J F E Z O G K T W S D J S E N Q D K Z R P S Z O O D V K K V E Q N K R D T
V V G N P I V H D S J D E S M O M C U G E G G Z E P D E T N I N N J H X I S I I Y H W A
W R L Y W A S S T E Q Y X J N D E A C G G H R X F X Z S D T F G V P C C V O B W E Z S K
G U K I X S L L A T I M Z F K C C E L Q H G B E J I J F A I I S Y A I H P K S M L V Z D
U X S U K A J G W Z H R R E O E O A S Y C H R Q S U V L L S C H G F R A S N M K Y O D J
M R T J X E R V K C L U Y G S H C N P L E J R O T S E H E B F T I T I O J A K J Q P F
L I E F P E R N U S O E M R C I D N F S V S A W X R I D F Z X E O A I I A Z E T C T L B
L V D S V A M T Q E C R E S T O Z M P O P V Y Q R S H O C X O F D R T J Q B B Q N H I A
D J W G T X R U S N P V R E J N G Z O H U W K O I C Y J N C Q I V S V H F J L H O Z B N
F K L Q Q R A X A C E T R E S A T C W P K N C X R X N V N W B E E U G A V I X E G W F R
F G Z K K R I I U R A O Y I L O M A V V F E D A W M Y O I R P U Y H N Z R S J F Y R V A
D R H R R T R C L O E L I X S A S U F V V C E V C L I G N V Q K A I Q W E I K K R B W N
S X C P Z A M V T H H V E O T X T W W I I S P R A T E A D D A W X G P L Q J A S B E T D
G Q L C V M D G T E G O J D P U J I T J E H B E A R S J E M V Z M X A S C A L B P X V O
D C Q O C F D U K D D Z P W O M D A O R N D O L R S I L U Q J L F C R J R T Z Q L A L M
H X C M H G W P O A B I B A S G G P Y N H Z E M I E E A R N F K S L F R V G J U J E A D
X C S K D B T W I E T R T O E E B E S F A R J D D R Q H B B R R W C K S H H F E R C F I
T T M N W Q K L F K L P L E N F V E E E R L A Q R I K K Q L A R P S Z E Z E J E H D P G
Z A K J C M J E S C G N W N M R P R R O Y T R A Y M U Y L L E R J S D I Y G N W I W J I
Z W A H I F I I F K S O O L U V B U C O P T I E I H H V O Z A Q S W A N C H O R S T C T
Q N L I N E A R R E G R E S S I O N V D P E E K S B M P P F P Z I I Y F S P S V V Y K D
Q H Q P O M Q R J Q U D H W B F O A D H L A K E H E I E T I D G R S S T L C H R D A Q I
M F D M P Z F G Z T T Y B R K S B Y D B T R Q X D B A B C I N W K H U D E E O L Z S P A
U S P X E L C Q K B W B W T R L X V U H E B W F L J P R O K D Z H G K R L P A R U T G L
N R J T C A S H B A C M P A L R L O D P H O I T C B W V C G M T R T V O V W P Q X I Z I
S X M H N D X M M T N J E Y C H D C O Q N C C U F G X G Z H G E P Z D N I E X E J N P N
V P C M I H H D I O K P R C X O P E N E N D E D I T E M D I D N X M R W M K Y K S U I G
O L I R K K K G J I C Z I M B D W S C A T T E R P L O T B S X E J J Q Y N I M Z H O W H
P A R T I A L L Y O P E N E N D E D I T E M W W U R J R D M N B S N B C Z C I E N Z I N
V D O S R O J F E Y C O R R E L A T I O N C O E F F I C I E N T I I I J A S J Q E U R P
F T E Y W B Z W G C L O S E D E N D E D I T E M O R W Y J R L Z Q L G P H C P F F A P F
W F D G A G Q A R R H R G C M X F R E S T R I C T I O N O F R A N G E N U Z B G R V S I
D B U Y N P V I F U S I X Y C E K V W G G H S V X X A I R E V E R S E C O D E D I T E M
```

survey	scatterplot	criterion variable
survey research design	data points	open-ended item
Likert scale	linear regression	partially open-ended item
double-barreled questions	positive correlation	restricted item
response set	negative correlation	theoretical generalization
bipolar scales	Pearson correlation coefficient	empirical generalization
anchors	covariance	confound variable
interviewer bias	outlier	reverse causality
response rate	restriction of range	reverse-coded item
correlational research design	regression	closed-ended item
correlation coefficient	predictor variable	random-digit dialing

ACROSS

3. a type of correlation in which the value of *r* is negative

6. the portion of participants who agree to complete a survey among all individuals who were asked to complete the survey

8. a score that falls substantially above or below most other scores in a data set

10. the extent to which the values of two factors vary together

11. an item that is scored by coding or entering responses for the item in reverse order from how they are listed

13. the extent to which results in a survey or other research study are consistent with data obtained in previous research studies

14. the tendency for participants to respond the same way to all items in a survey when the direction of ratings is the same for all items in the survey

16. a correlation coefficient for two factors on an interval or ratio scale of measurement

17. a numeric scale used to indicate a participant's rating for a survey item

18. a survey item that allows respondents to give any response in their own words, without restriction

20. a statistical procedure for the extent to which a regression equation can predict values of one factor, given known values of a second factor

21. a variable with values that are known and can be used to predict values of another variable

23. the best-fitting straight line to a set of data points

24. a statistic used to measure the strength and direction of the linear relationship between two factors

DOWN

1. a survey item that asks participants for one response to two different questions or statements

2. the tendency for the demeanor, words, or expressions of a researcher to influence the responses of a participant when the researcher and participant are in direct contact

4. a type of generalization for the extent to which results in a survey or other research study are consistent with predictions made by an existing theory

5. adjectives that are given to describe the end points of a rating scale to give the scale greater meaning

7. an unanticipated variable not accounted for in a research study that could be causing or associated with observed changes in one or more measured variables

9. a strategy for selecting participants in telephone interviews by generating telephone numbers to dial or call at random

12. a problem that arises when the direction of causality between two factors can be in either direction

15. a graphical display of discrete data points used to summarize the relationship between two factors

19. an item, question, or statement in a survey that includes a restricted number of answer options to which participants must respond

22. a series of questions or statements, called items, used in a questionnaire or interview to measure the self-reports or responses of respondents

Crossword Puzzle

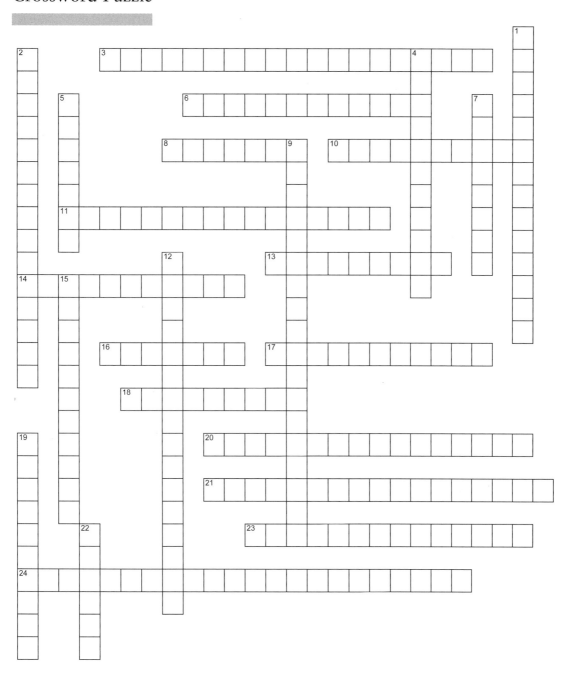

SECTION IV

Quasi-Experimental and Experimental Research Designs

9

Quasi-Experimental and Single-Case Experimental Designs

CHAPTER LEARNING OBJECTIVES

1. Define and identify a quasi-experiment and a quasi-independent variable.

2. Identify and describe two one-group quasi-experimental research designs: the posttest-only and pretest-posttest designs.

3. Identify and describe two nonequivalent control group quasi-experimental research designs: the posttest-only and pretest-posttest designs.

4. Identify and describe three time series quasi-experimental research designs: basic, interrupted, and control designs.

5. Identify and describe three developmental quasi-experimental research designs: longitudinal, cross-sectional, and cohort-sequential designs.

6. Define the single-case experimental design.

7. Identify and describe three types of single-case research designs: the reversal, multiple-baseline, and changing-criterion designs.

8. Identify in a graph the stability and magnitude of a dependent measure, and explain how each is related to the internal validity of a single-case design.

9. Identify three ways that researchers can strengthen the external validity of a result using a single-case design.

Chapter Summary

QUASI-EXPERIMENTAL DESIGNS

9.1 An Overview of Quasi-Experimental Designs

A **quasi-experimental research design** is the use of methods and procedures to make observations in a study that is structured similar to an experiment, but the conditions and experiences of participants lack some control because the study lacks random assignment, includes a preexisting factor (i.e., a **quasi-independent variable**), or does not include a comparison/control group. Hence a quasi-experiment does not demonstrate causality.

9.2 Quasi-Experimental Design: One-Group Designs

Two types of one-group quasi-experiments are the one-group posttest-only design and the one-group pretest-posttest design.

A **one-group posttest-only design**, also called the *one-shot case study*, is a quasi-experimental research design in which a dependent variable is measured for one group of participants following a treatment. The design lacks a comparison group and is prone to threats to internal validity, such as history effects (unanticipated events that can co-occur with the exam) and maturation effects (natural changes in learning), that make this design a poor research design.

A **one-group pretest-posttest design** is a quasi-experimental research design in which the same dependent variable is measured in one group of participants before and after a treatment is administered. The advantage of this design is that we can compare scores after a treatment to scores on the same measure in the same participants prior to a treatment. The disadvantage is that the one-group design does not include a no-treatment control group and therefore is still prone to many threats to internal validity associated with observing the same participants over time.

9.3 Quasi-Experimental Design: Nonequivalent Control Group Designs

Two types of nonequivalent control group quasi-experiments are the nonequivalent control group posttest-only design and the nonequivalent control group pretest-posttest design. A **nonequivalent control group** is a control group that is matched upon certain preexisting characteristics similar to those observed in a treatment group, but to which participants are not randomly assigned. Preexisting differences between groups or participants are called **selection differences**. In a quasi-experiment, a dependent variable measured in a treatment group is compared to that in the nonequivalent control group.

A **nonequivalent control group posttest-only design** is a quasi-experimental research design in which a dependent variable is measured following a treatment in one group and also in a nonequivalent control group that does not receive the treatment.

A **nonequivalent control group pretest-posttest design** is a quasi-experimental research design in which a dependent variable is measured in one group of participants before (pretest) and after (posttest) a treatment and that same dependent variable is also measured at pretest and posttest in another nonequivalent control group that does not receive the treatment.

9.4 Quasi-Experimental Design: Time Series Designs

Three types of time series quasi-experiments are the basic time series design, the interrupted time series design, and the control time series design. Time series quasi-experimental research designs include many observations made before and after a treatment.

A **basic time series design** is a quasi-experimental research design in which a dependent variable is measured at many different points in time in one group before and after a treatment that is manipulated by the researcher is administered. Using the basic time series design, the researcher manipulates or controls when the treatment will occur.

An **interrupted time series design** is a quasi-experimental research design in which a dependent variable is measured at many different points in time in one group before and after a treatment that naturally occurs—and so is not controlled or manipulated by a researcher. Using an interrupted time series design, the researcher does not manipulate or control when the treatment will occur.

A **control time series design** is a basic or interrupted time series quasi-experimental research design that also includes a nonequivalent control group that is observed during the same period of time as a treatment group, but does not receive the treatment.

9.5 Quasi-Experimental Design: Developmental Designs

Three types of quasi-experiments in developmental research are longitudinal design, cross-sectional design, and cohort-sequential design.

A **longitudinal design** is a quasi-experimental research design used to study changes across the life span by observing the same participants at different points in time and measuring the same dependent variable at each time. The advantage of this design is that changes in participant behavior can be recorded over long periods of time, even years. The disadvantage of the longitudinal design is that it is prone to all threats to internal validity associated with observing participants over time.

A **cross-sectional design** is a quasi-experimental research design in which participants are grouped by their age and participant characteristics are measured in each age group. Each age group is a **cohort,** which is any group of individuals who share common statistical traits or characteristics or experiences within a defined period. An advantage of the cross-sectional design is that participants are observed one time in each cohort; a disadvantage is the possibility of **cohort effects,** which occur if preexisting differences between members of a cohort can explain an observed result.

A **cohort-sequential design** is a quasi-experimental research design in which different cohorts of participants at different or overlapping ages are observed longitudinally over time. This design is a combination of the longitudinal and cross-sectional designs.

9.6 Ethics in Focus: Development and Aging

Ethical concerns related to age are often focused on those who are very young and those who are very old. Three rules to ensure that such groups or cohorts are treated in an ethical manner are to (1) obtain assent when necessary, (2) obtain permission from a parent, legal guardian, or other legally capable individual, such as a medical professional, when a participant is a minor or when a participant is functionally or legally incapable of providing consent, and (3) clearly show that the benefits of a study outweigh the costs.

SINGLE-CASE EXPERIMENTAL DESIGNS

9.7 An Overview of Single-Case Designs

A **single-case experimental design** is an experimental research design in which a participant serves as his or her own control and the dependent variable measured is analyzed for each individual participant and is not averaged across groups or across participants. The single-case design includes randomization, manipulation, and control, making it an experimental research design.

9.8 Single-Case Baseline-Phase Designs

Three types of single-case experimental research designs are reversal design, multiple-baseline design, and changing-criterion design.

A **reversal design**, or **ABA design**, is a single-case experimental design in which a single participant is observed before (A), during (B), and after (A) a treatment or manipulation. If the treatment in Phase B causes a change in the dependent variable, then the dependent variable should change from baseline to treatment, then return to baseline levels when the treatment is removed. To analyze the data, we look for two types of patterns that indicate that a treatment is causing an observed change: a *change in level* or a *change in trend*.

When it is not possible for a behavior to return to baseline levels, a **multiple-baseline design** can be used in which a treatment is successively administered over time to different participants, for different behaviors, or in different settings. The start of a treatment phase varies using the multiple-baseline design to determine if the changes in a dependent variable begin only after the baseline phases end.

For situations in which we administer many different treatments, a **changing-criterion design** can be used in which a baseline phase is followed by successive treatment phases where some criterion or target level of behavior is changed from one treatment phase to the next. The participant must meet the criterion of a treatment phase, before the next treatment phase is administered.

9.9 Validity, Stability, Magnitude, and Generality

The stability and magnitude of change across phases in a single-case design determine the extent to which a researcher has established control. The **stability** of a measure is indicated by the consistency in the pattern of change in each phase. The more stable a measure, the greater the control and the higher the internal validity in an experiment. The **magnitude** of change is the size of the change in a dependent measure observed between phases. The greater the magnitude of changes between phases, the greater the control and the higher the internal validity in a single-case experiment.

Generalizing across behaviors, generalizing across subjects/participants, or generalizing across settings can demonstrate external validity.

9.10 Ethics in Focus: The Ethics of Innovation

Single-case designs allow for the conduct of innovative research to rigorously evaluate potential, yet untested, treatments with small samples, thereby testing a treatment without exposing such a treatment to large groups of participants, particularly when the potential costs of implementing such a treatment are largely unknown or untested.

Chapter Summary Organized by Learning Objective

LO 1: Define and identify a quasi-experiment and a quasi-independent variable.

- A quasi-experimental research design is structured similar to an experiment, except that this design lacks random assignment, includes a preexisting factor (i.e., a variable that is not manipulated), or does not include a comparison/control group.
- A quasi-independent variable is a preexisting variable that is often a characteristic inherent to an individual, which differentiates the groups or conditions being compared in a research study. Because the levels of the variable are preexisting, it is not possible to randomly assign participants to groups.

LO 2: Identify and describe two one-group quasi-experimental research designs: the posttest-only and pretest-posttest designs.

- The **one-group posttest-only design** is a quasi-experimental research design in which a dependent variable is measured for one group of participants following a treatment.
- The **one-group pretest-posttest design** is a quasi-experimental research design in which the same dependent variable is measured in one group of participants before and after a treatment is administered.

LO 3: Identify and describe two nonequivalent control group quasi-experimental research designs: the posttest-only and pretest-posttest designs.

- A **nonequivalent control group** is a control group that is matched upon certain preexisting characteristics similar to those observed in a treatment group, but to which participants are not randomly assigned. When a nonequivalent control group is used, **selection differences** can potentially explain an observed difference between an experimental and a nonequivalent control group.
- The **nonequivalent control group posttest-only design** is a quasi-experimental research design in which a dependent variable is measured following a treatment in one group and is compared to a nonequivalent control group that does not receive the treatment.
- The **nonequivalent control group pretest-posttest design** is a quasi-experimental research design in which a dependent variable is measured in one group of participants before (pretest) and after (posttest) a treatment, and that same dependent variable is also measured at pretest and posttest in a nonequivalent control group that does not receive the treatment.

<u>LO 4</u>: Identify and describe three time series quasi-experimental research designs: basic, interrupted, and control designs.

- The **basic time series design** is a quasi-experimental research design in which a dependent variable is measured at many different points in time in one group before and after a treatment that is manipulated by the researcher is administered.
- The **interrupted time series design** is a quasi-experimental research design in which a dependent variable is measured at many different points in time in one group before and after a treatment that naturally occurs.
- A **control time series design** is a basic or interrupted time series quasi-experimental research design that also includes a nonequivalent control group that is observed during the same period of time as a treatment group, but does not receive the treatment.

<u>LO 5</u>: Identify and describe three developmental quasi-experimental research designs: longitudinal, cross-sectional, and cohort-sequential designs.

- A **longitudinal design** is a quasi-experimental research design used to study changes across the life span by observing the same participants over time and measuring the same dependent variable at each time.
- A **cross-sectional design** is a quasi-experimental research design in which participants are grouped by their age and participant characteristics are measured in each age group. Each age group is a **cohort,** so this design is prone to **cohort effects,** which occur when unique characteristics in each cohort can potentially explain an observed difference between groups.
- A **cohort-sequential design** is a quasi-experimental research design that combines longitudinal and cross-sectional techniques by observing different cohorts of participants over time at different or overlapping ages.

<u>LO 6</u>: Define the single-case experimental design.

- The **single-case experimental design** is an experimental research design in which a participant serves as his or her own control and the dependent variable measured is analyzed for each individual participant and is not averaged across groups or across participants. This design meets the three requirements to demonstrate cause and effect: randomization, manipulation, and comparison/control.

<u>LO 7</u>: Identify and describe three types of single-case research designs: the reversal, multiple-baseline, and changing-criterion designs.

- The **reversal design** is a single-case experimental design in which a single participant is observed before (A), during (B), and after (A) a treatment or manipulation.
- The **multiple-baseline design** is a single-case experimental design in which a treatment is successively administered over time to different participants, for different behaviors, or in different settings.
- The **changing-criterion design** is a single-case experimental design in which a baseline phase is followed by successive treatment phases in which some criterion or target level of behavior is changed from one treatment phase to the next. The participant must meet the criterion of one treatment phase, before the next treatment phase is administered.

<u>LO 8</u>: Identify in a graph the stability and magnitude of a dependent measure, and explain how each is related to the internal validity of a single-case design.

- The **stability** of a measure is the consistency in the pattern of change in a dependent measure in each phase of a design. The more stable or consistent changes in a dependent measure are in each phase, the higher the internal validity of a research design.
- The **magnitude** of change in a measure is the size of the change in a dependent measure observed between phases of a design. A measure can have a change in level or a change in trend. The larger the magnitude of change, the greater the internal validity of a research design.

<u>LO 9</u>: Identify three ways that researchers can strengthen the external validity of a result using a single-case design.

- A single-case design is typically associated with low population validity (a subcategory of external validity). However, three ways that researchers can strengthen the external validity of a result using a single-case design is to generalize across behaviors, across subjects or participants, and across settings.

Tips and Cautions for Students

The nonequivalent control group. One way that a nonequivalent control group can be distinguished from a standard control group is that a random assignment cannot be used to create or assign participants to a nonequivalent control group. Because random assignment cannot be used to assign participants to a nonequivalent control group, these types of controls are used with quasi-experiments. Indeed, anytime a nonequivalent control group is used, the study design cannot be experimental because random assignment is not used.

Using multiple cases with a single-case design. A single-case design implies that only one case, or only one participant, will be observed. However, some single-case designs actually require the use of multiple cases. Suppose, for example, we observe Case 1 and Case 2 using a single-case design. What makes this a single-case design? Keep in mind that a single-case design is associated with the analysis, not necessarily the observation, of a single case. Hence, this is a single-case design, if we will evaluate or analyze each case separately; this is evident when graphs depict the data for individual cases and not data that have been combined into one or more groups.

Practice Quiz

1. The quasi-experimental research design is structured similar to an experiment, except that this design:
   a. includes a quasi-independent variable
   b. lacks an appropriate or equivalent control group

   c. includes a variable that cannot be manipulated

   d. all of the above

2. One-group quasi-experimental research designs lack:

   a. participants

   b. a comparison group

   c. a dependent variable

   d. a hypothesis

3. An advantage of the one-group pretest-posttest design compared to the one-group posttest-only design is:

   a. the one-group pretest-posttest design includes a comparison in the value of a dependent variable before and after a treatment

   b. the one-group pretest-posttest design includes a posttest that actually follows a treatment

   c. the one-group pretest-posttest design includes a dependent variable that is measured in a group of participants

   d. the one-group pretest-posttest design can include more than one group of participants or observe one group of participants two or more times

4. Health assessment scores in a group of residents in Syracuse, New York, are compared to health assessment scores for residents in Buffalo, New York, which is a city that shares key similar demographics. Buffalo, New York, in this example is a(n):

   a. control group

   b. experimental group

   c. nonequivalent control group

   d. confound variable

5. Students register for an 8 a.m. or a 3 p.m. research methods course. Any preexisting differences between these classes of students are called:

   a. nonequivalences

   b. treatment effects

   c. controlled effects

   d. selection differences

6. A key difference between the nonequivalent control group posttest-only design and the nonequivalent control group pretest-posttest design is:

   a. only one design includes a nonequivalent control group

   b. only one design can compare changes in a dependent variable between an experimental and a nonequivalent control group

   c. only one design can compare changes in a dependent variable before and after treatment in both groups

   d. only one group includes a posttest that is observed in one group but not in the nonequivalent control group

7. Which of the following is a type of time series quasi-experimental design?

    a. basic

    b. interrupted

    c. control

    d. all of the above

8. A professor compares rates of class attendance in her class for five classes before and five classes after a university attendance policy was enacted. What type of time series design is described in this example?

    a. basic time series design

    b. interrupted time series design

    c. control time series design

    d. longitudinal time series design

9. The primary factor of interest for developmental research designs is:

    a. age

    b. health

    c. longevity

    d. gender

10. Using the cross-sectional design, each age group is considered a(n):

    a. manipulation

    b. independent variable

    c. cohort

    d. posttest

11. Which of the following is true about the cohort-sequential design?

    a. It combines the longitudinal and cross-sectional research designs.

    b. It is a type of time series experimental design.

    c. It cannot account for cohort effects.

    d. It does not control at all for threats to internal validity.

12. Which of the following explains why the single-case research design is regarded as an experimental research design?

    a. Only a single participant is observed.

    b. The sample size is small, which increases power.

    c. A dependent variable is measured.

    d. Researchers use randomization, manipulation, and control.

13. Which of the following is *not* a type of single-case research design?

    a. reversal design

    b. reverse causality design

c. multiple-baseline design

d. changing-criterion design

14. The following notation represents which type of single-case experimental design?

> A (baseline phase) → B (treatment phase) → A (baseline phase)

a. reversal design

b. multiple-baseline design

c. changing-criterion design

d. none of the above

15. Which of the following single-case experimental designs requires the observation of multiple cases?

a. reversal design

b. multiple-baseline design

c. changing-criterion design

d. all of the above

16. A researcher presents a child with positive reinforcements to reduce how often she bites her nails. The researcher successively increases the amount of reinforcement given to the child after an initial baseline phase. The successive treatments are administered until the child has reached a level where she is no longer biting her nails. What type of single-case experimental design was used in this example?

a. reversal design

b. multiple-baseline design

c. changing-criterion design

d. all of the above

17. The analysis of single-case experimental research designs is based largely on a _____ inspection of the data in a graph.

a. statistical

b. blind

c. parametric

d. visual

18. Which of the following can demonstrate high internal validity using a single-case experimental design?

a. a measure that is stable within each phase and has a large magnitude of change between phases

b. a measure that is unstable within each phase and has a large magnitude of change between phases

c. a measure that is stable within each phase and has a minimal magnitude of change between phases

d. a measure that is unstable within each phase and has a minimal magnitude of change between phases

19. The results in a single-case design can have high external validity in terms of generalizing across:

    a.   behaviors

    b.   settings

    c.   subjects or participants

    d.   all of the above

20. Which of the following is true about the graph of the single-case data below?

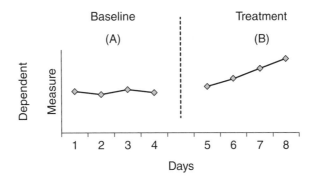

a. The graph shows data with low internal validity.

b. The graph shows a statistically significant effect.

c. The graph shows data with high internal validity.

d. The dependent variable was only measured in the baseline phase.

Key Term Word Search

```
C R O S S S E C T I O N A L D E S I G N Y I M L P K L T K Y M A D P I F Y C J N
U Y S X I F S K M M J M I R A W L V H Q M I W D T E C L U Y P K T N P T V L L M
M Q O H W N L W X Q Q P B Y B T Z Q C G L M F Q N E C L Q F E G P O C V N X N G
Z U F C R B G L P R I K X M R X P S Z O I K P Y O P L W M Z F T X N Z V F G O G
N A H I P M T T J G E Z E Q J B D E P Q N G S R P D C N C U X M G P C N I K M K
W S O B F E L X D D V O M T J R Q Q N P F R I M U U D B D W A I V Z T S X P T G
J I P I F M F K F Q I J L R Y I O Z O O E T Z V C R T Q Z F S S F A E E M K F Z
Y I Q Q S U F P W D C O H O R T E F F E C T S Y F O J J K E T M L D X Z J W F N
C N V U F H H Z R T I M E S E R I E S D E S I G N L N M D K T D L Z K P X Y F Y
B D Y T A J P J I J I W C O O E Z W S Y W Q U A G P T Y F A P A D N W F N G V D
M E E X M S I V C B O R D I F F S C T T J E D B U D L I O F S C G O J G M I F K
V P R S S J I J X R X C E I O Z S I E R N W T O Q N B Q I R C I L G I Q Y Z I E
U E D O T Z S E G X T C A H N V L U G Y R E R E O E T X E N S U D S S A V X X G
I N B V C L X X X I F O H J L I K W K I V G O T G L T V O E H M E W T N I H E A
H D O N N M V K Q P Q H Q A B N S T I D L F S L S L E W D H E D G H G P A W O G
Q E K W U I O N P C E F F A N B E S Q O L E X U K R Q E R H T Q J I B B T X V Q
V N H N W W D T U N H R T V V G J S R D T P Y F J N N M S S V L S V Z R L B Z S
J T B Y D Z U X H X T S I K V J I T C T K A W G R I G E E J G E V K O A S D V P
F V G O N N Q M O Z X A A M O P N N S G K B P T L H C T P D D P G H V D W E Q M
N A X V C P J I B C A Z P Q E O T O G X I H C E W N T B X L T J O U W J I G F W
P R E M U W I S U G Q W V R C N P C K C K M S M E S G U A L Q C H S X T A V S A
H I V E M F Z M B Z S K O T H P T I Z J R A O R O S Y N V F C U I V W D R I W J
V A V R J P W O T H P P N M U H E A N S B I E P Y A I X O F Z C P L S L I A W D
H B X B T A P X O I L E U O Z X L C L E J F T C I D I T I J J M K T G M A W S R
Y L I M L W O H D K L R R N T I M Y L R F S L E U S D Z D X L T B A T O C F D G
I E J V Q V C K J A T G G M Y V U P B I E J T T R Q O L F A B G Z B W M D N P Z
G K N F W D Z C V Y E M G L Q C I M D T P S I R K I B Q M C S D S E A H J V R S
O O U E R E D I E N R R N W H T M N E H J G E B X Q O Y B M X H B J O I X V R Q
T Q R X E H U H O Y V R Z C L A O R O K N W W A X J T N Y C A Q H T E K Z B S C
C S C C U Q C B V E T Q S U U I P R P O X P W B R D E P D A D G Z N Y Z Z Q P L
R V Z O E N A L A O X S M R T P F X L H E J N Y S C T P H E S X N C P P P N S S
H A O N S X N G H S H Y R C U S H C V D F V F E N A H Q W A S N E I B I F S Q J
I P O H G B G R B T E L E O G A P Q Z W W O W X S A Z D I C S I T E T G E N U M
U N Z Z L M O Z T H P L R G Y J K Y T R Z L E B V F L O E B M E G K V U V C M S
Z W Q S F G P A W N E G I S B Y W E G T Q X Q H B Z U J E S R N F N A B D H C T
M V L B U Z T P X S E A E N A X C X P L F G B M K K L E A C I R C O C F P E D K
R F F G R Q E V G N K A V B E V Q S M H Z U C J N P E I D T D G L K U I Q H J T
A G W L R V I X O D C N D Y L E Q B L K W K Q A G Z U S V N B S N A I D A Y V P
B T J Q C O Z P M U K N O N E Q U I V A L E N T C O N T R O L G R O U P I N Y Z
I A C T X G W Q K D S I N G L E C A S E E X P E R I M E N T A L D E S I G N T I
```

quasi-experimental research design
one-group pretest-posttest design
single-case experimental design
one-group posttest-only design
nonequivalent control group
quasi-independent variable
changing-criterion design
multiple-baseline design
cross-sectional design cohort

selection differences
longitudinal design
time series design
reversal design
cohort effects
magnitude
stability
baseline
cohort
phase

ACROSS

3. a time series design with a treatment that naturally occurs

4. a threat to internal validity in which differences in the characteristics of participants in different cohorts can alternatively explain an outcome

6. an experimental design in which data are analyzed for each individual participant and not averaged across groups

10. a quasi-experimental design in which the same dependent variable is measured in one group before and after treatment

12. a developmental design in which different cohorts of participants at different or overlapping ages are observed longitudinally

13. a single-case design in which a treatment is successively administered over time to different participants

15. the size of a change between each phase of a single-case design

16. a series of trials or observations made in one condition

17. a quasi-experimental design in which a dependent variable is measured for one group of participants following a treatment

18. a group of people who share common statistical traits or experiences in a defined period

19. a preexisting variable that differentiates groups in a research study

20. the consistency in the pattern of change in a dependent measure in each phase of a design

DOWN

1. a single-case design in which a single participant is observed before, during, and after a treatment

2. a nonequivalent control group _____ design is a quasi-experimental design in which one group is observed before and after a treatment and another group is a nonequivalent control

4. a developmental design in which participants are grouped by their age

5. a developmental design in which the same participants are observed over time

7. any differences, which are not controlled by the researcher, between individuals who are selected from preexisting groups

8. a time series design with a treatment that is manipulated by the researcher

9. a basic or interrupted time series design with a nonequivalent control group

11. a _____ control group design is a design in which a dependent variable is measured in a group that received a treatment and in another matched group that did not receive the treatment

14. a phase in which the treatment or manipulation is absent

Crossword Puzzle

10

Between-Subjects Experimental Designs

CHAPTER LEARNING OBJECTIVES

1. Delineate the between-subjects design and the between-subjects experimental design.

2. Distinguish between an experimental group and a control group.

3. Distinguish between a natural and a staged experimental manipulation.

4. Explain how random assignment, control by matching, and control by holding constant can make individual differences about the same between groups.

5. Explain why it is important to measure error variance in an experiment.

6. Identify the appropriate sampling method and test statistic for independent samples to compare differences between two group means.

7. Identify the appropriate sampling method and test statistic for independent samples to compare differences among two or more group means.

8. Identify and give an example of three types of measures for a dependent variable.

9. Name two advantages and one disadvantage of the between-subjects design.

10. Compute a two-independent-sample t test and a one-way between-subjects analysis of variance using SPSS.

Chapter Summary

10.1   Conducting Experiments: Between-Subjects Design

The **between-subjects design** is an experimental research design in which different participants are observed at one time in each group of a research study. Using this design, we manipulate the levels of a **between-subjects factor**, meaning that different participants are observed in each group or at each level of the factor. The **between-subjects experimental design** is when we manipulate the levels of a **between-subjects factor**, then randomly assign different participants to each group or to each level of that factor. Specifically, the between-subjects design is an experiment when it meets the three requirements for demonstrating cause and effect:

1. Randomization (random sampling and random assignment).

2. Manipulation (of variables that operate in an experiment).

3. Comparison/control (or a control group).

10.2   Experimental Versus Control Group

Research design can be distinguished by the level of control that is established by a researcher. **Control** in research design is (a) the manipulation of a variable and (b) holding all other variables constant. When control is low, neither criterion is met; when control is high, both criteria are met.

To establish control a researcher randomly assigns participants to an experimental group or a control group. The **experimental group** or **treatment group** is a condition in an experiment in which participants are treated or exposed to a manipulation, or level of the independent variable, that is believed to cause a change in the dependent variable. The **control group** is a condition in an experiment in which participants are treated the same as participants in a treatment group, except that the manipulation believed to cause a change in the dependent variable is omitted.

10.3   Manipulation and the Independent Variable

An **experimental manipulation** is the identification of an independent variable and the creation of two or more groups that constitute the levels of that variable. Experimental manipulations can be natural or staged. A **natural manipulation** is the manipulation of a stimulus that can be naturally changed with little effort (e.g., lighting in a room). A **staged manipulation** is the manipulation of an independent variable that requires the participant to be "set up" to experience some stimulus or event (e.g., the emotion of a participant).

An experimental manipulation allows researchers to create groups to which participants can be randomly assigned. Random assignment ensures that participants, and therefore the individual differences of participants, are assigned to groups entirely by chance. Hence, we can assume that the individual differences of participants in each group are about the same.

Restricted random assignment is a method of controlling differences in participant characteristics between groups in a study by first restricting a sample based on known participant characteristics, then using a random procedure to assign participants to each group. Two strategies of restricted random assignment are **control by matching** and **control by holding constant**.

To use **control by matching** we assess or measure the characteristic we want to control, group or categorize participants based on scores on that measure, and then use a random procedure to assign participants from each category to a group in the study. To use **control by holding constant** we limit which participants are included in a sample based on characteristics they exhibit that may otherwise differ between groups in a study.

10.4   Variability and the Independent Variable

Methodologically, the manipulation of the levels of an independent variable and the random assignment of participants to each level or group is how we control for the possibility that individual differences vary from one group to the next. Statistically, we can also control for individual differences numerically in terms of **error variance**. Random variation is measured by determining the extent to which scores in each group overlap. The more that scores in each group overlap, the larger the error variance; the less that scores overlap between groups, the smaller the error variance.

We measure this error variation, and differences between groups, using a **test statistic**, upon which we determine the extent to which differences observed between groups can be attributed to the manipulation used to create the different groups.

10.5   Ethics in Focus: The Accountability of Manipulation

Because the researcher creates or manipulates the levels of an independent variable in an experiment, he or she bears greater responsibility for how participants are treated in each group. Hence, manipulating the levels of an independent variable can be associated with greater ethical accountability on the part of the researcher.

10.6   Comparing Two Independent Samples

Using the between-subjects design different participants are observed in each group. When participants are observed in this way, the sample is called an **independent sample**. Selecting one sample from the same population and randomly assigning participants in the sample to two groups is commonly used in experiments because it allows researchers to use randomization, manipulation, and a comparison/control group.

Once participants have been assigned to groups, we conduct the experiment and measure the same dependent variable in each group. To compare differences between groups, we will compute a *test statistic*, which is a mathematical formula that allows us to determine whether the manipulation or error variance is likely to explain differences between the groups. When data are interval or ratio scale, the appropriate test statistic for comparing differences between two independent samples is the **two-independent-sample *t* test**. The numerator of the test statistic is the actual difference between the two groups. We divide the mean difference between two groups by the value for error variance in the denominator.

10.7   SPSS in Focus: Two-Independent-Sample *t* Test

SPSS can be used to compute a two-independent-sample *t* test using the **Analyze, Compare Means**, and **Independent-Samples T Test** options in the menu bar.

10.8   Comparing Two or More Independent Samples

Researchers use very similar sampling methods to select different participants to multiple groups. Selecting one sample from the same population and randomly assigning participants in the sample to multiple groups is commonly used in experiments because it allows researchers to use randomization, manipulation, and a comparison/control group.

Once participants have been assigned to groups, we conduct the experiment and measure the same dependent variable in each group. To compare differences between groups, we again compute a *test statistic*. When data are interval or ratio scale, the appropriate test statistic for comparing differences among two or more independent samples is the **one-way between-subjects analysis of variance** (**ANOVA**). The term *one-way* indicates the number of independent variables or factors in a design.

The one-way between-subjects ANOVA informs us only that at least one group is different from another group—it does not tell us which pairs of groups differ. For situations in which we have more than two groups in an experiment, we compute **post hoc tests**, or "after the fact" tests, to determine which pairs of groups are different. Post hoc tests are used to evaluate all possible **pairwise comparisons**, or differences between all possible pairings of two group means.

10.9   SPSS in Focus: One-Way Between-Subjects ANOVA

SPSS can be used to compute the one-way between-subjects ANOVA. Using the **One-Way ANOVA** command, select the **Analyze, Compare Means,** and **One-Way ANOVA** options in the menu bar.

10.10   Measuring the Dependent Variable

Three types of measures tend to be the most commonly used in experimentation: **self-report measures** (response scale items regarding a participant's actual or perceived experiences, attitudes, or opinions are recorded), **behavioral measures** (the actual behavior of participants is recorded), and **physiological measures** (the physical responses of the brain or body are recorded).

10.11   Advantages and Disadvantages of the Between-Subjects Design

The key advantage of using a between-subjects design is that it is the only research design that meets all three requirements for an experiment to demonstrate cause and effect (randomization, manipulation, and comparison/control). The key disadvantage of using a between-subjects design is that the sample size required to conduct a between-subjects design can be large, particularly with many groups.

Chapter Summary Organized by Learning Objective

<u>LO 1</u>: Delineate the between-subjects design and the between-subjects experimental design.

- A **between-subjects design** is a research design in which different participants are observed one time in each group of a research study.

- A **between-subjects experimental design** is an experimental research design in which the levels of a **between-subjects factor** are manipulated, then different participants are randomly assigned to each group or to each level of that factor, and observed one time. We follow six steps to use the between-subjects design in an experiment:

  1. Select a random sample.
  2. Create two or more groups by manipulating the levels of an independent variable.
  3. Use random assignment to select participants to a group.
  4. Measure the same dependent variable in each group.
  5. Use inferential statistics to compare differences between groups.
  6. Make a decision.

LO 2: Distinguish between an experimental group and a control group.

- An **experimental group** is a condition in an experiment in which participants are treated or exposed to a manipulation, or level of the independent variable, that is believed to cause a change in a dependent variable.
- A **control group** is a condition in an experiment in which participants are treated the same as participants in a treatment group, except that the manipulation believed to cause a change in the dependent variable is omitted.

LO 3: Distinguish between a natural and a staged experimental manipulation.

- An **experimental manipulation** is the identification of an independent variable and the creation of two or more groups that constitute the levels of that variable. Two types of experimental manipulations are the following:
  - In a **natural manipulation** we manipulate a stimulus that can be naturally changed with little effort.
  - In a **staged manipulation** we manipulate an independent variable that requires the participant to be "set up" to experience some stimulus or event.

LO 4: Explain how random assignment, control by matching, and control by holding constant can make individual differences about the same between groups.

- The random assignment of participants to different groups ensures that participants, and therefore the individual differences of participants, are assigned to groups entirely by chance. When we do this, we can assume that the individual differences of participants in each group are about the same.
- **Restricted random assignment** is a method of controlling differences in participant characteristics between groups in a study by first restricting a sample based on known participant characteristics, then using a random procedure to assign participants to each group. Two strategies of restricted random assignment are the following:

○ In **control by matching** we assess or measure the characteristic we want to control, group or categorize participants based on scores on that measure, and then use a random procedure to assign participants from each category to a group in the study.

○ In **control by holding constant** we limit which participants are included in a sample based on characteristics they exhibit that may otherwise differ between groups in a study.

LO 5: Explain why it is important to measure error variance in an experiment.

- **Error variance** or **error** is a numeric measure of the variability in scores that can be attributed to or are caused by the individual differences of participants in each group. We measure error variance to account for any overlap in scores between groups, which is an indication that differences are occurring by chance because participant behavior is overlapping between groups.

- To measure error variance, and differences between groups, we identify a **test statistic** that allows researchers to determine the extent to which differences observed between groups can be attributed to the manipulation used to create the different groups (i.e., groups are different), or can be attributed to error (i.e., people are different).

LO 6: Identify the appropriate sampling method and test statistic for independent samples to compare differences between two group means.

- Using the between-subjects design we select an **independent sample,** meaning that different participants are observed in each group. To select participants to an independent sample we can select two groups from different populations (a quasi-experimental method), or we can sample from a single population, then randomly assign participants to two groups (an experimental method).

- The appropriate test statistic for comparing differences between two group means for the between-subjects design is the **two-independent-sample t test.** Using this test statistic establishes statistical control of error or differences attributed to individual differences. The larger the value of the test statistic, the more likely we are to conclude that a manipulation, and not error, caused a mean difference between two groups.

LO 7: Identify the appropriate sampling method and test statistic for independent samples to compare differences among two or more group means.

- To select participants to an independent sample with two or more groups we can select groups from many different populations (a quasi-experimental method), or we can select groups from a single population, then randomly assign participants to two or more groups (an experimental method).

- The appropriate test statistic for comparing differences between two or more groups using the between-subjects design is the **one-way between-subjects ANOVA.** If significant, then at least one pair of group means are different, and we conduct **post hoc tests** to determine which pairs of group means are significantly different. The larger the value of the test statistic, the more likely we are to conclude that the manipulation, and not error, caused a mean difference between two groups. Using this statistical procedure establishes statistical control of error or differences attributed to individual differences.

LO 8: Identify and give an example of three types of measures for a dependent variable.

- Three types of measures for a dependent variable are **self-report measures** (e.g., items used in a survey), **behavioral measures** (e.g., speed and distance traveled by an athlete), and **physiological measures** (e.g., heart rate or body temperature).

LO 9: Name two advantages and one disadvantage of the between-subjects design.

- The key advantage of using a between-subjects design is that it is the only design that allows for the use of randomization, manipulation, and the inclusion of a comparison/control group, which are required to demonstrate cause and effect. A between-subjects design also places less of a burden on the participant and the researcher because participants are observed (or participate) only one time, and the researcher does not have to track participants over time.
- One disadvantage of a between-subjects design is that the sample size required to conduct this design can be large, particularly with many groups.

LO 10: Compute a two-independent-sample t test and a one-way between-subjects analysis of variance using SPSS.

- SPSS can be used to compute a two-independent-sample t test using the **Analyze, Compare Means,** and **Independent-Samples T Test** options in the menu bar. These actions will display a dialog box that allows you to identify the groups and run the test (for more details, see Section 10.7 in the book).
- SPSS can be used to compute the one-way between-subjects ANOVA. Using the **One-Way ANOVA** command, select the **Analyze, Compare Means,** and **One-Way ANOVA** options in the menu bar. These actions will display a dialog box that allows you to identify the variables, choose an appropriate post hoc test, and run the analysis (for more details, see Section 10.9 in the book).

Tips and Cautions for Students

Statistical and methodological control. From a methodological view, in an experiment the manipulation of the levels of an independent variable and the random assignment of participants to each level or group is the way we control for the possibility that individual differences vary from one group to the next. As an added measure of control, parametric tests for between-subjects designs (e.g., the t test and ANOVA, introduced in Chapter 10 of the book) also account for individual differences, as measured by error variance. Taken together, we can demonstrate *cause* in an experiment because individual differences between groups have been methodologically and statistically controlled before making decisions about differences between groups.

Practice Quiz

1. A between-subjects design means that:

   a. different participants are observed in each group

   b. the same participants are observed in each group

   c. each participant is assigned a different independent variable

   d. random assignment cannot be used to assign participants to groups

2. A factor in which different participants are assigned to each level of that factor is called a:

   a. within-subjects factor

   b. between-subjects factor

   c. control factor

   d. participant variable

3. Which of the following is *not* a requirement for establishing control in a research design?

   a. manipulate the levels of a variable

   b. observe preexisting variables

   c. hold all other variables constant

   d. control for confound variables

4. Participants are randomly assigned to rate the taste of a beverage that does or does not contain a sugar substitute. It is hypothesized that ratings for the beverage with the sugar substitute will be higher. In this example, the experimental group is:

   a. the group that rates the beverage with the sugar substitute

   b. the group that rates the beverage without the sugar substitute

   c. the taste ratings for a beverage

   d. the amount consumed of the beverage

5. A researcher measures sleep quality among participants given a drug to promote sleep. Which of the following would be an appropriate control group?

   a. a group that receives a higher dose of the sleep-promoting drug

   b. a group that receives no drug at all

   c. a group that receives a placebo or fake drug with no effects

   d. a group that does not sleep at all

6. Which of the following is a requirement for demonstrating cause and effect in an experiment?

   a. randomization

   b. manipulation of variables that operate in an experiment

   c. a control group

   d. all of the above

7. A researcher manipulates the size of a reward for mice in a behavior task as 1, 2, 4, or 8 drops of 0.1 ml water. What type of experimental manipulation is described in this example?

    a. staged manipulation

    b. participant manipulation

    c. natural manipulation

    d. randomized manipulation

8. The key advantage of random assignment is that it makes _____ about the same in each group.

    a. individual differences

    b. participant responses

    c. statistical data

    d. the levels of the independent variable

9. Which of the following is a type of restricted random assignment?

    a. control by matching

    b. control by holding constant

    c. control by withholding manipulation

    d. both a and b

10. To control for hunger, a researcher restricted a sample to include only those participants who reported not eating within 2 hours of the study. Which type of restricted random assignment did the researcher use?

    a. control by matching

    b. control by holding constant

    c. both a and b

11. Random variation not attributed to having different groups is measured by determining the extent to which scores in each group:

    a. match

    b. restrict

    c. overlap

    d. never change

12. The larger the value of a test statistic for a between-subjects experimental design, the more likely we are to decide:

    a. that a manipulation caused an effect

    b. that the difference between two groups is significant

    c. that the group means are different

    d. all of the above

13. Manipulating the levels of an independent variable can come with greater _____ on the part of the researcher.

   a. ethical responsibility

   b. irresponsibility

   c. unaccountability

   d. inactivity

14. Which of the following is a strategy for sampling two groups in a between-subjects experiment?

   a. select a sample from two different populations and select one group from each population

   b. select one sample from the same population and randomly assign participants in the sample to two groups

   c. none of the above

15. The parametric test statistic used in an experiment to compare two independent samples is called the _____; the test statistic used in an experiment to compare more than two independent samples is called the _____.

   a. one-way between-subjects ANOVA; two-independent-sample t test

   b. two-independent-sample t test; one-way between-subjects ANOVA

   c. one-way between-subjects ANOVA; one-way between-subjects ANOVA

   d. two-independent-sample t test; two-independent-sample t-test

16. What tests do we use following a significant ANOVA for more than two groups to determine which pairs of group means are significantly different?

   a. error variance tests

   b. between-subjects tests

   c. post hoc tests

   d. differential comparisons

17. Which of the following is a type of measure commonly used in an experiment?

   a. self-report measure

   b. behavioral measure

   c. physiological measure

   d. all of the above

18. Students completed a single-item measure that asked if they completed textbook reading assignments on a scale from 1 (*none*) to 5 (*all of the assigned material*). What type of measure was used in this example?

   a. self-report measure

   b. behavioral measure

   c. physiological measure

   d. none of the above

19. Which of the following is an example of a behavioral measure?
    a. Participants rate attitudes on a 5-point rating scale.
    b. The number of interruptions during a class is recorded.
    c. Arousal is measured using blood pressure measures.
    d. Participants respond to interview questions about their past experiences.

20. Which of the following is a key advantage of using the between-subjects design?
    a. The sample size required to conduct an experiment is typically very small.
    b. It places a greater burden on the participant and the researcher.
    c. It is the only design that can meet all three requirements of an experiment to demonstrate cause and effect.
    d. It is the only design that allows researchers to observe the same participants across many groups.

Key Term Word Search

```
O W I C H B L F P Z E S X E S G L V D M F B T V G Z F K E B C I B D U Z I X
N R S S W O T D J T Q Q O V X Q U G I R X D W A A L N U T Z P U D X J F B V
Z N Q W M C O W N J B U R R E C C L M M C O N T R O L G R O U P I T W P R W
C A U P C H O Z O V H Z V P F H G G Y V E P C C D Q Z Z V A O O I N P N K O
S S Q R O V H N W I X B E H A V I O R A L M E A S U R E G Y N C F L O B E N
K T A M N S M N T B N N J T B K O Y H N V E M H E Z I J S C S L I I F Y R E
V A R Z T T T R A R K D W G F E R T T S Q S H M F O T D T H R K T T P D R W
M C Y O R Z E H X T O G E Z V J T M W G O H V O T S X E A O R A X A O R O A
I Z L H O C N S O Y F L T P K P U W X O E U L O E C J U I K L Q R I M G R Y
N A Z I L B J E T C S K B K E Y H C E K V P J T I X B F I U F H B J W N V B
D A N H B S S R H S T E H Y G N D Y E E F I T T K L E H P Y V L N A M H A E
T L Y U Y T O Y L R T E L D M D D F S O N S P R I T H I J C U C D T G O R T
T J G M H A G S Z K N A S F G A D E B I E S Z S R T N O O B B L B W M Q I W
R P A G O G F V E E R U T T R J T J N L O W U H C A N P O S J W N J Q F A E
G U X L L E D U I I V L Y I S E Y C P T C L J B M U Q M Q P D B G C Q Y N E
I S R N D D Z C Y T X O A F S M P M H Z S R O L J C B F H L N L Q P C V C N
O G Z Z I M I H A E J F L P Y T A O M I L A A G G E X P F D R I G V Q X E S
Y F W S N A X H I E A E N V I S I X R P N R M N I Y C Z E I C B J M U A D U
U Y T Z G N D C Z D O Y W P T D Z C E T U G E P Y C C T V Z H S V P S E G B
C E I G C I S I I R S M U N R G S U F T M Q T L L S A X S N R E B W Q Z H J
M N A P O P V X V M O Y E N V R D J A Q E E U M T E M L P D E C C Z P H O E
X H R H N U O N A I U D X B X J N N Y B C I A U W U S V M K E G G B H R X C
Y C C L S L Z A R Z N E S Q X N V N N J O I W S W A Q T H E D S C N O Q Y T
P G N L T A E F J E R U M S K J H X K V N W M B U V C Z T V A O I P V O H S
K L B N A T T B P W N M E C K O Y L F E T W C U E R G E C E E S Y G C M B A
B I S M N I F E O G N H Q V H U G X P W R O V H P K E I V O S P U U N V A N
S E N O T O D F V C V N G W L G F B N U O D R U O R B X R K X T Z R S T M O
X E N S W N K F L V A V B N J M Y B U R L U I O U M W Y Y U I Z I L E R Q V
G T R N I B L L B E C E B S I I Y U E X P E R I M E N T A L G R O U P R N A
I M R L E O K A P A I R W I S E C O M P A R I S O N S A J F Q F V N W L A P
H S T Z L C W B E T W E E N S U B J E C T S F A C T O R I B C L S H I O W U
B O H F U O T E X P E R I M E N T A L M A N I P U L A T I O N V K F B P D X
E E N E Z L A A A K P E Z R A H T R X K I Y X P C S F D Q K R J E E Y Y X N
K E J P I Y A F E Z Y R E S V Q U H I O L S R H B V E J K Z D E C I S L U R
F S Q O F Q K U X C M R A D P P J Q V J C G S H Q O L C R Z F A T L L Q Z Q
V Z D Q Z V I N D E P E N D E N T S A M P L E D K A N K I C L D F D T K H P
J O F A S Z A P B N R Q O K I R N U P P O A X Z T H W A Q P M E Q F Z E C C
R J L J R E S T R I C T E D R A N D O M A S S I G N M E N T V G H I W C M F
```

one-way between-subjects
   ANOVA
restricted random assignment
two-independent-sample *t* test
control by holding constant
experimental manipulation
independent-sample *t* test
between-subjects design
between-subjects factor

physiological measure
natural manipulation
pairwise comparisons
staged manipulation
behavioral measure
control by matching
experimental group
independent sample

self-report measure
error variance
test statistic
control group
post hoc tests
control
placebo

ACROSS

1. a numeric measure of the variability in scores that can be attributed to or is caused by the individual differences of participants in each group

4. a _____ between-subjects ANOVA, or a statistical procedure used to test hypotheses for one factor with two or more levels concerning the variance among group means

5. a mathematical formula used to determine the extent to which differences observed between groups can be attributed to a manipulation

8. a sample in which different participants are observed in each group

12. a statistical procedure computed following a significant ANOVA to determine which pair or pairs of group means significantly differ

15. the group or condition in an experiment in which participants are treated or exposed to a manipulation

17. a type of manipulation of a stimulus that can be naturally changed with little effort

18. a type of measurement in which researchers record physical responses of the brain or body

DOWN

2. the group or condition in an experiment in which participants are treated the same as participants in a treatment group, except that the manipulation is omitted

3. a type of measurement in which participants are asked to respond to one or more questions or statements to indicate their actual or perceived experiences, attitudes, or opinions

6. a statistical comparison for the difference between two group means

7. a type of random assignment in which a sample is restricted based on known participant characteristics, then randomly assigned participants to groups

9. a type of restricted random assignment in which we separate participants into different categories, then randomly assign participants to groups

10. a type of measurement in which researchers directly observe and record the behavior of subjects or participants

11. an inert substance, surgery, or therapy that resembles a real treatment but has no real effect

13. a type of manipulation that requires the participant to be "set up" to experience some stimulus or event

14. a research design in which different participants are observed one time in each group

16. A two _____ sample t-test is a statistical procedure used to test hypotheses concerning the difference in interval or ratio scale data between two group means, in which the variance in the population is unknown

Crossword Puzzle

11

Within-Subjects Experimental Designs

CHAPTER LEARNING OBJECTIVES

1. Delineate the within-subjects design and the within-subjects experimental design.

2. Explain why it is important to control for time-related factors using a within-subjects experimental design.

3. Demonstrate the use of counterbalancing and control for timing using a within-subjects experimental design.

4. Identify three sources of variation and explain why one source is removed using the within-subjects design.

5. Identify the appropriate sampling method and test statistic for related samples to compare differences between two group means.

6. Identify the appropriate sampling method and test statistic for related samples to compare differences among two or more group means.

7. Apply a Solomon four-group design for the within-subjects experimental design.

8. Contrast the use of a between-subjects versus a within-subjects design for an experiment.

9. Compute a related-samples t test and a one-way within-subjects analysis of variance using SPSS.

Chapter Summary

11.1   Conducting Experiments: Within-Subjects Design

A **within-subjects design** is a research design in which the same participants are observed one time in each group of a research study. Using this design, a researcher manipulates a **within-subjects factor,** meaning that the same participants are observed in each group at each level of that factor. The **within-subjects experimental design** is when we manipulate the levels of a **within-subjects factor,** then observe the same participants in each group or at each level of the factor. To qualify as an experiment, the researcher must (1) manipulate the levels of the factor and include a comparison/ control group and (2) make added efforts to control for order and time-related factors.

Two common reasons that researchers observe the same participants in each group are to manage sample size and to observe changes in behavior over time, which is often the case for studies on learning or within-participant changes over time.

11.2   Controlling Time-Related Factors

Time-related factors include maturation, testing effects, regression toward the mean, attrition, and **participant fatigue.** To control for time-related factors, researchers make efforts to control for **order effects,** which occur when the order in which participants receive different treatments or participate in different groups causes changes in a dependent variable. To control for time-related factors that can threaten internal validity, researchers use two strategies:

1. Control order (counterbalancing, partial counterbalancing).

2. Control timing.

Counterbalancing is a procedure in which the order in which participants receive different treatments or participate in different groups is balanced or offset in an experiment. Two types of counterbalancing are complete and partial counterbalancing.

Complete counterbalancing is used to balance or offset the different orders in which participants could receive different treatments or participate in different groups.

Partial counterbalancing is used to balance or offset some, but not all, possible order sequences in which participants could receive different treatments or participate in different groups. This type of counterbalancing is often used when there are three or more groups. To ensure that the order sequences selected are representative of all order sequences, we must ensure that each treatment or group appears equally often in each position and that each treatment or group precedes and follows each treatment or group one time.

Researchers can control timing by controlling the interval between treatments or groups and the total duration of an experiment.

11.3   Ethics in Focus: Minimizing Participant Fatigue

To minimize risks related to participant fatigue, minimize the duration needed to complete an experiment, and allow for a reasonable time interval or rest period between treatment presentations.

11.4   Individual Differences and Variability

When the same participants are observed in each group, the individual differences of participants are also the same in each group. In a within-subjects design we can measure individual differences as **between-persons variability**; we measure the variability in participant responding within each group as **within-groups variability**. Both are measures of error. Because individual differences are the same in each group using a within-subjects design, we can assume that the value of the between-persons variability is zero. In a within-subjects design, then, we can represent the calculation of error, or variation not caused by the manipulation, as Error = Within-Groups Variability + 0.

11.5   Comparing Two Related Samples

Methodologically, we control for order and timing to control for time-related factors associated with observing the same participants in each group. Statistically, we add another level of control by using a test statistic to determine the likelihood that something other than the manipulation caused differences in a dependent measure between groups.

In a **related sample** the same or matched participants are observed in each group. We can select a sample from one population and observe that one sample of participants in each group. This type of sampling, called a *repeated-measures design*, can be used in an experiment only if we manipulate the levels of the independent variable and control for order effects. Another way to select related samples is called a **matched-samples design**, but this sampling design cannot be used in an experiment because groups are created based on preexisting characteristics of the participants and not on a manipulation made by the researcher.

Once participants have been selected, we observe the same participants in each group and also measure the same dependent variable in each group. The appropriate test statistic for comparing differences between two related samples is the **related-samples t test**. The numerator of the test statistic is the actual difference between the two groups. We divide the mean difference between two groups by the value for error in the denominator.

11.6   SPSS in Focus: Related-Samples t Test

SPSS can be used to compute a related-samples t test using the **Analyze, Compare Means,** and **Paired-Samples T Test** options in the menu bar.

11.7   Comparing Two or More Related Samples

We can also observe more than two groups using the within-subjects design. The appropriate test statistic for comparing differences among two or more related samples is the **one-way within-subjects analysis of variance (ANOVA)**. This test measures the variance of differences between groups divided by the variance attributed to error. In the one-way within-subjects ANOVA, we compute between-persons variability and remove it, thereby leaving only within-groups variability as a measure of error in the denominator of the test statistic.

The one-way within-subjects ANOVA informs us only that at least one group is different from another group—it does not tell us which pairs of groups differ. For situations in which we have more than two groups in an experiment, we compute post hoc tests, in the same way that we did for the between-subjects design.

11.8   SPSS in Focus: One-Way Within-Subjects ANOVA

SPSS can be used to compute the one-way within-subjects ANOVA using the **Analyze, General Linear Model,** and **Repeated Measures** options in the menu bar.

11.9   An Alternative for Pre-Post Designs: Solomon Four-Group Design

The **Solomon four-group design** is a combination of the one-group pretest-posttest design and the one-group posttest-only design, with two added control groups that can account for the possibility that confounding variables and extraneous factors have influenced the results. The strength of this design is that multiple comparisons can be made, which can eliminate the possibility that confounds or extraneous factors are causing differences from pre- to post-treatment; its main limitation is the complexity of the design itself.

11.10 Comparing Between-Subjects and Within-Subjects Designs

The between-subjects design allows researchers to use random assignment of participants to the levels of an independent variable; the within-subjects design does not. The advantage of using a within-subjects design is that fewer participants are required overall (economizing) because the same participants are observed in each group. Also, the test statistic for the within-subjects design has greater power to detect significant differences between groups.

Chapter Summary Organized by Learning Objective

LO 1: Delineate the within-subjects design and the within-subjects experimental design.

- A **within-subjects design** is a research design in which the same participants are observed one time in each group of a research study.
- A **within-subjects experimental design** is an experimental research design in which the levels of a **within-subjects factor** are manipulated, then the same participants are observed in each group or at each level of the factor. To qualify as an experiment, the researcher must (1) manipulate the levels of the factor and include a comparison/control group, and (2) make added efforts to control for order and time-related factors.

LO 2: Explain why it is important to control for time-related factors using a within-subjects experimental design.

- When we observe the same participants over time, factors related to observing participants over time can also vary between groups. When time-related factors covary with the levels of the independent variable (the manipulation), it can threaten the internal validity of an experiment.

- Time-related factors include maturation, testing effects, regression toward the mean, attrition, **participant fatigue**, and **carryover effects**. For a study to be an experiment each of these time-related factors must be controlled for, or be the same between groups, such that only the levels of an independent variable are different between groups.

LO 3: Demonstrate the use of counterbalancing and control for timing using a within-subjects experimental design.

- For the **counterbalancing** procedure, the order in which participants receive different treatments or participate in different groups is balanced or offset in an experiment. Two types of counterbalancing are as follows:
  - o Complete counterbalancing in which all possible order sequences are included in an experiment.
  - o Partial counterbalancing in which some, but not all, possible order sequences are included in an experiment. One example of partial counterbalancing is the **Latin square**.
- We can also control for order effects by controlling timing. We can control the interval between treatments or groups and the total duration of an experiment. As a general rule, increasing the interval between treatments and minimizing the total duration of an experiment is often the most effective strategy to minimize threats to internal validity that are associated with observing the same participants over time.

LO 4: Identify three sources of variation and explain why one source is removed using the within-subjects design.

- In a within-subjects design we can measure individual differences as **between-persons variability**. We measure the mean difference caused by the manipulation as **between-groups variability**. We measure variability in participant responding within each group as **within-groups variability**.
- When the same participants are observed in each group, we assume that the individual differences of participants are also the same in each group. We therefore measure and remove the between-persons variability because we will assume that the value of the between-persons variability is zero—that there is no difference in the individual differences in each group; the individual differences between persons are the same.

LO 5: Identify the appropriate sampling method and test statistic for related samples to compare differences between two group means.

- Using a within-subjects design, the same participants are observed in each group. When participants are observed in this way, the sample is called a **related sample**. There are two ways to select related samples:
  - o The **repeated-measures design** in which we select a sample from one population and observe that one sample of participants in each group. This type of sampling can be used in an experiment when researchers control for order effects and manipulate the levels of the independent variable.

o The **matched-samples design** in which participants are matched, experimentally or naturally, based on characteristics or traits that they share. This type of sampling cannot be used in an experiment because groups are created based on preexisting characteristics of the participants and not on a manipulation made by the researcher.

- The appropriate test statistic for comparing differences between two group means using the within-subjects design is the **related-samples *t* test**. Using this *t* test, we divide the mean difference between groups by the value for within-groups error. Because individual differences are the same in each group, the between-persons error is removed by reducing the data to difference scores before computing the test statistic. The larger the value of the test statistic, the more likely we are to conclude that the manipulation, and not error, caused a mean difference between two groups.

LO 6: Identify the appropriate sampling method and test statistic for related samples to compare differences among two or more group means.

- The repeated-measures design is used to observe participants in more than two groups. Using a repeated-measures design, participants are selected from a single population and observed in multiple groups in an experiment.
- The appropriate test statistic for comparing differences between two or more group means using a within-subjects design is the **one-way within-subjects ANOVA**. If the ANOVA is significant, then we conduct *post hoc tests* to determine which pairs of group means are significantly different. Using this test, we divide the variability between groups by the value for within-groups error. Because individual differences are the same in each group, the between-persons error is measured and removed from the value for error placed in the denominator. The larger the value of the test statistic, the more likely we are to conclude that the manipulation, and not error, caused a mean difference between groups.

LO 7: Apply a Solomon four-group design for the within-subjects experimental design.

- The Solomon four-group design is a combination of the one-group pretest-posttest design and the one-group posttest-only design, with two added control groups that can account for the possibility that confounding variables and extraneous factors have influenced the results.
- To apply the Solomon four-group design, two groups are given a treatment, and two groups are given no treatment. In one treatment group, participants are given a pretest, a treatment, and a posttest; in the other treatment group, participants are given a treatment and a posttest. In one no-treatment group, participants are given a pretest and a posttest without a treatment; in the other no-treatment group, participants are given a posttest only without a treatment. In all, we make five comparisons to demonstrate evidence that a treatment caused changes in a posttest measure.
- Because the Solomon four-group design includes appropriate control groups, it is regarded as an experimental design, so long as the researcher manipulates the treatment and randomly assigns participants to the different groups. The strength of the

design is that it is capable of controlling for threats to internal validity; its main limitation is the complexity of the design itself.

LO 8: Contrast the use of a between-subjects versus a within-subjects design for an experiment.

- A between-subjects design allows for the use of random assignment; a within-subjects design does not. The advantage of using random assignment is that we do not need to control for order effects using a between-subjects design; however, we do need to control for order effects using a within-subjects design.
- An advantage of using a within-subjects design is that fewer participants are required overall (economizing) because the same participants are observed in each group. A second advantage of using the within-subjects design is that the test statistic for this design has greater power to detect an effect between groups.

LO 9: Compute a related-samples *t* test and a one-way within-subjects ANOVA using SPSS.

- SPSS can be used to compute a related-samples *t* test using the **Analyze, Compare Means,** and **Paired-Samples T Test** options in the menu bar. These actions will display a dialog box that allows you to identify the groups and run the test (for more details, see Section 11.6 in the book).
- SPSS can be used to compute the one-way within-subjects ANOVA using the **Analyze, General Linear Model,** and **Repeated Measures** options in the menu bar. These actions will display a dialog box that allows you to identify the variables, choose an appropriate post hoc test, and run the analysis (for more details, see Section 11.8 in the book).

Tips and Cautions for Students

Statistical and methodological control. Methodologically, we control for order and timing to control for time-related factors associated with observing the same participants in each group. As an added measure of control, parametric tests for within-subjects designs (e.g., the *t* test and ANOVA, introduced in Chapter 11 of the book) also account for individual differences, as measured by error variance. Hence, we can demonstrate cause in an experiment, then, because order and time-related factors have been controlled methodologically and individual differences are statistically accounted by error before making decisions about differences between groups.

Counterbalancing. Remember that when we observe the same participants over time, we need to account for the fact that time varies systematically with the levels of an independent variable. Counterbalancing allows us to control for many factors associated with observing the same participants over time. By making time-related factors the same or about the same in each group (by using counterbalancing), we can be more confident that the actual manipulation of the levels of the independent variable, and not the order in which we observed participants, was causing an observed effect.

Practice Quiz

1. A within-subjects design means that:

   a. different participants are observed in each group

   b. the same participants are observed in each group

   c. each participant is assigned a different independent variable

   d. random assignment can be used to assign participants to groups

2. A factor in which the same participants are assigned to each level of that factor is called a:

   a. within-subjects factor

   b. between-subjects factor

   c. control factor

   d. participant variable

3. Which of the following is a time-related factor that can threaten the internal validity of an experiment?

   a. participant fatigue

   b. maturation

   c. testing effects

   d. all of the above

4. Researchers make efforts to control for _____ by specifically controlling for time-related factors.

   a. group assignment

   b. individual differences

   c. order effects

   d. selection effects

5. In a within-subjects experiment, children performed two tasks, yet researchers discovered that they used knowledge about one task to help them complete the second task. What type of effect is described in this example?

   a. carryover effect

   b. cohort effect

   c. selection bias

   d. factorial effect

6. What is the name of a procedure in which the order in which participants receive different treatments or participate in different groups is balanced or offset in an experiment?

   a. ordered manipulation

   b. experimental differentiation

c. counterbalancing

d. counterintuition

7. A researcher observes the same participants in each of four groups. To counterbalance the order in which participants experience each group, the researcher uses a Latin square procedure. Which type of counterbalancing was used in this example?

a. complete counterbalancing

b. partial counterbalancing

c. foreign counterbalancing

d. none; a Latin square is not a counterbalancing procedure

8. Counterbalancing _____ order effects such that order effects are equal or the same in each treatment or group.

a. balances

b. eliminates

c. enhances

d. creates

9. Researchers can control for the timing of a manipulation by:

a. controlling the interval between treatments or groups

b. controlling the total duration of an experiment

c. both a and b

10. Minimizing the duration needed to complete an experiment and allowing for a reasonable time interval or rest period between treatment presentations are two ways to:

a. ensure that participants do not complete a study

b. reward participants for doing a good job

c. make the tasks in each group more demanding

d. minimize risks related to participant fatigue

11. Using a within-subjects design, we can assume that the individual differences of participants are _____ in each group.

a. the same

b. different

c. variable

d. enhanced

12. Which of the following is a statistical measure for individual differences that is removed from the error term in the formula of the test statistic for a within-subjects design?

a. between-groups variability

b. between-persons variability

    c. within-groups variability

    d. all of the above

13. For a within-subjects experimental design, between-groups variability is a measure of:

    a. variability associated with individual differences

    b. variability attributed to participant responding within each group

    c. the mean difference caused by a manipulation

    d. the variability attributed to error

14. Which of the following is a strategy for sampling two or more groups in a within-subjects experiment?

    a. select a sample from two or more different populations and select one group from each population

    b. select one sample from the same population and randomly assign participants in the sample to each group

    c. select one sample from the same population and observe the same participants in each group

    d. none of the above

15. Which of the following designs cannot be used in an experiment?

    a. repeated-measures design

    b. pre-post design

    c. within-subjects design

    d. matched-samples design

16. The parametric test statistic used in an experiment to compare two related samples is called the _____; the test statistic used in an experiment to compare more than two related samples is called the _____.

    a. one-way within-subjects ANOVA; related-samples t test

    b. related-samples t test; one-way within-subjects ANOVA

    c. one-way between-subjects ANOVA; one-way within-subjects ANOVA

    d. related-samples t test; two-independent-sample t test

17. What tests do we use following a significant ANOVA for more than two groups to determine which pairs of group means are significantly different?

    a. error variance tests

    b. between-subjects tests

    c. post hoc tests

    d. differential comparisons

18. The experimental research design in which different participants are assigned to each of four groups in such a way that comparisons can be made to determine if a treatment causes

changes in posttest measure, and to control for possible confounds or extraneous factors related to giving a pretest measure and observing participants over time, is called the:

   a. Solomon four-group design

   b. pre-post design

   c. between-subjects design

   d. within-subjects design

19. The advantage of using a within-subjects design is that:

   a. fewer participants are required overall because the same participants are observed in each group

   b. participants are not randomly assigned to each group or treatment

   c. a different dependent variable is measured in each group and compared to standardized norms

   d. it can control for threats to validity without needing to control for order effects

20. The test statistic for a within-subjects design has _____ power to detect significant differences between groups compared to the test statistic for a between-subjects design.

   a. less

   b. greater

   c. no

   d. absolute

Key Term Word Search

```
T I P Q P R N X W E S E U I G S G Q P R Y E C S A A R H E L K E T F
O I Z X Q A C L Q I Q S V H Y Y B W L Y S A T M C W U V G V T S H H
P R S V L O R A B D T C O F K W K K D J P C P Z S Y V U S D U B I Q
C K W F A V Y T E E B H X K P M H X I N E D A Y T J T X F O G V R E
O J I I R R V F I D T P I Y Q F S W M F X T R I K S O T J V G M Z V
M I T O E K A Y E A M W P N U H Z S F H S N L J E B B A N S N C U O
P T H Q L S H U F Q L U E W G W C E A E G I T T A V L G N O W Z S R
L N I H M L X W D L F C X E J R R O T Y B F T P E U I E R W O M H I
E C N U E K N K I L O P O D N E O T U A B S R S A S I W I C A B I E
T M S F R Q C F Z T W J G U D P S U I N E W F K E I M T R V F V P I
E E U L X Y I G A O H O F R N E E R P L T B O D L S T H Z F C B N W
C X B W X G L B I K A I O U L T A R P S S E S B E N K U L D C Y P N
O G J P L I S P Z D D R N P P V E M S Q V E R L Y M E R B J E C F Q
U W E C X X X H L A B O M S S V A R H O L A P B J J Z A U P Y I E L
N P C Z O K Q H X Y C A U P U S M Q B P N M R V A C Y X J Z X X I T
T A T P Q B F W J P S H U K D B Z W M A A S I I V L K D D V B N J Q
E R S T N D L C I D C O V E O S J A J S L N V M A T A N I H H D J U
R T D A X R C R E F R A R S C H S E D R P A H A I B Z N W Y O Z G V
B I E W N U B T O G L I F W X D W E C R J B N L R S I V C L P Z F F
A C S W U X A V N C A E D Z E T T U B T N K H C H I L L Y I D A F I
L I I P V L E E S P D P R H I A W T B S S P X K I T A F I L N N Y R
A P G J E C E C B R A A C K L P P X E K X F A F Z N G B W T G G S O
N A N R A W R B S Y G T P E Z L G U Q A V V A Q I L G L I L Y D H J
C N Y Y T G S V V S A T R T Y D H O Z X U B C C E F P W H L N N O G
I T F E X R G F Q M A Y I L A T I N S Q U A R E T X S E H A I W Z G
N F B L U Z M X Z D I V C J V V D V C M C O D D A O D G O J G T P W
G A Z M C Q I S T T P K C U R L H I E R T Y L A Q P R B M U H V Y N
I T I Y R W Z X O N E W A Y W I T H I N S U B J E C T S A N O V A J
C I P E C A R R Y O V E R E F F E C T S U O J Q B E N E W Y L J D M
F G Z C M F D D F K T O L X Y S R O S Q W R P F R M A N V E D X U I
F U I O Z U O K I T V V R H H U J U T T P J X B L C W G T P M X T V
V E M K Q N Y H X K I O F B U B A J C G A L H D T L O Q T K O D W J
D U Y M S E P Y J O V X I N A U K S E P T O Z J C W M O D S W P M A
K G C X G J X Y R I J B F G Q I E R D P S L Q K L V U C Y R J U P Z
```

between-persons variability

one-way within-subjects ANOVA

between-groups variability

complete counterbalancing

partial counterbalancing

paired-samples *t* test

participant fatigue

carryover effects

counterbalancing

within-groups variability

matched samples design

within-subjects design

within-subjects factor

related-samples *t* test

related samples

order effects

Latin square

ACROSS

2. a _____ within-subjects ANOVA is used to test hypotheses for one factor with two or more levels

4. a source of variance in a dependent measure that is attributed to observing different participants in each group

5. a state of physical or psychological exhaustion resulting from intense research demands

6. a within-subjects design in which participants are matched, experimentally or naturally, based on shared traits

8. a type of sample in which the same or matched participants are observed in each group

9. a _____ samples t test is used to test hypotheses concerning two related samples in which the variance in one population is unknown

10. a type of research design in which the same participants are observed one time in each group

12. a type of counterbalancing in which some, but not all, possible order sequences are counterbalanced

13. a matrix design used to partially counterbalance order sequences

14. an experimental design in which different participants are assigned to each of four groups such that comparisons can be made to determine if a treatment causes changes in a posttest measure and control for possible confounds related to giving a pretest measure and observing participants over time

15. a procedure used to balance the order that participants receive different treatments or participate in different groups

16. a threat to internal validity in which participation in one group "carries over" or causes changes in performance in a second group

DOWN

1. a source of variance in a dependent measure that is caused by or associated with the manipulation of the levels or groups of an independent variable

2. a threat to internal validity in which the order in which participants receive different treatments or participate in different groups causes changes in the dependent variable

3. a source of variance in a dependent measure that is caused by or associated with individual differences or differences in participant responses across all groups

7. a type of counterbalancing in which all possible order sequences in which participants receive different treatments or participate in different groups are balanced or offset in an experiment

11. a source of variance that cannot be attributed to having different groups or treatments

Crossword Puzzle

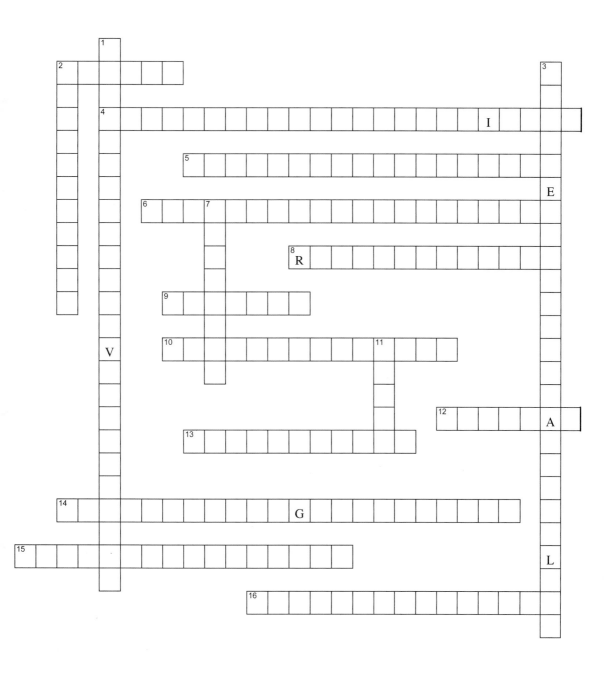

12

Factorial Experimental Designs

CHAPTER LEARNING OBJECTIVES

1. Delineate the factorial design from the factorial experimental design.

2. Identify the appropriate sampling method for a factorial design used in an experiment.

3. Identify and describe three types of factorial designs.

4. Distinguish between a main effect and an interaction.

5. Identify main effects and interactions in a summary table and in a graph.

6. Identify the implications of using a quasi-independent factor in a factorial design.

7. Explain how a factorial design can be used to build on previous research, control for threats to validity, and enhance the informativeness of interpretation.

8. Describe the higher-order factorial design.

9. Compute a factorial analysis of variance for the between-subjects, within-subjects, and mixed factorial design using SPSS.

Chapter Summary

12.1   Testing Multiple Factors in the Same Experiment

A **factorial design** is a research design in which participants are observed across the combination of levels of two or more factors. The combination of levels for two factors creates unique groups to be observed. The **factorial experimental design** is when we create groups by manipulating the levels of two or more factors, then observe the same or different participants in each group using experimental procedures of randomization (for a between-subjects factor) and using control for timing and order effects (for a within-subjects factor).

12.2   Selecting Samples for a Factorial Design in Experimentation

The sampling procedures for a factorial design follow a similar form for an experiment: We select one sample from the same population, then assign the same or different participants to groups created by combining the levels of two or more factors or independent variables. For a between-subjects factor, we use random assignment to observe different participants in each group. For a within-subjects factor, we observe the same participants in each group and control for order effects.

12.3   Types of Factorial Designs

Three types of factorial designs introduced in this section are:

Between-subjects design (a design in which all factors are between-subjects factors). For this design to be an experiment, we must manipulate the levels of each factor, cross the levels of the two factors to create the groups, and randomly assign different participants to each group.

Within-subjects design (a design in which all factors are within-subjects factors). For this design to be an experiment, we must manipulate the levels of each factor, cross the levels of the two factors to create the groups, and control for order effects due to observing the same subjects or participants in each group.

Mixed factorial design (a design with at least one between-subjects factor and one within-subjects factor). For this design to be an experiment, we must manipulate the levels of each factor, cross the levels of the two factors to create the groups, randomly assign different participants to each level of the between-subjects factor, and control for order effects due to observing the same participants at each level of the within-subjects factor.

12.4   Ethics in Focus: Participant Fatigue and Factorial Designs

Two concerns are of particular importance for a factorial design: The larger the number of levels combined to create the groups, the greater the demands on the participants, and the greater the demands in each group, the greater the burden on the participants.

12.5   Main Effects and Interactions

The test statistic used for a factorial design is the **two-way analysis of variance** (ANOVA), which is a statistical procedure used to analyze the variance in a dependent variable between groups created by combining the levels of two factors.

When the levels of two factors (A and B) are combined to create groups, the design is called a **two-way factorial design**. We can identify three sources of variation using this design:

1. Two main effects (one for Factor A and one for Factor B). A **main effect** is a source of variation associated with mean differences across the levels of a single factor.

2. One interaction (the combination of levels of Factors A and B). An **interaction** is a source of variation associated with how the effects of one factor are influenced by, or depend on, the levels of a second factor.

3. Error variance (variability attributed to individual differences). Error variance is a measure of individual differences or a measure to account for the fact that people are different or behave as individuals, regardless of the group to which they are assigned.

12.6   Identifying Main Effects and Interactions in a Graph

A main effect is evident in the row and column means of a table summary. An interaction is evident in the cell means of a table summary. Keep in mind, however, that even if a graph shows a possible main effect or interaction, the use of a test statistic is still needed to determine whether a main effect or an interaction is significant. In other words, we use the test statistic to determine if a manipulation of two factors or error caused an observed pattern that is plotted in a graph. Refer to Figure 12.2 and Figure 12.3 in Chapter 12 of the book to see how main effects and interactions appear graphically.

12.7   Including Quasi-Independent Factors in an Experiment

The factorial design can be used when we include preexisting or quasi-independent factors. When all factors in a factorial design are quasi-experimental, then the design is not an experiment because no factor is manipulated.

When at least one factor in a factorial design is manipulated (an independent variable), then the design is typically called an experiment, even if a quasi-independent factor is included in the design. The quasi-independent factor is typically a **participant variable** or demographic characteristic (i.e., characteristics of the participants in a study). However, an effect of a quasi-independent variable shows that the factor is related to changes in a dependent variable; it does not demonstrate cause and effect because the factor is preexisting.

12.8   Reasons for Including Two or More Factors in an Experiment

Three common reasons to add factors in an experiment:

- To build on previous research. Not only is it important to replicate previous findings; it is also important to build on or add to what those findings showed.
- To control for threats to validity. We can control for just about any other threat to internal validity by including it as a factor in a factorial design.
- To enhance the informativeness of interpretation. Factorial designs are more informative in that they allow us to observe the interaction of two or more factors.

12.9   Higher-Order Factorial Designs

A **higher-order factorial design** is a research design in which the levels of more than two factors are combined or crossed to create groups. One consequence of adding factors is that the number of possible effects we could observe increases, so we could observe a **higher-order interaction**, which is an interaction for the combination of levels of three or more factors in a factorial design.

Interpreting a higher-order interaction can be challenging, particularly when the interaction is for four or more factors. For this reason, researchers will often limit the number of factors in a factorial design to two or three to avoid the possibility of observing higher-order interactions with four or more factors.

12.10 SPSS in Focus: General Instructions for Conducting a Factorial ANOVA

SPSS can be used to analyze factorial designs that include only between-subjects factors by using the **Analyze, General Linear Model,** and **Univariate** options in the menu bar.

SPSS can also be used to analyze factorial designs that include at least one within-subjects factor by using the **Analyze, General Linear Model,** and **Repeated Measures** options in the menu bar.

Chapter Summary Organized by Learning Objective

LO 1: Delineate the factorial design from the factorial experimental design.

- A **factorial design** is a research design in which participants are observed in groups created by combining the levels of two or more factors.
- A **factorial experimental design** is a research design in which groups are created by manipulating the levels of two or more factors, then the same or different participants are observed in each group using experimental procedures of randomization (for a between-subjects factor) and using control for timing and order effects (for a within-subjects factor).

LO 2: Identify the appropriate sampling method for a factorial design used in an experiment.

- The appropriate sampling method for a factorial design used in an experiment is to select one sample from the same population, then randomly assign the same or different participants to groups created by combining the levels of two or more factors. This type of sampling is used in experiments because we can include randomization, manipulation, and a comparison or control group.

LO 3: Identify and describe three types of factorial designs.

- **Between-subjects design** (a design in which all factors are between-subjects factors). Using this design we manipulate the levels of both factors, cross the levels of each factor to create groups, and randomly assign different participants to each group.

- **Within-subjects design** (a design in which all factors are within-subjects factors). Using this design we manipulate the levels of both factors, cross the levels of each factor to create groups, and control for order effects due to observing the same participants in each group.
- **Mixed factorial design** (a design with at least one between-subjects factor and one within-subjects factor). Using this design we manipulate the levels of both factors, cross the levels of each factor to create groups, randomly assign different participants to each level of the between-subjects factor, and control for order effects due to observing the same participants at each level of the within-subjects factor.
- We identify any type of factorial design by the number of levels of each factor. We find the number of groups in a factorial design by multiplying the levels of each factor. For example, a 3 × 4 factorial design has two factors, one with three levels and one with four levels, and with 3 × 4 = 12 groups. How participants are assigned to each group depends on whether we manipulate the levels of a within-subjects factor or the levels of a between-subjects factor.

LO 4: Distinguish between a main effect and an interaction.

- A **main effect** is a source of variation associated with mean differences across the levels of a single factor. In a two-way factorial design there are two possible main effects (one for each factor).
- An **interaction** is a source of variation associated with the variance of group means across the combination of levels of two factors. In a table summary, an interaction is a measure of how cell means at each level of one factor change across the levels of a second factor.
- The test statistic used to analyze the main effects and interactions in a **two-way factorial design** is the **two-way analysis of variance**. The two-way ANOVA is used for factorial designs that measure data on an interval or a ratio scale.

LO 5: Identify main effects and interactions in a summary table and in a graph.

- The group means in a table summary can be graphed to identify a main effect, an interaction, or both. A main effect is evident when changes in a dependent variable vary across the levels of a single factor. An interaction is evident when changes in a dependent variable across the levels of one factor depend on which level of the second factor you analyze. Note that even if a graph shows a possible main effect or interaction, only the test statistic can determine if a main effect or an interaction is significant.

LO 6: Identify the implications of using a quasi-independent factor in a factorial design.

- The factorial design can be used when we include quasi-independent factors. When all factors in a factorial design are quasi-experimental, the design is not an experiment because no factor is manipulated; the design is a quasi-experiment. When at least one factor in a factorial design is manipulated (i.e., an independent variable), then the design is typically called an experiment; however, any effects involving the quasi-independent variable cannot demonstrate cause—only effects of the experimentally manipulated variable can demonstrate cause.

LO 7: Explain how a factorial design can be used to build on previous research, control for threats to validity, and enhance the informativeness of interpretation.

- A factorial design can be used to replicate a previous finding and also in the same design demonstrate a novel or new finding. While it is important to determine whether a previous finding can be replicated, that alone is redundant, so it is important to also build on previous research findings.
- A factorial design can be used to control for possible threats to validity. One way to control for possible threats to validity is to add these possible threats as factors in a factorial design.
- A factorial design can enhance the informativeness of interpretation. The factorial design is more informative because it allows us to analyze the effects of two or more factors simultaneously, which leads to the analysis of an effect that is unique to the factorial design: the interaction. In this way, an analysis using a factorial design is more informative than research designs that analyze the effects of only one factor at a time.

LO 8: Describe the higher-order factorial design.

- A **higher-order factorial design** is a research design in which the levels of more than two factors are combined or crossed to create groups. The higher-order factorial design allows researchers to analyze **higher-order interactions** for the combination of levels of three or more factors. Because a higher-order interaction is difficult to interpret, researchers will often try to limit the number of factors in a factorial design to two or three, if possible.

LO 9: Compute a factorial analysis of variance for the between-subjects, within-subjects, and mixed factorial design using SPSS.

- SPSS can be used to analyze factorial designs that include only between-subjects factors by using the **Analyze, General Linear Model,** and **Univariate** options in the menu bar. These actions will display a dialog box that allows you to identify the variables, choose an appropriate post hoc test for the main effects, and run the analysis (for more details, see Section 12.10 in the book).
- SPSS can be used to analyze factorial designs that include at least one within-subjects factor by using the **Analyze, General Linear Model,** and **Repeated Measures** options in the menu bar. These actions will display a dialog box that allows you to identify the variables, choose an appropriate post hoc test for the main effects, and run the analysis (for more details, see Section 12.10 in the book).

Tips and Cautions for Students

A × B between-subjects ANOVA. To simplify the notation of the two-way ANOVA, we label the factors alphabetically (e.g., A × B ANOVA), then refer to the levels of each factor in the design (e.g., 3×2 ANOVA). Notice that we know the number of groups by multiplying the levels of each factor, as indicated in the notation for the design. For example, a 3×2 factorial design has six groups. Because each number indicates the levels of a factor, we also know that the levels for two factors were observed, so this notation is rather informative.

   Interactions and main effects. Keep in mind that main effects are effects caused by a single factor. In a table summary, a main effect is a measure of how the row and column means differ across the levels of a single factor. An interaction, on the other hand, is an effect caused by the combination of two factors. In a table summary, an interaction is a measure of how cell means at each level of one factor change across the levels of a second factor. In this way, you can distinguish between main effects and interactions, particularly when data are summarized in a table.

Practice Quiz

1. The factorial experimental design includes the manipulation of:

   a. two or more groups

   b. one independent variable

   c. two or more independent variables

   d. multiple dependent variables

2. A _____ factorial design is one in which each level of one factor is combined or crossed with each level of the other factor, with participants observed in each cell or combination of levels.

   a. quasi-

   b. partial

   c. complete

   d. differential

3. Different participants are observed across the levels of a(n) _____, whereas the same participants are observed across the levels of a(n) _____.

   a. within-subjects factor; between-subjects factor

   b. between-subjects factor; within-subjects factor

   c. quasi-independent variable; independent variable

   d. independent variable; quasi-independent variable

4. Which of the following is a type of factorial experimental design that includes at least one between-subjects factor and at least one within-subjects factor?

   a. mixed factorial design

   b. between-subjects design

   c. within-subjects design

   d. matched-samples design

5. Participants taste and rate each of four beverages that vary based on the type of flavor (familiar, unfamiliar) and sugar content (low, high). Assuming the type of flavor and sugar content are the two manipulated factors in this study, which type of factorial experimental design is illustrated in this example?

   a. mixed factorial design

   b. between-subjects design

   c. matched-samples design

   d. within-subjects design

6. Which of the following is *not* a requirement for a between-subjects factorial design to qualify as an experiment?

   a. manipulate the levels of each factor

   b. cross the levels of the two factors to create the groups

   c. randomly assign different participants to each group

   d. control for order effects due to observing the same subjects in each group

7. A researcher has participants rate two vignettes. Half of the participants are randomly assigned to rate a vignette describing a man eating a healthy food and then a second vignette describing a woman eating a healthy food. The other half of participants are assigned to rate the same vignettes, except the man and woman are described as eating an unhealthy food in each vignette. In this example, the within-subjects factor is:

   a. healthfulness of the food (healthy, unhealthy)

   b. gender of person described in the vignette (man, woman)

   c. ratings given for each vignette

   d. none; only between-subjects factors are described in this example

8. A mixed factorial design has a between-subjects factor with four levels and a within-subjects factor with two levels. If 12 participants are observed in each group, then how many total participants were observed in the study?

   a. 12 participants

   b. 24 participants

   c. 48 participants

   d. 96 participants

9. Which of the following factorial experimental designs involve(s) the manipulation of a between-subjects factor?

   a. mixed factorial design

   b. between-subjects design

    c. within-subjects design

    d. both a and b

10. How many main effects are possible in a two-way factorial design?

    a. 0

    b. 1

    c. 2

    d. at least 2

11. A researcher found that variations in the effects of one factor are influenced by, or depend on, the levels of a second factor. What type of effect did the researcher find?

    a. interaction

    b. main effect

    c. two main effects

    d. none of the above

12. In a 2 × 2 table summary, where do you look to identify the main effects?

    a. row means

    b. column means

    c. cell means

    d. either a or b

13. In the 2 × 2 table summary below, which set of means reflects the interaction between the two factors, A and B?

Factor A

	A1	A2	
B1	1	5	3
B2	3	9	6
	2	7	

(Factor B labels the rows)

    a. 1, 5, 3, and 9 in cells

    b. 3 and 6 in row totals

    c. 2 and 7 in column totals

    d. none; an interaction cannot be identified in a 2 × 2 table summary

14. The researcher looks at the number of tasks participants completed after being exposed to different types of settings (clustered, organized) for different durations of time (short, long).

The graph below depicts the results of the study. In this graph, which of the following effects is/are likely to be significant?

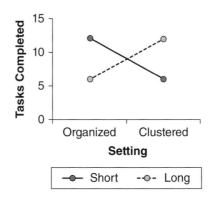

a. a main effect of setting and a main effect of duration only

b. a main effect of duration and a Setting × Duration interaction

c. a Setting × Duration interaction only

d. a main effect of setting and a Setting × Duration interaction

15. A researcher manipulates the type of color used in a product line (bright, dark) and tests if preference ratings for the product vary by gender (man, woman). In this example, the quasi-independent participant variable is:

a. gender

b. the product

c. type of color

d. preference ratings

16. How are the conclusions we can draw in a factorial design limited when the design includes at least one quasi-independent factor?

a. We do not show cause and effect for any effect that involves the quasi-independent factor.

b. We do not demonstrate cause and effect for any factors, regardless of whether the factor is an independent or a quasi-independent factor.

c. We can only make conclusions similar to those made in a nonexperiment.

d. No limitations; a quasi-independent variable is never included in a factorial research design.

17. Which of the following is a common reason for adding factors to an experiment?

a. to build on previous research

b. to control for threats to validity

c. to enhance the informativeness of interpretation

d. all of the above

18. Factorial designs are more informative than one-factor designs because:
    a. they allow us to observe a single main effect
    b. they allow us to observe the interaction of two or more factors
    c. they allow us to identify the difference between two group means
    d. they allow us to analyze the significance of an effect

19. Which of the following identifies a higher-order interaction assuming that each letter identifies a factor?
    a. A × B interaction
    b. A × B × C interaction
    c. B × C interaction
    d. both b and c

20. The "way" of a factorial design indicates:
    a. the number of groups in the design
    b. the number of participants in the design
    c. the number of factors in the design
    d. the number of effects in the design

Key Term Word Search

```
Y Z D X E Q I C M I X E D F A C T O R I A L D E S I G N I V N A M R I G
E Z F U S Z M I P P A R T I C I P A N T V A R I A B L E S G S M S C B Z
I H G M Y D Y Z U L L T Q X O Z C H L S Z D S D C U F K I N S L E O O O
Q H Q B I F J G W D V J Q W Q C I P Y J T Q L U K X H S G E P R U F P Y
I M P I W R D B J S S D H Z O V A L P V Q H E K G P E H C B K T Z K Z J
Q Z G D M Z M D P X C Q B A S G X M M X D I N U C D R M O T Z W F O N B
T H I B H R B R K G L X G R N M E Z X U R O N T L R I X I P A O F U M R
W E H O X L H Q O G I E S X N C T M Y B D Y G A I U O F U E O W A G U U
I O M I C Z L Y P P F U Z R I G O M D F B V I R W T V Y O P R A F C R J
S W F E B D G R Q G Z O L J A S K T O V N R F B P B N S X N J Y A O J T
P C L C M U X K W G J L C M C H B O P X O O W D Q Z N B I A M A C M M W
M V P X P J L I A M T W O W A Y F A C T O R I A L D E S I G N N T P M N
L T D X C G Y T V K O C T X S V C K C V N J O V N X N K X P U A O L N N
T V Q Z E J N O E L P F I Z E I B A X F K A J S E O T W S O E L R E O J
S E G L M D N D F Q B A W Y G K F N E V Q F M T I H Q U M O Y Y I T F D
A K K O G W B P U D A T K J W S L J G J L L A T T I L S P Q V S A E N N
D U H B X R E W N W K T P F T U L P M A W A C C I C D T S L H I L F O D
N G V R E F X I G L H T L C D B O D W B W A F W C E W S Y A U S D A W G
L H E G G H C G H I N T E R A C T I O N R L A V L R U B Y T V O E C V U
R V N A P A T V P L B J A N T A V J S E Z Y N I U C V W O B R F S T T E
M P I U M L C Y B S B Y Z M V R U S T O Y A A Q I K M P N R M V I O D L
I X Z Z M Y H I D U T J O P A I N N T K E I S Y E T I O W B U A G R X H
G R I A B F X U S T U I N J Z I I V R C T G F R I D K E Q J N R N I T O
Z D H I E H I N B W V Z U L G R N L P H W W X O P T B J G Q D I C A Z X
G C U H W D E S A V Z E A L E G Z E Y Y Y D S P Y O A D F B H A Z L R A
F Z X G L E V F N W G Q P D S P C A F M F U X G A G J W Y S O N P D U D
B P T E W O Y V R W S R R H F T F L W F F N O N P H U R I A N C Q E J D
S I I T Y Q A G Q K H O S U L W H N V D E M S B I F L O U W M E O S Y R
Q C E M A P N P R N R I R I E R D N N Y I C M I F V M K T R C G D I H K
G B O X H R Q W N E R B Z H U I H Y A A I G T L T B A W Y H P M L G F A
Y S F W J E A U H J J U P R P Z I W F O C F S M M J S F O O U P L N G R
M I V C Q Y N G H Y K E X F E M Y C T J Y E Z W D C H N B F Z S M A H T
Q T V P A J I V J F A Q L X D Q Q I H M B O K G U E G C B Q L W Y Z T Z
R H X J W H I G H E R O R D E R F A C T O R I A L D E S I G N I V L A M
R S W I T H I N S U B J E C T S F A C T O R I A L D E S I G N Y H Q Y G
E P J O E V C D S B Y J G Z J N E L M W G X R G L P D F R I Z Y W X C W
```

interaction	participant variables
two-way analysis of variance	within-subjects factorial design
complete factorial design	mixed factorial design
higher-order interaction	main effect
higher-order factorial design	two-way factorial design
between-subjects factorial design	factorial design

ACROSS

3. a source of variation associated with mean differences across the levels of a single factor

4. a source of variation associated with how the effects of one factor are influenced by, or depend on, the levels of a second factor

5. a research design in which participants are observed across the combination of levels of two or more factors

6. a _____ factorial design, or a factorial design in which each level of one factor is combined or crossed with each level of the other factor, with participants observed in each combination of levels

10. a _____ factorial design, or a research design in which the levels of more than two factors are combined or crossed to create groups

11. a _____ factorial design, or a research design in which the levels of two or more within-subjects factors are combined to create groups

12. a _____ factorial design, or a research design in which the levels of two or more between-subjects factors are combined to create groups

DOWN

1. a two-way _____ design, or a research design in which participants are observed in groups created by combining or crossing the levels of two factors

2. a quasi-independent or preexisting variable that is related to or characteristic of the personal attributes of a participant

7. a _____ analysis of variance, or a statistical procedure used to analyze the variance in a dependent variable between groups created by combining the levels of two factors

8. a _____ interaction, or an interaction for the combination of levels of three or more factors in a factorial design

9. a _____ factorial design, or a research design in which different participants are observed at each level of a between-subjects factor and then repeatedly observed across the levels of the within-subjects factor

Crossword Puzzle

SECTION V

Analyzing, Interpreting, and Communicating Research Data

13

Analysis and Interpretation: Exposition of Data

CHAPTER LEARNING OBJECTIVES

1. State two reasons why it is important to summarize data.

2. Define descriptive statistics and explain how they are used to describe data.

3. Identify and construct tables and graphs for frequency distributions.

4. Identify and appropriately use the mean, median, and mode to describe data.

5. Identify and appropriately use the variance and standard deviation to describe data.

6. Define and apply the empirical rule.

7. Identify and construct graphs used to display group means and correlations.

8. Use Cronbach's alpha and Cohen's kappa to estimate reliability.

9. Compute the mean, median, mode, variance, and standard deviation using SPSS.

10. Compute two measures of reliability using SPSS: Cronbach's alpha and Cohen's kappa.

Chapter Summary

13.1   Descriptive Statistics: Why Summarize Data?

To report research data, you typically summarize a general picture of the data because that is a clearer way to present them. A clear presentation of the data is necessary because it allows the reader to critically evaluate the data you are reporting. Two common reasons that we summarize data using descriptive statistics is to clarify what patterns were observed in a data set at a glance, and to be concise.

To describe data, we use **descriptive statistics**, which are procedures used to summarize, organize, and make sense of a set of scores, typically presented graphically, in tabular form (in tables), or as summary statistics (single values). Descriptive statistics summarize data to make sense or meaning of the measurements we make.

13.2   Frequency Distributions: Tables and Graphs

A **frequency** is the number of times or how often a category, score, or range of scores occurs. One way to describe frequency data is in a **frequency distribution table**. We can summarize the frequency of a continuous variable, a discrete variable, and a categorical variable, either grouped into intervals or listed as individual scores or categories.

Frequencies can also be presented graphically. To present frequency data graphically, we list the categories or scores on the x-axis (the horizontal axis) and the frequency of each category or score on the y-axis (the vertical axis) of a graph. Continuous data are often summarized graphically using a **histogram**. Discrete data are often summarized using a **bar chart** or a **pie chart**. Frequencies are often converted to percentages when presented in a pie chart.

13.3   Measures of Central Tendency

Measures of **central tendency** are single values that have a "tendency" to be at or near the "center" of a distribution. Three measures of central tendency are the mean, median, and mode.

The **sample mean** is the sum of all scores ($\sum x$) divided by the number of scores summed (n) in a sample, or in a subset of scores selected from a larger population. The sample mean is the balance point of a distribution and is typically used to describe data that are normally distributed and measured on an interval or ratio scale of measurement. A **normal distribution** is a distribution with data that are symmetrically distributed around the mean, the median, and the mode.

The **median** is the middle value in a distribution of data listed in numeric order. The median is an appropriate measure of central tendency to describe data that have a skewed distribution and are measured on an ordinal scale of measurement. A **skewed distribution** is a distribution of scores that includes outliers, or scores that fall substantially above or below most other scores in a data set. The **mode** is the value in a data set that occurs most often or most frequently. So long as a distribution has a value that occurs most often (i.e., a mode), the mode can be used to describe that value or values. Modal distributions can have a single mode, such as a normal distribution (the mode and mean are reported together) or a skewed distribution (the mode and median are reported together). The mode is also used to describe nominal data.

13.4 Measures of Variability

Variability is a measure of the dispersion or spread of scores in a distribution and ranges from 0 to $+\infty$. Measures of variability include variance and standard deviation. Variability can be 0 or greater than 0; a negative variability is meaningless.

The **sample variance**, represented as s^2, is a measure of the average squared distance that scores deviate from the mean. The formula for sample variance is the **sum of squares (SS)** divided by the **degrees of freedom for sample variance:**

$$s^2 = \frac{SS}{df}, \text{ where } df = n - 1$$

The **sample standard deviation (SD)** is a measure of variability for the average distance that scores in a sample deviate from the sample mean and is computed by taking the square root of the sample variance. The formula for the sample standard deviation can be represented as follows:

$$SD = \sqrt{s^2} = \sqrt{\frac{SS}{df}}$$

The standard deviation is the most informative measure of variability for the normal distribution because of the **empirical rule**. The empirical rule identifies each of the following:

- At least 68% of all scores fall within one standard deviation of the mean.
- At least 95% of all scores fall within two standard deviations of the mean.
- At least 99.7% of all scores fall within three standard deviations of the mean.

13.5 SPSS in Focus: Central Tendency and Variability

SPSS can be used to compute the mean, median, mode, variance, and standard deviation. Each measure is computed using the **Analyze, Descriptive Statistics,** and **Frequencies** options in the menu bar.

13.6 Graphing Means and Correlations

We can graph a mean for one or more groups using a graph with lines or bars to represent the means. By convention, we use a bar graph when the groups on the x-axis (horizontal axis) are represented on a nominal or ordinal scale; we use a line graph when the groups on the x-axis are represented on an interval or ratio scale.

A correlation is graphed using a **scatterplot**, which is a graphical display of discrete data points (x, y). The relationship between two factors can be evident by the pattern of data points plotted in a scatterplot.

13.7 Using Correlation to Describe Reliability

Cronbach's alpha is a measure of internal consistency that estimates the average correlation for every possible way that a measure can be split in half. The formula for Cronbach's alpha is as follows:

$$\text{Cronbach's alpha} = \left(\frac{n}{n-1} \right) \left(\frac{\sigma_X^2 - \sum \sigma_Y^2}{\sigma_X^2} \right)$$

Cohen's kappa is a measure of interrater reliability that estimates the level of agreement between two raters, while taking into account the probability that the two raters agree by chance or error. The following is the formula for Cohen's kappa, in which P_A is the percent agreement and P_E is the percent expected by error:

$$\text{Cohen's kappa} = \frac{P_A - P_E}{1 - P_E}$$

13.8   SPSS in Focus: Cronbach's Alpha and Cohen's Kappa

SPSS can be used to compute Cronbach's alpha by using the **Analyze, Scale,** and **Reliability Analysis** options in the menu bar.

SPSS can be used to compute Cohen's kappa by using the **Analyze, Descriptive Statistics,** and **Crosstabs** options in the menu bar.

13.9   Ethics in Focus: Deception Due to the Distortion of Data

Presenting data is an ethical concern when the data are distorted in any way, which can occur by accident or intentionally. Distortion of descriptive statistics can occur for data presented graphically or as summary statistics. Anytime you read a claim about results in a study, it is important to refer back to the data to confirm the extent to which the data support the claim being made by the author of a study.

Chapter Summary Organized by Learning Objective

<u>LO 1</u>: State two reasons why it is important to summarize data.

- It is important to summarize data in order (1) to clarify what patterns were observed in a data set at a glance and (2) to be concise.
- It is more meaningful to present data in a way that makes the interpretation of the data clearer. Also, when publishing an article, many journals have limited space, which requires that the exposition of data be concise.

<u>LO 2</u>: Define descriptive statistics and explain how they are used to describe data.

- **Descriptive statistics** are procedures used to summarize, organize, and make sense of a set of scores or observations. Descriptive statistics are presented graphically, in tabular form (in tables), or as summary statistics (e.g., mean, median, mode, variance, and standard deviation).

LO 3: Identify and construct tables and graphs for frequency distributions.

- A **frequency distribution table,** which lists scores or categories in one column and the corresponding frequencies in a second column, can be used to summarize (1) the frequency of each individual score or category in a distribution or (2) the frequency of scores falling within defined ranges or intervals in a distribution.

- A frequency distribution table can be presented graphically by listing the categories, scores, or intervals of scores on the x-axis (the horizontal axis) and the frequency in each category, for each score, or in each interval on the y-axis (the vertical axis) of a graph.

- The type of graph we use to describe frequency data depends on whether the factors being summarized are continuous or discrete. Continuous data are displayed in a **histogram.** Discrete and categorical data are displayed in a **bar chart** or **pie chart.** To summarize data as percents, a **pie chart** can be a more effective display than a bar chart.

LO 4: Identify and appropriately use the mean, median, and mode to describe data.

- The **sample mean** is the sum of all scores (Σx) divided by the number of scores summed (n) in a sample. The mean is used to describe data that are normally distributed and on an interval or ratio scale of measurement.

- The **median** is the middle value in a distribution of data listed in numeric order. The median is used to describe data that are skewed and data on an ordinal scale of measurement.

- The **mode** is the value that occurs most often or at the highest frequency in a distribution. The mode is used to describe distributions with one or more modes and categorical data on a nominal scale of measurement.

LO 5: Identify and appropriately use the variance and standard deviation to describe data.

- The **sample variance** is a measure of variability for the average squared distance that scores in a sample deviate from the sample mean. The sample variance is associated with $n - 1$ **degrees of freedom** (*df*) and is computed by dividing the **sum of squares** (SS) by *df*. The larger the sample variance, the farther that scores deviate from the mean, on average. One limitation of sample variance is that the average distance of scores from the mean is squared. To find the deviation or distance of scores from the mean we take the square root of the variance, called the **standard deviation.**

LO 6: Define and apply the empirical rule.

- For normal distributions, the **empirical rule** states that 68% of scores fall within one standard deviation, 95% of scores fall within two standard deviations, and 99.7% of scores fall within three standard deviations of the mean.

LO 7: Identify and construct graphs used to display group means and correlations.

- We can graph a mean for one or more groups using a graph with lines or bars to represent the means. By convention, we use a bar graph when the groups on the x-axis (horizontal axis) are represented on a nominal or ordinal scale; we use a line graph when the groups on the x-axis are represented on an interval or ratio scale.

- We graph correlations using a scatterplot. To plot a data point, you first move across the x-axis, and then move up or down the y-axis to mark or plot each pair of (x, y) data points. In a scatterplot, the pattern of a positive correlation appears as an ascending line; the pattern of a negative correlation appears as a descending line.

LO 8: Use Cronbach's alpha and Cohen's kappa to estimate reliability.

- **Cronbach's alpha** is a measure of internal consistency that estimates the average correlation for every possible way that a measure can be split in half. The higher the value of Cronbach's alpha, the stronger the correlation or relationship between items on the same measure.

- **Cohen's kappa** is a measure of interrater reliability that measures the level of agreement between two raters, while taking into account the probability that the two raters agree by chance or error. The higher the value of Cohen's kappa, the stronger the interrater reliability.

LO 9: Compute the mean, median, mode, variance, and standard deviation using SPSS.

- SPSS can be used to compute the mean, median, mode, variance, and standard deviation by using the **Analyze, Descriptive Statistics,** and **Frequencies** options in the menu bar. These actions will bring up a dialog box that will allow you to identify the variable and select the **Statistics** option to select each descriptive statistic (for more details, see Section 13.5 in the book).

LO 10: Compute two measures of reliability using SPSS: Cronbach's alpha and Cohen's kappa.

- SPSS can be used to compute Cronbach's alpha by using the **Analyze, Scale,** and **Reliability Analysis** options in the menu bar. These actions will display a dialog box that allows you to identify items on the scale and choose the **Statistics** option to identify the value of Cronbach's alpha for the **Scale** and **Scale if item deleted** (for more details, see Section 13.8 in the book).

- SPSS can be used to compute Cohen's kappa by using the **Analyze, Descriptive Statistics,** and **Crosstabs** options in the menu bar. These actions will display a dialog box that allows you to identify the raters and run the analysis. A **weight cases** option must also be selected from the menu bar (for more details, see Section 13.8 in the book).

Tips and Cautions for Students

Variability. Keep in mind that variability, to include variance and standard deviation, can never be negative. As stated in the chapter, the variability of scores can never be negative; variability ranges from 0 to $+\infty$. If four students receive the same scores of 8, 8, 8, and 8 on some assessment, then their scores do not vary because they are all the same value; the variability is 0. However, if the scores are 8, 8, 8, and 9, then they do vary because at least one of the scores differs from the others. Thus, scores can either not vary (variability is 0) or vary (variability is greater than 0). A negative variability is meaningless.

Graphing correlations. When graphing a correlation, the regression line can tell you a lot about the strength and direction of the relationship between two factors. A negative correlation is evident when the regression line is descending; a positive correlation is evident when the regression line is ascending. The strength of the correlation is evident by how far the data points fall from the regression line. When data points are generally close to the regression line, the strength of the correlation is likely strong; when data points are generally far from the regression line, the strength of the correlation is likely weak. In this way, graphing a correlation can inform you of both the strength and the direction of the correlation being depicted.

Practice Quiz

1. Anytime you conduct a study, it is important to _____ the data in a way that is useful or accessible to the reader.
   a. rescind
   b. report
   c. reuse
   d. recycle

2. A common reason that we summarize data using descriptive statistics is:
   a. to be concise
   b. to clarify what patterns were observed in a data set at a glance
   c. to provide a clear summary of the data
   d. all of the above

3. Descriptive statistics are used with:
   a. quantitative data
   b. qualitative data
   c. both quantitative and qualitative data
   d. none of the above

4. A researcher constructs the following simple frequency distribution. How many scores were measured in this study?

Scores (x)	Frequency
12–14	8
9–11	12
6–8	4
3–5	6
0–2	10

   a. between 0 and 14 scores

   b. 14 scores

   c. 40 scores

   d. It depends on which interval has the most scores.

5. A researcher measures the following scores: 0, 2, 2, 2, 2, 2, 4, 4, 4, 4, 0, 0, 0, 0, 0, 0, 0, 2, 2, 2, 2, 2, 4, 4, 4, 4, 4, 4, 4, 4, 4, 4, 0, 2, 4, 2, 2, 4, 4, 4, 4, 4, and 0. Should these data be grouped?

   a. yes, because so many scores were measured

   b. yes, because the range of values is small

   c. no, because the data are categorical

   d. no, because the number of different scores is small

6. A researcher measures the number of votes submitted for each of three candidates. What type of graph (shown below) was used to summarize these data? Is it appropriate?

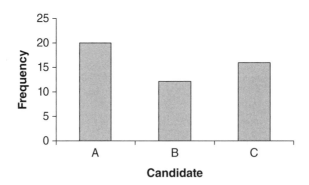

   a. bar chart; yes, because the data are continuous

   b. bar chart; yes, because the data are categorical

   c. bar chart; no, because the data are categorical

   d. histogram; yes, because the data are continuous

7. Which of the following is *not* a measure of central tendency?

   a. mode

   b. median

   c. variance

   d. mean

8. The mean is the balance point of a distribution, which means that it is:

   a. always equal to 0

   b. used to measure the extent to which objects balance

   c. equal to the score in the middle of a distribution

   d. not always located at the center of a distribution

9. A researcher records the following times (in seconds) that children in a sample play with an unfamiliar toy: 12, 14, 10, 6, 8, 10, 13, 12, 4, 12, and 6. Which measure of central tendency (the mean, the median, or the mode) is largest?

   a. mean

   b. median

   c. mode

   d. All measures for central tendency are equal.

10. Suppose that at least 68% of scores in a normal distribution fall between a score of 7 and 10. Using the empirical rule, what is the approximate mean and standard deviation of these data?

    a. mean = 7, standard deviation = 10

    b. mean = 8.5, standard deviation = 3

    c. mean = 8.5, standard deviation = 1.5

    d. mean = 10, standard deviation = 7

11. The _____ is the square root of the _____.

    a. median; mean

    b. mean; median

    c. variance; standard deviation

    d. standard deviation; variance

12. The sample variance is an unbiased estimator of the population variance when we:

    a. divide SS by $(n - 1)$

    b. divide SS by N

    c. multiply SS by $(n - 1)$

    d. multiply the sample variance by the population variance

13. The standard deviation is most informative for describing what type of distribution?

    a. normal distribution

    b. skewed distribution

   c. bimodal distribution

   d. nonmodal distribution

14. The following graph displays data for the relationship between time spent training (in hours per week) and time to complete a short-distance run (in minutes). What type of data is displayed in this graph?

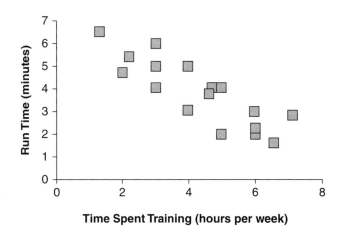

   a. group means

   b. grouped data

   c. correlational data

   d. both a and b

15. By convention, we use a bar graph to display group means that are represented on _____ scale; we use a line graph to display group means that are represented on _____ scale.

   a. a nominal or interval; an ordinal or ratio

   b. a nominal or ordinal; an interval or ratio

   c. an interval or ratio; a nominal or ordinal

   d. an ordinal or ratio; a nominal or interval

16. The analysis to test for internal consistency is _____; the analysis to test for interrater reliability is _____.

   a. Cronbach's alpha; Cronbach's alpha

   b. Cohen's kappa; Cronbach's alpha

   c. Cohen's kappa; Cohen's kappa

   d. Cronbach's alpha; Cohen's kappa

17. Cronbach's alpha describes:

   a. the extent to which two pairs of group means are similar

   b. the extent to which a set of items consistently measures the same phenomena

    c. the percent agreement between two raters, while taking into account error

    d. the level of confidence for the interval of a set of scores

18. In the formula for Cohen's kappa, what does P_E represent?

    a. percent agreement

    b. percent eliminated

    c. percent expected by error

    d. percent of effect size

19. Cohen's kappa measures the percent agreement between two raters, while taking into account _____.

    a. error

    b. effect size

    c. significance

    d. indecisiveness

20. Which of the following is *not* a common distortion of data to look for in graphs?

    a. displays with the scales standardized to indicate differences along the same scale for all measures

    b. displays with one axis altered in relation to the other axis

    c. displays with an unlabeled axis

    d. displays in which the vertical axis does not begin with 0

Key Term Word Search

```
Y  J  Y  M  O  D  E  H  Q  U  B  V  H  M  E  D  I  A  N  V  V  A  R  V  Z  F  Y  X
K  F  C  O  H  E  N  S  K  A  P  P  A  T  U  E  F  N  V  M  R  B  B  G  K  U  M  Z
G  W  G  Y  L  I  I  I  G  R  O  A  K  A  J  S  B  K  K  Z  Z  O  T  I  Z  B  J  N
B  D  J  V  F  R  E  Q  U  E  N  C  Y  D  I  S  T  R  I  B  U  T  I  O  N  S  E  X
A  E  S  D  N  S  N  Y  Z  S  B  D  X  R  W  V  D  A  Y  G  E  C  K  D  J  I  J  V
R  S  X  A  W  I  U  O  J  R  P  M  D  Q  S  G  S  H  S  U  S  I  X  Z  F  L  C  P
G  C  B  C  M  S  S  J  R  F  N  H  L  C  A  E  X  M  M  Y  X  Z  U  I  D  W  S  D
R  R  O  E  M  P  R  K  J  M  R  A  M  M  D  P  A  R  N  G  N  X  F  I  E  D  U  E
A  I  O  N  C  K  L  T  E  L  A  C  L  H  J  R  I  C  Z  O  B  L  S  H  G  Y  M  P
P  P  A  T  U  E  T  E  W  W  P  L  K  P  G  P  M  E  G  C  C  I  V  D  R  G  O  V
H  T  Q  R  C  G  W  J  S  F  E  B  D  O  P  R  B  Y  C  M  M  T  G  G  E  F  F  Y
O  I  X  A  B  R  E  R  W  T  C  D  T  I  X  F  L  A  V  H  P  X  B  C  E  R  S  V
R  V  Q  L  H  M  O  Q  S  Q  A  S  D  L  S  O  N  T  R  Z  A  T  Y  G  S  E  Q  C
A  E  E  T  P  I  G  N  H  S  I  N  G  I  P  T  S  B  S  C  C  R  P  J  O  Q  U  S
Q  S  M  E  B  Y  J  Y  B  H  T  D  D  Y  S  H  R  F  Z  L  H  D  T  M  F  U  A  C
T  T  P  N  Z  V  K  G  E  A  S  H  C  A  B  T  G  I  W  P  U  A  Z  O  F  E  R  A
L  A  I  D  Y  C  E  N  H  J  C  N  B  G  R  R  R  M  B  U  S  N  R  I  R  N  E  T
I  T  R  E  M  P  I  F  C  U  E  H  W  V  S  D  J  I  E  U  N  C  C  T  E  C  S  T
Q  I  I  N  H  R  Q  I  H  U  N  B  S  K  R  A  D  N  B  Q  T  L  Y  N  E  Y  W  E
O  S  C  C  W  C  G  E  Q  N  C  W  R  A  B  M  M  E  K  U  M  I  Y  R  D  F  Y  R
U  T  A  Y  Q  R  C  E  Q  U  O  B  N  P  L  G  O  P  V  T  T  R  O  H  O  Q  B  P
O  I  L  H  C  F  R  X  J  U  V  F  C  X  U  P  N  F  L  I  F  I  U  N  M  K  T  L
M  C  R  T  C  F  F  J  S  J  U  A  U  X  W  F  H  O  Y  E  A  P  O  J  O  U  S  O
C  S  U  X  V  V  D  H  W  D  O  I  H  D  Q  W  P  A  U  U  M  T  O  N  O  N  Z  T
G  S  L  N  C  S  A  M  P  L  E  V  A  R  I  A  N  C  E  U  X  E  I  W  V  M  A  W
I  C  E  Y  Q  G  Z  V  N  V  C  V  A  R  I  A  B  I  L  I  T  Y  A  O  D  V  X  I
Z  Z  H  P  M  O  W  L  P  U  I  H  D  V  R  C  X  X  F  M  M  W  F  N  N  H  Y  A
C  R  G  X  O  T  U  R  I  N  N  U  C  P  Y  P  M  W  T  Z  M  K  X  L  T  H  Y
```

mode	histogram	sum of squares	normal distribution
median	sample mean	Cronbach's alpha	skewed distribution
bar chart	variability	sample variance	descriptive statistics
bar graph	Cohen's kappa	central tendency	frequency distribution
frequency	scatterplot	frequency polygon	sample standard
pie chart	empirical rule	degrees of freedom	deviation

ACROSS

2. the square root of the sample variance

5. the _____ for sample variance that is one less than the sample size

6. a graphical display used to summarize the frequency of continuous data that are distributed in numeric intervals using bars connected at the upper limits of each interval

7. a measure of variability for the average squared distance that scores in a sample deviate from the sample mean

8. a measure of interrater reliability

11. a graphical display used to summarize the frequency of discrete and categorical data using bars to represent each frequency

12. a graphical display in the shape of a circle that is used to summarize the relative percent of discrete and categorical data into sectors

13. the middle value in a distribution of data listed in numeric order

14. statistical measures for locating a single score that is most representative or descriptive of all scores in a distribution

15. a measure of the dispersion or spread of scores in a distribution

16. a value that describes the number of times or how often a category, score, or range of scores occurs

17. the sum of all scores divided by the number of scores summed in a sample

18. a rule for normally distributed data that states that at least 99.7% of data fall within three standard deviations of the mean; at least 95% of data fall within two standard deviations of the mean; and at least 68% of data fall within one standard deviation of the mean

DOWN

1. procedures used to summarize, organize, and make sense of a set of scores or observations, typically presented graphically, in tabular form, or as summary statistics

2. a distribution of scores that includes outliers or scores that fall substantially above or below most other scores in a data set

3. a summary display table for a distribution of data organized or summarized in terms of how often a category, score, or range of scores occurs

4. a graphical display of discrete data points used to summarize the relationship between two variables

7. the sum of the squared deviations of scores from the mean, in the numerator of the sample variance formula

9. a measure of internal consistency

10. the value in a data set that occurs most often or most frequently

Crossword Puzzle

14

Analysis and Interpretation: Making Decisions About Data

CHAPTER LEARNING OBJECTIVES

1. Define inferential statistics and explain why they are necessary.

2. Describe the process of null hypothesis significance testing (NHST).

3. Distinguish between Type I and Type II errors and define power.

4. Distinguish between parametric and nonparametric tests and choose an appropriate test statistic for research designs with one and two factors.

5. Distinguish between a chi-square goodness-of-fit test and a chi-square test for independence.

6. Identify and describe the following effect size measures: Cohen's *d,* eta squared, the coefficient of determination, and Cramer's *V.*

7. Distinguish between a point estimate and an interval estimate and explain how estimation relates to the significance and effect size of an outcome.

8. Distinguish between the precision and the certainty of an interval estimate.

9. Compute a chi-square goodness-of-fit test and a chi-square test for independence using SPSS.

Chapter Summary

14.1   Inferential Statistics: What Are We Making Inferences About?

Inferential statistics are procedures that allow researchers to *infer* or generalize observations made with samples to the larger population from which they were selected. We use inferential statistics to make decisions about characteristics in a population based on data measured in a sample.

Inferential statistics include a diverse set of tests of statistical significance known as *null hypothesis significance testing* (NHST). To use NHST, we state a **null hypothesis**, which is a statement about a population parameter, such as the population mean, that is assumed to be true. The null hypothesis is a starting point. We test whether the value stated in the null hypothesis is likely to be true.

We then state a criterion for making a decision about the null hypothesis, called the **level of significance**, which is a criterion of judgment upon which a decision is made regarding the value stated in a null hypothesis. The criterion is based on the probability of obtaining a sample statistic if the value stated in the null hypothesis is true.

To determine the likelihood or probability of obtaining a sample outcome, if the value stated in the null hypothesis is true, we compute a **test statistic**. A test statistic is used to find the p **value**, which is the actual probability of a sample outcome if the null hypothesis is true. When $p \leq .05$, we reject the null hypothesis and state that an effect or difference reached **significance**.

14.2   Types of Error and Power

When we decide to retain the null hypothesis, we can be correct or incorrect. When we correctly retain the null hypothesis, we call the decision a null finding. When we incorrectly retain the null hypothesis, we call the decision a **Type II error**.

When we decide to reject the null hypothesis, we can be correct or incorrect. When we correctly reject the null hypothesis, we call the decision the **power** because deciding to reject a false null hypothesis is when we learn the most about populations by accurately rejecting false notions of truth. When we incorrectly reject the null hypothesis, we call the decision a **Type I error**.

14.3   Parametric Tests: Applying the Decision Tree

Parametric tests are significance tests that are used to test hypotheses about parameters in a population in which the data in the population are normally distributed and measured on an interval or ratio scale of measurement.

We use the *t* tests and analysis of variance (ANOVA) tests for studies in which participants are assigned to one or more groups. Choosing an appropriate parametric test depends largely on how participants are observed (between subjects or within subjects) and how many factors and groups are included in a research design.

We also use parametric tests concerning the extent to which two factors are related (correlation) and the extent to which we can use known values of one factor to predict values of a second factor (linear regression). For a parametric test, we use the *Pearson correlation coefficient* for data measured on an interval or ratio scale. The Spearman, point-biserial, and phi correlation coefficients—which are used for data on different scales of measurement—are mathematically equivalent to the Pearson correlation coefficient.

14.4 Nonparametric Tests: Applying the Decision Tree

Nonparametric tests are significance tests used to test hypotheses about data that can have any type of distribution and to analyze data on a nominal or ordinal scale of measurement. Nonparametric tests are used as alternatives to parametric tests for situations in which the levels of one factor are used to create groups, but the data are ordinal or are not normally distributed. Although the introduction to nonparametric tests for ordinal data goes beyond the scope of the book, these tests can be readily computed in SPSS by using the **Analyze, Nonparametric Tests,** and **Legacy Dialogs** options in the menu bar.

Nonparametric tests can also be used to analyze nominal or categorical data. For one categorical factor, we can analyze the extent to which frequencies observed fit well with frequencies expected using the **chi-square goodness-of-fit test**. We can analyze the extent to which frequencies observed across the levels of two nominal (categorical) factors are related or independent using the **chi-square test for independence**.

14.5 SPSS in Focus: The Chi-Square Tests

The chi-square goodness-of-fit test is computed using the **Analyze, Nonparametric Tests,** and **Chi-square** options in the menu bar.

The chi-square test for independence is computed using the **Analyze, Descriptive Statistics,** and **Crosstabs** options in the menu bar.

14.6 Effect Size: How Big Is an Effect in the Population?

An **effect** is a mean difference or discrepancy between what was observed in a sample and what was expected to be observed in the population (stated by the null hypothesis). When we reject the null hypothesis, an effect is significant; when we retain the null hypothesis, an effect is not significant. **Effect size** is a statistical measure of the size or magnitude of an observed effect in a population, which allows researchers to describe how far scores shifted in a population, or the percent of variance in a dependent variable that can be explained by the levels of a factor.

Cohen's d is an effect size measure used with the one-sample, two-independent-sample, and related-samples t tests. Eta squared is used to estimate effect size as the proportion of variance in a dependent variable that can be explained or accounted for by the levels of a factor with an ANOVA test. When a correlation or regression is used to analyze data, the coefficient of determination, R^2, is used to estimate effect size. Cramer's V is used to estimate effect size when data are analyzed using the chi-square test for independence.

14.7 Estimation: What Are the Possible Values of a Parameter?

Estimation is a statistical procedure in which a sample statistic is used to estimate the value of an unknown population parameter. Two types of estimation are point estimation and interval estimation.

A **point estimate** is a sample mean for one group or mean difference between two groups. We use the sample mean (the statistic) to estimate the population mean (the parameter). An **interval estimate**, called the **confidence interval**, is the range of possible values for the parameter stated within a given **level of confidence**, which is the likelihood that a population mean is contained within that given interval.

14.8   Confidence Intervals, Significance, and Effect Size

The process of computing a confidence interval is related to the process we used to retain or reject a null hypothesis using NHST. In fact, we can apply the following rules to identify the significance of an outcome: If the null hypothesis were inside a confidence interval, the decision would have been to retain the null hypothesis (not significant). If the null hypothesis were outside the confidence interval, the decision would have been to reject the null hypothesis (significant).

14.9   Issues for Interpretation: Precision and Certainty

The *precision* of an estimate is determined by the range of a confidence interval: The smaller the range of a confidence interval, the more precise the estimate. The *certainty* of an estimate is determined by the level of confidence: The larger the level of confidence, the more certain the estimate. In terms of the level of confidence, decreasing the level of confidence increases the precision of an estimate; increasing the level of confidence increases the certainty of an estimate.

14.10 Ethics in Focus: Full Disclosure of Data

When reporting statistical results, it is important to report data as thoroughly, yet concisely, as possible. Always fully disclose data and do not selectively omit data. To avoid problems in trusting the outcomes reported in a paper, the simple solution is to always fully disclose data.

Chapter Summary Organized by Learning Objective

<u>LO 1</u>: Define inferential statistics and explain why they are necessary.

- **Inferential statistics** are procedures that allow researchers to *infer* or generalize observations made with samples to the larger population from which they were selected.
- Inferential statistics allow researchers to use data recorded in a sample to draw conclusions about the larger population of interest—this would not be possible without inferential statistics.

<u>LO 2</u>: Describe the process of null hypothesis significance testing (NHST).

- To use NHST, we begin by stating a **null hypothesis**, which is a statement about a population parameter, such as the population mean, that is assumed to be true but contradicts the research hypothesis. We then state a criterion upon which we will decide to retain or reject the null hypothesis.

- To establish a criterion for a decision, we state a **level of significance** for a test. The level of significance for most studies in behavioral science is .05. To determine the likelihood or probability of obtaining a sample outcome, if the value stated in the null hypothesis is true, we compute a **test statistic**. A test statistic is used to find the p value, which is the actual probability of obtaining a sample outcome if the null hypothesis is true. We reject the null hypothesis when $p \leq .05$; an effect reached **significance**. We retain the null hypothesis when $p > .05$; an effect failed to reach significance.

<u>LO 3</u>: Distinguish between Type I and Type II errors and define power.

- A **Type I error** is the probability of rejecting a null hypothesis that is actually true. Researchers control for this type of error by stating a level of significance, which is typically set at .05. A **Type II error** is the probability of retaining a null hypothesis that is actually false, meaning that the researcher reports no effect in the population, when in truth there is an effect.
- **Power** is the probability of rejecting a false null hypothesis. Specifically, power is the probability that we will detect an effect if it actually exists in a population.

<u>LO 4</u>: Distinguish between parametric and nonparametric tests and choose an appropriate test statistic for research designs with one and two factors.

- **Parametric tests** are significance tests that are used to test hypotheses about parameters in a population in which the data are normally distributed and measured on an interval or ratio scale of measurement.
- **Nonparametric tests** are significance tests that are used to test hypotheses about data that can have any type of distribution and to analyze data on a nominal or ordinal scale of measurement.
- Choosing an appropriate parametric and nonparametric test can depend largely on how participants were observed (between subjects or within subjects), how many factors and groups were included in a research design, and the type of research question being asked.

<u>LO 5</u>: Distinguish between a chi-square goodness-of-fit test and a chi-square test for independence.

- A **chi-square goodness-of-fit test** is a statistical procedure used to determine whether observed frequencies at each level of one categorical variable are similar to or different from the frequencies we expected at each level of the categorical variable. If frequencies observed fit well with frequencies expected, the decision will be to retain the null hypothesis; if frequencies observed do not fit well with frequencies expected, the decision will be to reject the null hypothesis.
- A **chi-square test for independence** is a statistical procedure used to determine whether frequencies observed at the combination of levels of two categorical variables are similar to frequencies expected. If two factors are independent, the decision will be to retain the null hypothesis; if two factors are related, the decision will be to reject the null hypothesis.

LO 6: Identify and describe the following effect size measures: Cohen's *d*, eta squared, the coefficient of determination, and Cramer's *V*.

- **Effect size** is a statistical measure of the size of an observed effect in a population, which allows researchers to describe how far scores shifted in a population, or the percent of variance in a dependent variable that can be explained by the levels of a factor.

- **Cohen's *d*** is a measure of effect size in terms of the number of standard deviations that mean scores shift above or below a population mean. The larger the value of *d*, the larger the effect in the population. Cohen's *d* is an effect size measure used with the one-sample, two-independent-sample, and related-samples *t* tests.

- When ANOVA is used to analyze data, **eta squared** (η^2) is used to estimate effect size as the proportion of variance in a dependent variable that can be explained or accounted for by the levels of a factor. When a correlation or regression is used to analyze data, the **coefficient of determination** (R^2) is used to estimate effect size. The coefficient of determination is mathematically equivalent to eta squared.

- **Cramer's *V*** is used to estimate effect size when data are analyzed using the chi-square test for independence and is interpreted the same as the coefficient of determination.

LO 7: Distinguish between a point estimate and an interval estimate and explain how estimation relates to the significance and effect size of an outcome.

- To use **estimation**, we set limits for the possible values of a population parameter within which the parameter is likely to be contained. Two types of estimates are a **point estimate** (a sample mean or mean difference) and an **interval estimate** (the range of possible values for a parameter stated with a given level of confidence).

- An effect would be significant if the value stated in a null hypothesis were outside the limits of a confidence interval; an effect would not be significant if contained within the limits of a confidence interval.

- The effect size for a confidence interval is stated as a range or interval, in which the lower effect size estimate is the difference between the value stated in a null hypothesis and the lower confidence limit; the upper effect size estimate is the difference between the value stated in a null hypothesis and the upper confidence limit. Effect size can then be interpreted in terms of a shift in the population when the value of the null hypothesis is outside a specified confidence interval.

LO 8: Distinguish between the precision and the certainty of an interval estimate.

- The precision of an estimate is determined by the range of the confidence interval. The certainty of an estimate is determined by the level of confidence. To be more certain that an interval contains a population parameter, we typically give up precision.

LO 9: Compute a chi-square goodness-of-fit test and a chi-square test for independence using SPSS.

- SPSS can be used to compute the chi-square goodness-of-fit test using the **Analyze, Nonparametric Tests,** and **Chi-square** options in the menu bar. These actions will display a dialog box that allows you to identify the groups and run the test. A **Weight Cases** option must also be selected from the menu bar (for more details, see Section 14.5 in the book).

- SPSS can be used to compute the chi-square test for independence using the **Analyze, Descriptive Statistics,** and **Crosstabs** options in the menu bar. These actions will display a dialog box that allows you to identify the groups and run the analysis. A **Weight Cases** option must also be selected from the menu bar (for more details, see Section 14.5 in the book).

Tips and Cautions for Students

Stating the hypotheses in NHST. In null hypothesis significance testing, note that the alternative hypothesis always restates the question as a truth. For example, suppose the hypothesis is that test scores are higher than 85% if you eat breakfast prior to an exam. The alternative hypothesis reflects the hypothesis that scores are higher than 85%. The null hypothesis will state what is thought to be true in the population—that the average score is equal to 85%.

Effect size and Cohen's d. Cohen's d indicates the number of standard deviations that an effect shifts in the population. The sample standard deviation is used as an estimate of the population standard deviation, which is unknown. Note that Cohen's d uses the sample standard deviation in the denominator of the formula, and not sample size, which is why the value of Cohen's d (effect size) is not affected by changes in sample size.

Precision and certainty of confidence intervals. The two key characteristics of confidence intervals, precision and certainty, are related in that to increase one, we must decrease the other. To have more *precision*, and thus a *narrower* confidence interval, we reduce the certainty of the estimate. Likewise, to be more certain, we must give up precision (i.e., the confidence interval is widened). Because of this give-and-take relationship, certainty and precision are characteristics that we try to balance.

Practice Quiz

1. In science, we systematically record data, and based upon these data, we:
    a. make decisions about samples
    b. make decisions about populations
    c. make decisions about the participants in a study
    d. rarely make decisions

2. A researcher observes 30 students who are enrolled at a local university. If students at the university are the group of interest to the researcher, then which group constitutes the sample?

   a. the parents of the students

   b. all students at the university

   c. the 30 students observed by the researcher

   d. the sample is not clearly identified in this example

3. Which type of statistics allows researchers to make decisions about a population based upon the limited data observed in a sample that was selected from that population?

   a. inferential statistics

   b. descriptive statistics

   c. central tendency

   d. summary statistics

4. Tests of statistical significance are more formally known as:

   a. IRB

   b. COBRA

   c. NHST

   d. USMC

5. Using NHST, researchers test their hypothesis against the _____, which is a statement about a population parameter and is assumed to be true but contradicts the researcher's hypothesis.

   a. alternative hypothesis

   b. sample hypothesis

   c. theoretical hypothesis

   d. null hypothesis

6. What decisions can be made using NHST?

   a. retain or reject the null hypothesis

   b. retain or accept the null hypothesis

   c. retain or reject the alternative hypothesis

   d. retain or accept the alternative hypothesis

7. A researcher computes a test statistic and finds that this outcome is associated with $p = .02$. What is the decision for this test if the level of significance is set at .05?

   a. the effect reached significance

   b. reject the null hypothesis

   c. the likelihood that the effect was due to chance or error is less than .05

   d. all of the above

8. If the level of significance is set at .05, then which of the following p values would lead to a decision to retain the null hypothesis?

   a. $p = .021$

   b. $p = .402$

   c. $p = .012$

   d. $p = .006$

9. Is it possible that a decision made using NHST could be wrong?

   a. yes, there is always some probability that a decision is wrong

   b. yes, a decision could be wrong but in most cases the probability is 0 that a decision is wrong

   c. no, a decision can never be wrong

   d. no, researchers do not make decisions using NHST

10. A Type II error occurs when researchers:

    a. incorrectly decide to reject the null hypothesis

    b. incorrectly decide to retain the null hypothesis

    c. correctly decide to reject the null hypothesis

    d. correctly decide to retain the null hypothesis

11. Which of the following decisions describes the power of the decision-making process?

    a. incorrectly decide to reject the null hypothesis

    b. incorrectly decide to retain the null hypothesis

    c. correctly decide to reject the null hypothesis

    d. correctly decide to retain the null hypothesis

12. Which of the following is an example of a parametric hypothesis test?

    a. one-sample t test

    b. one-way ANOVA

    c. related-samples t test

    d. all of the above

13. What are the scales of measurement for data that are measured using a parametric test?

    a. nominal or ordinal

    b. ordinal or interval

    c. interval or ratio

    d. nominal, ordinal, interval, or ratio

14. Which parametric test is used for studies in which participants are observed in more than two groups created by manipulating the levels of a single factor?

    a. one-way analysis of variance test

    b. related-samples t test

   c. independent-sample *t* test

   d. higher-order factorial analysis of variance test

15. Which of the following correlation coefficients is used for data measured on an interval or ratio scale of measurement?

   a. Pearson correlation coefficient

   b. phi correlation coefficient

   c. Spearman correlation coefficient

   d. point-biserial correlation coefficient

16. Nonparametric tests can be used when:

   a. data in the population have any type of distribution

   b. data are measured on a nominal or ordinal scale of measurement

   c. both a and b

17. Which of the following is a type of nonparametric hypothesis test?

   a. one-sample sign test

   b. Mann-Whitney *U* test

   c. Wilcoxon signed-ranks *t* test

   d. all of the above

18. Which of the following is a nonparametric test for nominal data?

   a. *t* tests

   b. chi-square tests

   c. ANOVA tests

   d. all of the above

19. To determine if an effect is significant we use a(n) _____; the size of an effect is measured by a(n) _____.

   a. effect size; test statistic

   b. test statistic; effect size

   c. descriptive statistic; summary statistic

   d. summary statistic; descriptive statistic

20. Which of the following measures of effect size are used only to estimate the size of an effect following a *t* test?

   a. proportion of variance

   b. coefficient of determination

   c. Cohen's *d*

   d. Cramer's *V*

21. Based on conventions, a value of .28 would be a ____ effect if it represented the value of Cohen's *d*, whereas .28 would be a ____ effect if it represented the value of eta squared.

    a. small; small

    b. small; large

    c. medium; medium

    d. medium; large

22. The value of the coefficient of determination is equal to which value?

    a. Cohen's *d*

    b. eta squared

    c. Cramer's *V*

    d. all of the above

23. An alternative to NHST in which researchers use a sample mean or mean difference to estimate the value of a population parameter is called:

    a. sampling

    b. variation

    c. estimation

    d. significance testing

24. A researcher reports the following 95% confidence interval: 95% CI 0.23 to 0.69. What is the point estimate for this confidence interval?

    a. 0.23

    b. 0.46

    c. 0.69

    d. 95%

25. A researcher reports the following 95% confidence interval: 95% CI 2.00 to 4.00 points for the mean difference between two groups. If the null hypothesis is that the groups did not differ (mean difference = 0), then what is the effect size for this confidence interval?

    a. between 2 and 4 points

    b. 2 points

    c. 4 points

    d. none; effect size cannot be interpreted from a confidence interval

26. Increasing the level of confidence increases the _____ of an estimate.

    a. certainty

    b. precision

    c. significance

    d. proportion of variance

Key Term Word Search

```
N W D Z E I C Z C Q J I Z W E T A S Q U A R E D S P K R C D F Z D E S T V
U Q R N W F P I L J P R O P O R T I O N O F V A R I A N C E C P O T Z N W
L S C K W U A H G K A U L S B A X D U B N C R A M E R S V T Q B S X M K G
L Z N W S E R N F P D X E J D C K K J L K W U D W K N G M O U E B X U Z W
H N V B O W A G M A N L R F N P B Q P Y V Y Y G C S A Y L P T G K B V L Q
Y I T N V P M C O P I N F E R E N T I A L S T A T I S T I C S Y W F R I S
P Z M E Z L E U K S A W L X M F Z H E N P M I H U B R F I A E R Q T P N L
O L X F A B T U Z D C S B N I J N C P B D A G S D B P R S W T F G K K O M
T F X U X O R T H C E O W I C O N C V I S H F P M S T I P Y W X F C O N V
H D B B P G I K N A O J N R D A S Y K D B Y V K O E Q C X N U X A E D N D
E U J F F F C R E P S E Y F C E Y I E B Z T A A M I E P Z N C K F C C W T
S Z I A L Z T C X H I S F I I D A T H C L Y M A X E N J L Q A R V L S T E
I G V A Z J E I N U F T F F N D A G T H W H R O L X X T J T O X A D V E S
S V G W F P S W P R M I H B I M E L C F S A L D Z B N B E V E V T J T T T
S R V R M Z T P C R N V S V I C R N Y A P A Q T N O R T M S R K K F X M F
T K J B B Q S T G G J I T T H O I A C N E A S H D G V N F E T A S J Z M O
H U D H M Q R C I O C N S X F I C E O E P O X M R Y T H T D W I O X V M R
M H U L J W G S I J O E J W G B E N N I L D P X G F W N I Z F P M K B H I
Y B Z I C L F J Z M L D E T I G U L F T K I G J S X I H Z Y I V H A Y W N
Y M I V G O J R E A T M N A I M A E C J O F M T X E U O I G S Z P H T I D
C V H L L T A J V S I Z V E S R C I Z P W F A I C E Q J A V E N Y R E E E
G Q L E J A N R S P G P F C S N T E P L I Y D N T R A P H X Q W Z Z U G P
J R V C T J E M N Y S O T W E S K V C K C V E E X S L Q J Z C H I C Y G E
M E U Q J T Y X U E N W K D I C O H E N S D Y F T P I C D F O S I N Y W N
L J C G N O S H A I J V I T J B D F P I I V Z H J E X C E Z T J H S J E D
G P Z I I U D N L S P F A X Z C R G F F Q L S T N W R X T C M T S L R R E
Z W G W Y Q F V J H N T C A H L Y V N I V N K N P Q E M E P W M I S Q I N
T A L L G V B R D O S L U F B J U O J A T D N U T T V F I G E V C S A Q C
M E L N X H W F C T D L C E T S C O V U Y T J T I N F I U N H J S C S O E
J J Q J E S F F S W R R P G M P V A L U E E E I L E C K U G A U Q O S R D
Q N N K T G O E T E L Z Y P A N S U A W Q O R S Z G L S C O Z T C Q T T L
R S O F L L T Q W J N I R A X O D C Q O I L I Y T L Z E A D A U I D N S V
G S B L E B B O K W G C J P S I G N I F I C A N C E L E V E L B Y O Z B J
S R W V H X P Y I M A W S S B P L Q A W Q L E A G D X T E T X V I T N X Q
D B E A T C M E V Z N Q Y T L G E U M O L U H K Q M O X Q F R P R U N Z M
V L W I X G M R P R E S T I M A T I O N F C Q V M H Q O E B F Z I Y A R B
B S I E F K B R X X S Y T S K V L G J U Y V S I G N I F I C A N C E R E S
```

power	eta squared	interval estimate	test for independence
effect	significance	goodness-of-fit test	proportion of
p value	point estimate	level of confidence	variance
Cohen's *d*	test statistic	significance level	inferential statistics
Cramer's *V*	null hypothesis	confidence interval	coefficient of
effect size	parametric test	nonparametric test	determination
estimation	confidence limit	level of significance	

ACROSS

4. a mathematical formula to determine the likelihood of obtaining a sample outcome if the null hypothesis is true

11. the chi-square _____ is used to determine if frequencies observed fit well with frequencies expected

12. the probability of obtaining a sample outcome, if the value stated in the null hypothesis is true

13. the discrepancy between what was observed in a sample and what was expected in the population

15. significance tests for data that can have any type of distribution and are on a nominal or ordinal scale of measurement

16. the likelihood that an interval estimate will contain an unknown population parameter

18. procedures that allow researchers to generalize observations made with samples to a larger population

19. the upper and lower boundaries of a confidence interval given within a specified level of confidence

20. an effect size estimate for the chi-square test for independence

21. a sample statistic used to estimate a population parameter

DOWN

1. a criterion of judgment upon which a decision is made regarding the value stated in a null hypothesis

2. when we reject the null hypothesis, we say that we have reached this

3. significance tests for data that are normally distributed and measured on an interval or ratio scale of measurement

5. a statement about a population parameter that is assumed to be true

6. the interval within which an unknown population parameter is likely to be contained

7. a statistical measure of the size or magnitude of an observed effect in a population

8. the chi-square _____ test is used to determine if observed frequencies are similar to or different from expected frequencies across the levels of two categorical factors

9. the probability of rejecting a false null hypothesis

10. a measure of effect size in terms of the percent of variability in a dependent variable that can be explained by the levels of a factor

13. a statistical procedure in which a sample statistic is used to estimate the value of an unknown population parameter

14. a measure of effect size for the mean shift in scores from the population mean stated by the null hypothesis

17. a proportion of variance used to describe effect size for data analyzed using an ANOVA

Crossword Puzzle

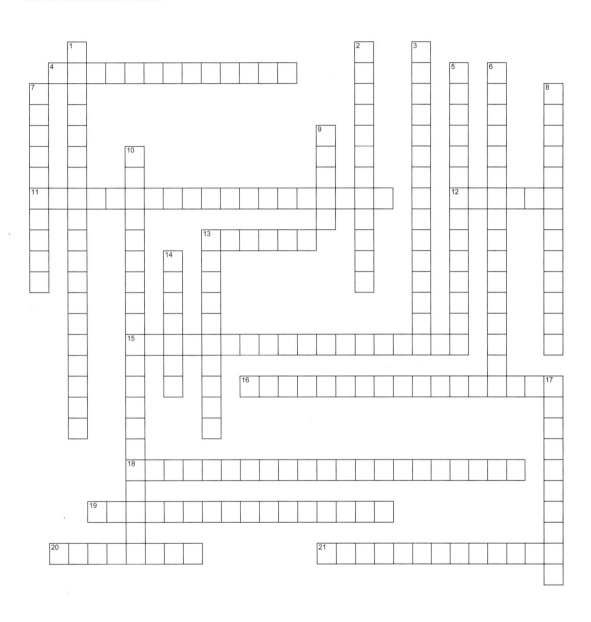

15

Communicating Research: Preparing Manuscripts, Posters, and Talks

CHAPTER LEARNING OBJECTIVES

1. Identify three methods of communication among scientists.

2. Describe three elements of communication.

3. Apply APA writing style and language guidelines for writing a manuscript.

4. Apply APA formatting requirements for writing a manuscript.

5. Apply APA guidelines for writing and organizing a literature review article.

6. Delineate how results are reported for a qualitative versus a quantitative research design.

7. State APA guidelines for identifying the authorship of published scientific work.

8. Identify guidelines for effectively presenting a poster.

9. Identify guidelines for effectively giving a professional talk.

Chapter Summary

15.1   Elements of Communication

Writing a manuscript for publication, presenting a poster, and preparing a talk are three key methods of communication among scientists. Three elements of communication are the speaker/author, the audience, and the message.

The speaker at a talk or poster session, or the author of a manuscript, is the key to any communication. For a manuscript, it is important to communicate using the following guidelines: Use first person and third person appropriately; use past, present, and future tense appropriately; use an impersonal writing style; reduce biased language; and give credit where appropriate.

The audience is any individual or group with whom you intend to communicate. For any scientific work, the author should consider the following audiences who are likely to read their report: scientists and professionals, college students, and the general public.

The author, or speaker, communicates the message, which is any information regarding the design, analyses, interpretations, and new ideas contributed by a completed research project or literature review. To effectively communicate a message, the message should be novel, interesting, and informative.

15.2   Writing a Manuscript: Writing Style and Language

A **peer review** is a procedure used by scientific journals in which a manuscript or work is sent to peers or experts in that area to review the work and determine its scientific value regarding publication. Upon acceptance from peer reviewers, a work can be published in a peer-reviewed journal. To submit a work for consideration for publication in a peer-reviewed journal, we prepare a document called an **APA-style manuscript,** which is any document created using the formatting style described in the *Publication Manual of the American Psychological Association* (2009).

Four general writing guidelines for using APA style are be accurate; be comprehensive, yet concise; be conservative; and be appropriate. Accuracy is important because it reflects the credibility of the author. To be comprehensive, yet concise, a manuscript should clearly state all essential information in as few words as possible. Being conservative means that you do not generalize your claims or interpretations beyond the data or overstate your conclusions. Finally, be appropriate by following APA guidelines for using unbiased and appropriate language.

15.3   Elements of an APA-Style Manuscript

An APA-style manuscript is organized into the following major sections:

- **Title page.** The title page is always the first page and includes the running head, title, author or authors, affiliations, and author note with the contact information of the primary author.
- **Abstract.** The abstract is always the second page and provides a brief written summary of the purpose, methods, and results of a work or published document in 150 to 250 words.

- **Main body.** The main body most often includes the following subheadings: (1) an introduction section that includes a literature review and identification of research hypotheses, (2) a method section that describes the participants, surveys and materials, procedures, and analyses, (3) a results section that fully discloses the data measured and statistical outcomes observed, and (4) a discussion section that provides an evaluation of the design, the data, and the hypotheses.
- **References.** The references page always follows the main body on a new page. All sources cited in the manuscript are listed in APA format in this section.
- **Footnotes** (if any). Footnotes are used to provide additional content or acknowledge copyright permissions.
- **Tables** (if any). Tables can be included, often to summarize participant data or data analyses. Each table is given on a separate page after the references section. Table captions should be included with each table.
- **Figures** (if any). Figures can be included, often to summarize data analyses or illustrate a research procedure. Each figure is given on a separate page following the tables. Figure captions should be included with each figure.
- **Appendices** (if any). In some cases there may be supplemental materials, such as surveys, or illustrations or instructions for using complex equipment.

15.4   Literature Reviews

A **literature review article** is a written comprehensive report of findings from previously published works about a problem in the form of a synthesis of previous articles or as a meta-analysis. To write a literature review, we include a title page, an abstract, a literature review (main body), and references.

To write the main body of a literature review, identify the problem and how it will be evaluated; integrate the literature to identify the state of the research; identify how findings and interpretations in the published literature are related or are inconsistent, contradictory, or flawed; and consider the progress made and potential next steps toward clarifying the problem. In all, a literature review organizes, integrates, and evaluates published works about a problem and considers progress made toward clarifying that problem.

15.5   Reporting Observations in Qualitative Research

The following are two key differences in writing an APA-style manuscript for qualitative versus quantitative research: The introduction and methods sections in a qualitative report argue ways of examining a problem in a way that often leaves open many alternatives that were anticipated or not anticipated by the authors. Also, in a qualitative report, a narrative is constructed in an analysis section to describe what was observed, instead of a summary of statistical outcomes reported in a results section of a quantitative report.

15.6   Ethics in Focus: Credit and Authorship

Authors listed on the title page of a manuscript should be listed in order of their "relative scientific or professional contributions" (APA, 2010, p. 11) to the work being submitted to an editor and not based on their status or institutional position. The APA suggests that to resolve any concerns regarding authorship, all potential authors should talk about publication credit as early as possible.

15.7 Presenting a Poster

A **poster** is a concise description of a research study in the form of a display of text boxes, figures, and tables on a single large page that is typically presented in a **poster session** at a conference or professional meeting. The APA does not provide specific guidelines for creating posters. Some guidelines are as follows: Keep the title short; do not use small font size and use a constant font type; use colorful figures and borders; display the logo for your school affiliation (optional); place each text box or section in a logical order; make sure the poster takes less than five minutes to read; avoid technical jargon; always stand near the poster, but not directly in front of it; and bring supportive materials, such as reprints or a printed copy of the poster itself, to give to attendees.

15.8 Giving a Professional Talk

The following is a list of eight suggestions for giving a great talk: Arrive early and be prepared, dress appropriately, introduce yourself, begin with an attention-grabber, use technology to facilitate your talk (do not read from it), keep the talk focused, follow through with questions, and always end a presentation with references and acknowledgements.

Chapter Summary Organized by Learning Objective

LO 1: Identify three methods of communication among scientists.

- Three methods of communication among scientists are to publish a manuscript, present a poster, and give a talk.

LO 2: Describe three elements of communication.

- Three elements in communication are the speaker or author, the audience, and the message. The speaker or author uses first person and third person appropriately; uses past, present, and future tense appropriately; uses an impersonal writing style; reduces biased language; and gives credit where appropriate. The audience includes scientists and professionals, college students, and the general public. The message should be novel (contribute new findings or new ideas), interesting (to the readership of the work), and informative.

LO 3: Apply APA writing style and language guidelines for writing a manuscript.

- To submit a work for consideration for publication in a peer-reviewed journal, we prepare an **APA-style manuscript** using the writing style format described in the *Publication*

Manual. Four writing and language guidelines for writing an APA-style manuscript are to be accurate; comprehensive, yet concise; conservative; and appropriate. To be comprehensive, yet concise, apply the following suggestions: Abbreviate where appropriate, display data in a figure or table, keep the writing focused, and do not repeat information.

LO 4: Apply APA formatting requirements for writing a manuscript.

- An APA-style manuscript is formatted or organized into the following major sections: title page, abstract, main body (includes introduction, methods, results, and discussion), references, footnotes (if any), tables (if any), figures (if any), and appendices (if any).
- A title page is on page 1 and includes the title, authors, affiliations, and author note. On page 2, the abstract provides a brief written summary of the purpose, methods, and results of a work or published document in 150 to 250 words. On page 3, the main body begins with the title on line 1, and the introduction begins on line 2. The introduction states a problem and why it is important to address, reviews the pertinent literature, and states how the problem will be addressed. The "Method" section is divided into four main subheadings: "Participants," "Procedures" (can be further divided into subheadings), "Data Analyses" (may be optional), and "Results." The "Discussion" section evaluates and interprets how the outcomes in a study relate to the problem that was tested. The "References" section, which begins on a new page, is an alphabetical list of all sources cited in a manuscript.

LO 5: Apply APA guidelines for writing and organizing a literature review article.

- A **literature review article** is a written comprehensive report of findings from previously published works about a problem in the form of a synthesis of previous articles or as a meta-analysis. To write the main body of a literature review:
  - Identify the problem and how it will be evaluated.
  - Integrate the literature to identify the state of the research.
  - Identify how findings and interpretations in the published literature are related or consistent, or are inconsistent, contradictory, or flawed.
  - Consider the progress made in an area of research and potential next steps toward clarifying the problem.

LO 6: Delineate how results are reported for a qualitative versus a quantitative research design.

- The "Results" section is replaced with an "Analysis" section in a qualitative research study, which provides a series of interpretations and contributes a new perspective or generates the possibility that many different perspectives can explain the observations made. The "Analysis" section is written as a narrative and not as a report of statistical outcomes.

- In a qualitative report the introduction and the "Method" section argue ways of examining a problem in a way that often leaves open many alternatives that were anticipated or not anticipated by the authors. In the "Analysis" section a narrative is used to describe what was observed, and the "Discussion" section evaluates possible explanations for those observations with little effort to generalize beyond the specific observations made.

LO 7: State APA guidelines for identifying the authorship of published scientific work.

- According to the APA, authors listed on the title page of a manuscript should be listed in order of their "relative scientific or professional contributions." The APA suggests that to resolve any concerns regarding authorship, all potential authors should talk about publication credit as early as possible.

LO 8: Identify guidelines for effectively presenting a poster.

- A **poster** is a concise description of a research study in the form of a display of text boxes, figures, and tables on a single large page. A poster is presented at a conference or professional meeting in a **poster session**, which is a 1- to 4-hr time slot during which many authors stand near their poster ready and open to answer questions or talk about their work with interested attendees.
- The APA does not provide specific guidelines for creating and presenting posters; however, using the following suggestions is advisable: Keep the title short, do not use small font size and use a constant font type, use colorful figures and borders, display the logo for your school affiliation, place each text box or section in a logical order, make sure the poster takes less than five minutes to read, avoid technical jargon, always stand near the poster but not directly in front of it, and bring supportive materials.

LO 9: Identify guidelines for effectively giving a professional talk.

- Giving a professional talk can be a great way to promote your research and get people excited about your work. The following is a list of eight suggestions for giving an effective talk: Arrive early and be prepared, dress appropriately, introduce yourself, begin with an attention-grabber, use technology to facilitate your talk, keep the talk focused, follow through with questions, and always end with references and acknowledgements.

Tips and Cautions for Students

APA writing and formatting style. Keep in mind that APA style is more than just a writing style; it is a formatting style as well. For example, there are requirements for a title page, margins, headings, and other features related to the formatting of an APA-style paper. APA style also has many guidelines for writing, many of which are described in the chapter. However, note that the formatting is just as important, and many students lose needless points on mistakes made in formatting, although the guidelines for formatting are rather straightforward. Keep the formatting requirements for writing according to APA style in mind as much as the writing guidelines, and this will serve you well as you prepare APA-style papers for your class. Refer also to the GPS guide in this workbook to help with your grammar, punctuation, and spelling.

Practice Quiz

1. Which of the following is a method of communication commonly used among scientists?
   a. publish a peer-reviewed article
   b. give an oral presentation to peers
   c. present a poster at a conference
   d. all of the above

2. Which of the following statements about tense use are correct?
   a. use only past tense in an article
   b. use only future tense in an article
   c. use only present tense in an article
   d. use past, present, and future tense, but do so appropriately

3. Which of the following should be avoided using APA-style writing?
   a. present tense
   b. third-person tone of voice
   c. literary devices
   d. citations in text

4. The audience of a scientific work is:
   a. limited mostly to those in the scientific community
   b. of interest to a diverse audience of scientists, professionals, and laypersons
   c. of interest only to college professors and research scientists
   d. rarely interested at all in what scientists have to say

5. The audiences with which we share our ideas and works are often ____ than we recognize.
   a. larger
   b. smaller
   c. less intelligent
   d. more distracted

6. Which of the following is true about the message of a work or communication using APA-style writing?

    a. The message should be novel.

    b. The message should be interesting.

    c. The message should be informative.

    d. all of the above

7. A procedure used by scientific journals in which a manuscript or work is sent to peers or experts in that area to review the work and determine its scientific value or worth regarding publication is called:

    a. randomization

    b. peer review

    c. scientific method

    d. citation bias

8. A typical rejection rate of works submitted to peer-reviewed journals is:

    a. less than 50%

    b. 10% to 15%

    c. 75% or greater

    d. close to 0%; a manuscript submitted for publication is typically accepted the first time it is submitted

9. Which of the following is the meaning of the abbreviation APA?

    a. American Psychological Association

    b. American Philanthropic Association

    c. American Publication Association

    d. Aggregation of Psychological Acquaintances

10. Accuracy in writing is important because it reflects the _____ of the author.

    a. kindness

    b. credibility

    c. popularity

    d. age

11. Which of the following is a strategy used to be comprehensive, yet concise, when using APA-style writing?

    a. abbreviate when appropriate

    b. display data in a figure or table

    c. do not repeat information

    d. all of the above

12. Conclusions made about a study should be based upon _____.

    a. the author's opinions

    b. data from anonymous sources

    c. the data in that study

    d. statements that appeal to the authority of the author

13. Which of the following is the correct order of the five major sections in an APA paper?

    a. title, abstract, main body, references, tables, and figures

    b. title, abstract, tables, figures, main body, and references

    c. title, abstract, main body, tables, figures, and references

    d. title, abstract, figures, tables, main body, and references

14. Which of the following is a subheading in the main body of an APA manuscript?

    a. "Discussion"

    b. "Method"

    c. "Results"

    d. all of the above

15. Using APA style, an abstract should be how long?

    a. 1 to 2 pages

    b. at least 250 words

    c. 150 to 250 words

    d. up to 1 page

16. Two sections in a literature review that differ from a manuscript or report of primary research are the:

    a. references and footnotes

    b. abstract and main body

    c. title and abstract

    d. main body and references

17. In a qualitative analysis, researchers evaluate the _____ of their observations.

    a. trustworthiness

    b. internal validity

    c. external validity

    d. construct validity

18. A poster is an eye-catching and engaging display that is typically presented during a _____ at a professional conference.

    a. poster session

    b. manuscript reading

   c. peer-debate session

   d. references check

19. Which of the following is not a strategy for creating a noteworthy poster?

   a. use colorful figures and borders

   b. include as much text, in place of graphs and figures, as possible

   c. do not use small font size and use a constant font type

   d. always stand near the poster, but not directly in front of it

20. When giving a professional talk, the speaker should:

   a. arrive early and be prepared

   b. begin the talk with an attention-grabber

   c. keep the talk focused

   d. all of the above

Key Term Word Search

```
T  S  R  E  A  X  X  B  U  B  Q  X  L  T  O  B  J  Z  H
L  K  P  P  H  O  S  G  A  O  H  T  Z  Q  K  P  X  O  L
E  F  H  Y  S  N  K  P  T  A  A  C  N  P  I  R  N  Z  I
G  K  Z  O  T  W  A  P  H  G  Y  O  A  M  V  U  S  H  T
P  T  X  K  Z  S  Z  I  X  H  I  C  C  Q  Y  S  V  Y  E
R  B  K  W  Y  J  I  D  U  S  O  J  T  H  Q  M  F  O  R
Z  O  R  E  L  N  D  H  S  V  M  M  Y  G  R  M  M  J  A
A  P  A  S  T  Y  L  E  M  A  N  U  S  C  R  I  P  T  T
S  C  Z  K  H  A  S  F  Z  R  Q  U  X  Q  W  O  W  L  U
H  O  N  N  S  R  I  E  X  F  G  P  F  S  F  E  D  U  R
O  P  J  Q  E  F  M  J  J  S  L  H  U  C  I  F  M  N  E
P  D  V  T  I  G  C  U  Q  H  V  V  Y  V  B  J  L  O  R
H  D  S  C  M  W  T  O  S  L  I  F  E  I  S  X  K  T  E
S  O  W  S  N  X  O  F  V  M  R  R  W  J  Z  U  H  I  V
P  S  I  S  P  O  S  T  E  R  R  N  O  P  U  U  D  D  I
T  R  T  W  R  D  P  O  V  E  W  A  K  G  R  E  N  O  E
L  E  V  Y  I  A  A  J  E  Q  T  E  V  Z  T  P  B  W  W
E  R  I  V  B  T  N  P  P  B  R  A  N  S  X  N  N  H  M
O  V  X  L  A  T  A  F  I  H  U  X  A  B  C  B  Y  K  U
```

APA-style manuscript   poster session   poster
literature review   peer review

ACROSS

3. a document that is created using the writing style format detailed in the *Publication Manual of the American Psychological Association*

5. a 1- to 4-hr timeslot during which time many authors stand near their poster ready and open to answer questions or talk about their work with interested attendees

DOWN

1. a written comprehensive report of findings from previously published works about a problem in the form of a synthesis of previous articles or as a meta-analysis

2. a procedure used by scientific journals in which a manuscript or work is sent to peers or experts in that area to review the work and determine its scientific value or worth regarding publication

4. a concise description of a research study in the form of a display of text boxes, figures, and tables on a single large page

Crossword Puzzle

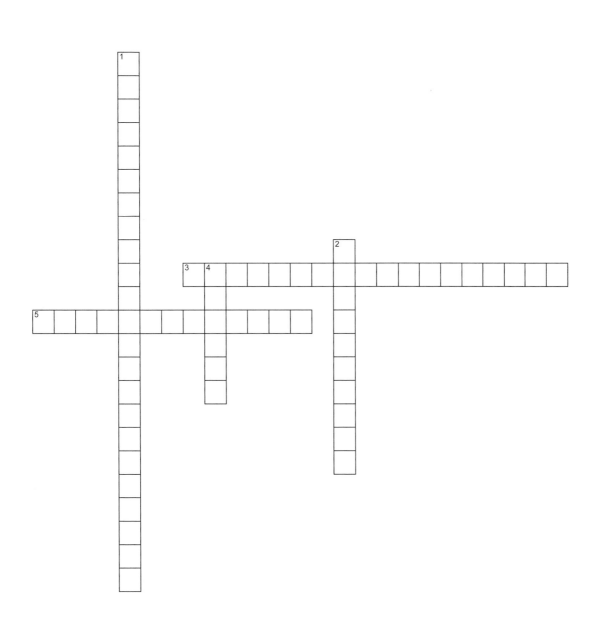

SPSS in Focus Exercises
With General Instructions

SPSS in Focus: One-Sample *t* Test

Exercise 5.1

An example for computing the one-sample *t* test appears in Chapter 5, Section 5.9, of the book. Complete and submit the SPSS grading template and a printout of the output file.

Exercise 5.1: Change in Mood Following a Romantic Movie Clip

A researcher asked participants to watch a short romantic movie clip. The movie clip depicted a romantic scene ending with two long-lost lovers embracing in a kiss. After the short romantic movie clip, participants were asked to indicate how the romantic movie clip affected their mood on a bipolar scale ranging from −3 (*much worse mood*) to +3 (*much better mood*), with 0 indicating no change in mood. The results are given below. It was assumed that the average participant would give a rating of 0 if there were no change in mood. Test whether or not participants reported a significant change in mood at a .05 level of significance (compute a two-tailed test).

−3	−2	3
0	−1	2
−2	−1	2
0	0	3
2	0	3
2	1	0
3	1	−2
1	−2	0
1	0	0
1	2	3
0	3	3
0	3	2

With regard to the SPSS exercise answer the following questions:

Based on the table shown in SPSS, state the following values for the sample:

Sample size   _____

Sample mean   _____

Sample standard deviation   _____

Estimated standard error   _____   (labeled "Std. Error Mean")

Based on the table shown in SPSS, state the following values associated with the test statistic:

Mean difference   _____   (This is the numerator for the test statistic.)

t obtained(t)   _____

Degrees of freedom (df)   _____

Significance (two-tailed)   _____

Based on the value of the test statistic, what is the decision for a one-sample t test? (Circle one)

Not Significant   Significant

Compute Cohen's d (show your work) and state the size of the effect as small, medium, or large. In a sentence, also state the number of standard deviations that scores shifted in the population.

Note: SPSS does *not* give Cohen's d. To compute: Cohen's $d = \dfrac{M - \mu}{SD}$, where M is the sample mean, μ is the null hypothesis for the value of the population mean, and SD is the sample standard deviation.

SPSS in Focus: Two-Independent-Sample *t* Test

Exercise 10.1

An example for computing the two-independent-sample *t* test appears in Chapter 10, Section 10.7, of the book. Complete and submit the SPSS grading template and a printout of the output file.

Exercise 10.1: Sitting Down to Measure Attraction

A researcher had participants sit in a "waiting area" prior to participating in a study. In the waiting area was an attractive or unattractive woman sitting in one of the chairs. In fact, the same woman was present in the waiting area and manipulated to look either attractive or unattractive (relatively speaking). The woman was a confederate in the study, meaning that, unbeknownst to participants, she was a coresearcher in the study. Participants were asked to sit in the waiting area until called upon. One group waited in the room with the attractive confederate; the other group waited in the room with the unattractive confederate. The distance (in feet) that participants sat from the confederate was considered a measure of attraction. The results are given below. It was hypothesized that if this was actually measuring attraction, then participants should sit closer (in feet) to the attractive versus the unattractive confederate. Test this hypothesis at a .05 level of significance (compute a two-tailed test).

Attractiveness of Confederate	
Attractive	Unattractive
1.3	6.8
2.2	5.7

Attractiveness of Confederate	
Attractive	Unattractive
3.5	4.9
0.7	8.5
2.3	9.2
2.1	8.4
4.0	6.7
6.0	4.3
2.3	1.3
5.8	6.3
6.8	8.8
5.3	9.2
8.4	5.7
3.5	7.3
0.4	2.6
7.9	2.1
8.2	6.0
1.6	3.4

With regard to the SPSS exercise answer the following questions:

Based on the table shown in SPSS, state the following values for each sample. Make sure you label each sample in each column in the space provided:

	Sample 1:	Sample 2:
	_____	_____
Sample size	_____	_____
Sample mean	_____	_____
Sample standard deviation	_____	_____
Estimated standard error	_____	_____

Based on the table shown in SPSS, state the following values associated with the test statistic (assume equal variances):

Mean difference	_____
t obtained	_____
Degrees of freedom	_____
Significance	_____
Estimated standard error for the difference	_____

Based on the value of the test statistic, what is the decision for a two-independent-sample t test? (Circle one)

Not Significant   Significant

Compute Cohen's d and state the size of the effect as small, medium, or large. (Show your work.) In a sentence, also state the number of standard deviations that scores have shifted in the population.

Note: SPSS does *not* give Cohen's d. To compute: Cohen's $d = \dfrac{M_1 - M_2}{\sqrt{s_P^2}}$, where M_1 and M_2 are the sample means for each group, and $\sqrt{s_P^2}$ is the pooled or weighted sample standard deviation.

SPSS in Focus: Related-Samples *t* Test

Exercise 11.1

An example for computing the related-samples *t* test appears in Chapter 11, Section 11.6, of the book. Complete and submit the SPSS grading template and a printout of the output file.

Exercise 11.1: Enhancing Recall With Color

A researcher wanted to test whether color could influence recall of words in a list. To test this, the researcher displayed 20 words on a computer screen. Ten words were in color, and 10 words were in black. All words were presented on a white background. Participants were given one minute to view the list; then the list was taken away, and participants were allowed one additional minute to write down as many words as they could recall. The researcher recorded the number of colored versus black words accurately recalled. The results are given below. Test whether the color of words in the list influenced recall at a .05 level of significance (compute a two-tailed test).

Participant	Type of Word	
	Color	Black
1	7	4
2	8	4
3	4	6
4	6	4
5	4	6

(Continued)

(Continued)

Participant	Type of Word	
	Color	Black
6	8	2
7	6	3
8	7	3
9	5	6
10	6	9
11	4	5
12	6	7
13	5	5
14	8	3
15	9	0
16	10	0
17	6	8
18	4	6
19	2	6
20	8	4
21	6	2
22	4	1

With regard to the SPSS exercise answer the following questions:

Based on the table shown in SPSS, state the following values for the sample. Make sure you label each sample in the space provided:

	Sample 1:	Sample 2:
Group Name:	_____	_____
Sample size	_____	_____
Sample mean	_____	_____
Sample standard deviation	_____	_____
Estimated standard error	_____	_____

Based on the table shown in SPSS, state the following values associated with the difference scores:

Mean difference	_____
Standard deviation	_____
Estimated standard error for difference scores	_____

Based on the table shown in SPSS, state the following values associated with the test statistic:

t obtained (t)	_____
Degrees of freedom (df)	_____
Significance (two-tailed)	_____

Based on the value of the test statistic, what is the decision for a related-samples t test? (Circle one)

Not Significant   Significant

Compute Cohen's d and state the size of the effect as small, medium, or large. (Show your work.) In a sentence, also state the number of standard deviations that scores have shifted in the population.

Note: SPSS does *not* give Cohen's d. To compute: Cohen's $d = \dfrac{M_D}{s_D}$, where M_D is the sample mean difference, and S_D is the sample standard deviation for the difference.

SPSS in Focus: One-Way Between-Subjects ANOVA

Exercise 10.2

An example for computing the one-way between-subjects ANOVA appears in Chapter 10, Section 10.9, of the book. Complete and submit the SPSS grading template and a printout of the output file.

Exercise 10.2: Reinforcing Behavior in the Workplace

A local business was having difficulty keeping its office workers on task at work. To help improve this situation, the business asked a psychologist to provide consultation. The psychologist noted that the company mostly used punishment to keep employees on task (for example, by docking pay or firing employees for not being on task). The psychologist proposed that employees would stay on task more if the company put more emphasis on reinforcing employees for staying on task (rather than simply punishing them for getting off task). To test this, the researcher assigned employees to one of three conditions. In one condition, the employees met as a group at the start of their shift, at which time the researcher praised them for the things they did well (group reinforcement). In the second condition, this feedback was provided individually to each employee at the start of his or her shift (individual reinforcement). In the third control condition, employees did not receive any type of reinforcement (no reinforcement). The amount of time spent on task (in minutes) during the last two hours of work was recorded (the data are given by group below). Test whether the reinforcement improved time spent on task at a .05 level of significance.

Type of Reinforcement		
Group	Individual	None
55	87	76
43	95	59

	Type of Reinforcement	
Group	Individual	None
100	48	43
105	32	46
95	103	60
93	99	88
50	108	90
83	110	30
86	112	65
59	100	92
60	66	34
110	60	56
100	76	45
92	60	82
108	65	94
84	85	80
75	97	50
60	91	40

With regard to the SPSS exercise answer the following questions:

Based on the output shown in SPSS, complete the following F table:

Sources of variation	SS	df	MS	F statistic	Sig.
Between-Groups					
Error					
Total					

Based on the value of the test statistic, what is the decision for the one-way between-subjects ANOVA? (Circle one)

Not Significant   Significant

Based on the F table you just completed, state the following values:

Total sample size	_____
Sample size per group	_____
Number of groups (k)	_____
Degrees of freedom numerator	_____
Degrees of freedom denominator	_____
Significance	_____

Based on your decision, is it appropriate to conduct a post hoc test? Explain. Note: If it is not necessary to conduct a post hoc test, then skip the next question only.

Based on the SPSS output table, state the means for each pair of groups that significantly differed using a Fisher's LSD post hoc test. Hint: SPSS places an asterisk next to each significant difference in the "Mean Difference" column of the output table.

Compute proportion of variance using eta squared or omega squared, and state the size of the effect as small, medium, or large. In a sentence, also state the proportion of variance in the dependent variable that can be explained by the factor. Note: SPSS reports eta squared as "R Squared" and reports omega squared as "Adjusted R Squared."

State the conclusions for this test in APA format. In your conclusions, report the test statistic, the effect size, and each significant post hoc comparison. Provide an interpretation for the statistics you report.

SPSS in Focus: One-Way Within-Subjects ANOVA

Exercise 11.2

An example for computing the one-way within-subjects ANOVA appears in Chapter 11, Section 11.8, of the book. Complete and submit the SPSS grading template and a printout of the output file.

Exercise 11.2: Getting Children to Like Toys

A researcher noticed that many products sold in the United States depict famous people or characters. To determine whether this actually influences how much children like these products, the researcher gave children a block of wood. On the top of the block of wood was a sticker of either a superhero, a parent, a teacher, or no person at all (just a plain colored sticker). Children were allowed to handle each block of wood for two minutes, and then asked to rate how much they liked each block of wood on a pictorial scale similar to the one shown below (adapted from Bradley & Lang, 1994). These types of scales are typically used with children. Higher ratings indicated greater liking (the ratings are given by group below). Test whether the stickers influenced liking for the block of wood at a .05 level of significance.

Type of Reinforcement			
Superhero	Parent	Teacher	None
4	5	5	3
3	5	4	1
4	4	5	3
4	4	5	5

(Continued)

(Continued)

5	3	4	5
5	4	3	3
4	5	5	1
3	4	3	1
4	2	4	3
5	4	3	4
4	5	4	3
5	4	3	4
4	4	5	1
5	5	4	5

<u>An example of a pictorial scale for liking used with children:</u>

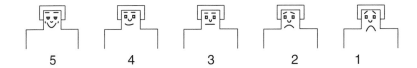

<u>Reference</u>: Bradley, M. M., & Lang, P. J. (1994). Measuring emotion: The Self-Assessment Manikin and the semantic differential. *Journal of Behavior Therapy & Experimental Psychiatry, 25,* 49–59. doi:10.1016/0005-7916(94)90063-9

With regard to the SPSS exercise answer the following questions:

Based on the output given in SPSS, complete the following *F* table (assume sphericity):

Sources of variation	SS	*df*	MS	*F* statistic	Sig.
Between-Groups					
Error					
Total					

Based on the value of the test statistic, what is the decision for the one-way within-subjects ANOVA? (Circle one)

Not Significant   Significant

Based on the table, the sum of squares for error is _____. Is this the total error in this study? If not, then what additional source of error is omitted?

Based on the *F* table you just completed, state the following values:

Sample size (*n*)   _____

Number of groups (*k*)   _____

Degrees of freedom numerator   _____

Degrees of freedom denominator   _____

Significance   _____

Based on your decision, is it appropriate to conduct a post hoc test? Explain. Note: If it is not necessary to conduct a post hoc test, then skip the next question only.

Based on the SPSS output table, state the means for each pair of groups that significantly differed using a Fisher's LSD post hoc test. Hint: SPSS places an asterisk next to each significant difference in the "Mean Difference" column of the output table.

Compute proportion of variance using partial eta squared, and state the size of the effect as small, medium, or large. In a sentence, also state the proportion of variance in the dependent variable that can be explained by the factor.

State the conclusions for this test in APA format. In your conclusions, report the test statistic, the effect size, and each significant post hoc comparison. Provide an interpretation for the statistics you report.

SPSS in Focus: Two-Way Between-Subjects ANOVA

Exercise 12.1

$\mathbf{A}$n example for computing the two-way between-subjects ANOVA appears in Chapter 12, Section 12.10, of the book. Complete and submit the SPSS grading template and a printout of the output file.

Exercise 12.1: Relationship Status, Gender, and Forgiveness

A hypothetical study investigated the extent to which heterosexual men and women were willing to forgive an opposite-sex partner for transgressions in a relationship. Men and women participants completed a questionnaire in which they read five different scenarios about an opposite-sex partner who transgressed in a relationship. After each scenario, participants rated their willingness to forgive on a scale from 1 (*not forgive at all*) to 7 (*definitely forgive*). Hence, total ratings could range from 5 (*all 1s recorded*) to 40 (*all 7s recorded*). The table lists the data for this hypothetical between-subjects study. Test whether gender and relationship status influenced forgiveness at a .05 level of significance.

		Relationship Status	
		Short-term	Long-term
Gender	Men	18	8
		24	22
		12	20
		9	11
		12	5
		29	21
		13	25

		Relationship Status	
		Short-term	Long-term
Gender	Men	9	30
		32	28
		36	28
	Women	28	18
		34	32
		22	27
		19	21
		14	14
		27	32
		28	25
		28	24
		31	25
		20	25

With regard to the SPSS exercise answer the following questions:

Based on the output shown in SPSS, complete the following *F* table (label each factor in the space provided in the first column):

Sources of variation	SS	*df*	MS	*F* statistic	Sig.
A					
B					
AB					
Error					
Total					

Based on the value of the test statistics, what is the decision for each factor in the two-way between-subjects ANOVA? (Circle one)

Factor A: Not Significant   Significant

Factor B: Not Significant   Significant

A × B Interaction: Not Significant   Significant

Based on the *F* table you just completed, state the following values:

Total sample size   _____
Sample size per cell   _____
Number of levels for Factor A (*p*)   _____
Number of levels for Factor B (*q*)   _____
p value for each test: Factor A   _____
                                Factor B   _____
                                A × B Interaction   _____

Based on your decision(s), what is the next appropriate step? Note: Simple effect tests are necessary when the interaction is significant.

If the interaction is significant, then reorganize the data and compute simple effect tests. Otherwise, compute post hoc tests on the main effects and state the means for each pair of groups that significantly differed.

Compute proportion of variance using eta squared for each *significant* effect, and state the size of the effect as small, medium, or large. In a sentence, also state the proportion of variance in the dependent variable that can be explained by the factor.

State the conclusions for this test in APA format. In your conclusions, report the test statistic, the effect size, and each significant simple main effect or post hoc comparison test. Provide an interpretation for the statistics you report.

SPSS in Focus: Two-Way Within-Subjects ANOVA

Exercise 12.2

An example for computing the two-way within-subjects ANOVA appears in Chapter 12, Section 12.10, of the book. Complete and submit the SPSS grading template and a printout of the output file.

Exercise 12.2: The Effect of Music Tempo and Scale on Mood

A hypothetical study investigated whether the tempo and scale of music can differentially enhance mood. Participants wore sound-canceling headphones through which four different types of music were played to each participant: music with a slow tempo–minor scale, fast tempo–minor scale, slow tempo–major scale, and fast tempo–major scale. After listening to each type of music, participants rated their change in mood on a scale from −3 (*more negative mood*) to +3 (*more positive mood*), with 0 representing no change in mood. The order in which music types were played was counterbalanced. The table below lists the data for this hypothetical within-subjects study. Test whether music tempo and scale influenced mood change at a .05 level of significance.

		Tempo	
		Slow	Fast
Scale	Minor	1	2
		2	1
		−3	1
		0	0
		2	2

(Continued)

(Continued)

		Tempo	
		Slow	Fast
Scale	Minor	0	0
		−1	2
		0	1
	Major	0	2
		1	3
		1	3
		2	2
		−3	3
		0	3
		2	1
		−1	3

With regard to the SPSS exercise answer the following questions:

Based on the output shown in SPSS, complete the following F table (label each factor in the space provided in the first column):

Sources of variation	SS	df	MS	F statistic	Sig.
A (scale)					
Error A (scale)					
B (tempo)					
Error B (tempo)					
AB (scale × tempo)					
Error (scale × tempo)					

Based on the value of the test statistics, what is the decision for each factor in the two-way within-subjects ANOVA? (Circle one)

Factor A:	Not Significant	Significant
Factor B:	Not Significant	Significant
A × B Interaction:	Not Significant	Significant

Based on the *F* table you just completed, state the following values:

Total sample size   _____

Sample size per cell   _____

Number of levels for Factor A (*p*)   _____

Number of levels for Factor B (*q*)   _____

p value for each test: Factor A   _____

                                   Factor B   _____

                                   A × B Interaction   _____

Based on your decision(s), what is the next appropriate step? Note: Simple effect tests are necessary when the interaction is significant.

If the interaction is significant, then reorganize the data and compute simple effect tests. Otherwise, compute post hoc tests on the main effects and state the means for each pair of groups that significantly differed.

Compute proportion of variance using eta squared for each *significant* effect, and state the size of the effect as small, medium, or large. In a sentence, also state the proportion of variance in the dependent variable that can be explained by the factor.

State the conclusions for this test in APA format. In your conclusions, report the test statistic, the effect size, and each significant simple main effect or post hoc comparison test. Provide an interpretation for the statistics you report.

SPSS in Focus: Two-Way Mixed Factorial ANOVA

Exercise 12.3

An example for computing the two-way mixed factorial ANOVA appears in Chapter 12, Section 12.10, of the book; refer also to the GIG for specific instructions on how to compute this type of factorial ANOVA. Complete and submit the SPSS grading template and a printout of the output file.

Exercise 12.3: Attitudes Toward Working on Group Projects Among Traditional and Nontraditional College Students

A hypothetical study tested the extent to which college students (traditional, nontraditional) have positive attitudes toward working on group projects with other traditional versus nontraditional college students. In this study, traditional and nontraditional students read two vignettes: One vignette described a nontraditional student who had been assigned to work with the participant on a group project; a second vignette described a traditional student who had been assigned to work with the participant on a group project. Ratings of how positively a participant viewed working with the student described in the vignette were recorded; the data are given in the table below. The order in which vignettes were read was counterbalanced. Test if the type of student (traditional, nontraditional; between-subjects factor) influenced ratings of the person described in the vignette (traditional, nontraditional; within-subjects factor) at a .05 level of significance.

		Type of Student Described in the Vignette	
		Traditional	Nontraditional
	Traditional	0	1
		1	1

		Type of Student Described in the Vignette	
		Traditional	Nontraditional
College Student	Traditional	1	3
		3	0
		3	3
		1	2
		3	3
		2	1
	Nontraditional	2	2
		0	3
		0	0
		−2	−2
		1	2
		−3	−3
		0	2
		−1	1

With regard to the SPSS exercise answer the following questions:

Based on the output shown in SPSS, complete the following F table (label each factor in the space provided in the first column):

Sources of variation	SS	df	MS	F statistic	Sig.
A (vignette)					
A (vignette × student)					
Error A (vignette)					
B (student)					
Error B (student)					

Based on the value of the test statistics, what is the decision for each factor in the two-way mixed factorial ANOVA? (Circle one)

Factor A:	Not Significant	Significant
Factor B:	Not Significant	Significant
A × B Interaction:	Not Significant	Significant

Based on the *F* table you just completed, state the following values:

Total sample size	_____
Sample size per group	_____
Number of levels for Factor A (*p*)	_____
Number of levels for Factor B (*q*)	_____
p value for each test:	Factor A _____
	Factor B _____
	A × B Interaction _____

Based on your decision(s), what is the next appropriate step? Note: Simple effect tests are necessary when the interaction is significant.

If the interaction is significant, then reorganize the data and compute simple effect tests. Otherwise, compute post hoc tests on the main effects and state the means for each pair of groups that significantly differed.

Compute proportion of variance using eta squared for each *significant* effect, and state the size of the effect as small, medium, or large. In a sentence, also state the proportion of variance in the dependent variable that can be explained by the factor.

State the conclusions for this test in APA format. In your conclusions, report the test statistic, the effect size, and each significant simple main effect or post hoc comparison test. Provide an interpretation for the statistics you report.

SPSS in Focus: Pearson Correlation Coefficient

Exercise 8.1

An example for computing the Pearson correlation coefficient appears in Chapter 8, Section 8.11, of the book. Complete and submit the SPSS grading template and a printout of the output file.

Exercise 8.1: Notebook Computer Use and Grades

A professor notices that more and more students are using their notebook computers in class, presumably to take notes. He wonders if this may actually improve academic success. To test this, the professor records the number of times each student uses his or her computer during a class for one semester and records his or her final grade in the class (out of 100 points). If notebook computer use during class is related to academic success, then a positive correlation between these two factors should be evident. The data are given in the table. Test whether notebook computer use and grades are related at a .05 level of significance.

Notebook Computer Use	Final Grade for Course
30	86
23	88
6	94
0	56
24	78
36	72

(Continued)

(Continued)

Notebook Computer Use	Final Grade for Course
10	80
0	90
0	82
8	60
12	84
18	74
0	78
32	66
36	54
12	98
8	81
18	74
22	70
38	90
5	85
29	93
26	67
10	80

With regard to the SPSS exercise answer the following questions:

Based on the value of the correlation coefficient, is there a significant relationship? (Circle one)

Not Significant   Significant

Based on the SPSS output, state the following values:

Pearson correlation   _____
Coefficient of determination   _____
Sample size   _____
Significance (two-tailed)   _____

State the conclusions for this test using APA format. In your conclusions, describe the correlation coefficient (r) in words, and interpret and give the value of the coefficient of determination (R^2).

SPSS in Focus: Analysis of Regression

Exercise 8.2

A n example for computing an analysis of regression appears in Chapter 8, Section 8.11, of the book. Complete and submit the SPSS grading template and a printout of the output file.

Exercise 8.2: Attitudes and Eco-Friendly Behaviors

A researcher noted that many individuals who eat organic foods also tend to behave in ways that benefit the planet (referred to as eco-friendly behaviors). This researcher wanted to see if the attitudes people have toward organic food consumption can be used to predict eco-friendly behaviors among college students. To test this, the researcher had college students complete two surveys. The first assessed their attitudes toward organic foods and people who consume organic foods. This organic attitudes survey was scored between 0 and 50, with higher scores indicating more positive attitudes toward organic food consumption. The second survey assessed the students' current eco-friendly behaviors (such as the extent to which they recycle, reuse, and conserve energy). This survey was also scored between 0 and 50, with higher scores indicating greater eco-friendly behaviors. Compute an analysis of regression to determine the extent to which attitudes toward organic consumption can predict eco-friendly behaviors at a .05 level of significance.

Attitudes Toward Organic	Eco-Friendly Behaviors
38	40
50	46
28	30
16	12

(Continued)

(Continued)

Attitudes Toward Organic	Eco-Friendly Behaviors
10	19
13	20
34	38
45	40
42	10
30	36
26	28
28	21
32	32
18	20
22	28
40	31
29	40
14	48
44	42
12	20

With regard to the SPSS exercise answer the following questions:

Based on the output shown in SPSS, complete the following regression table:

Sources of variation	SS	df	MS	F statistic	Sig.
Regression					
Residual (Error)					
Total					

Based on the value of the test statistic, what is the decision for the analysis of regression? (Circle one)

Not Significant   Significant

Based on the regression table you just completed, state the following values:

Sample size   _____

Standard error of estimate   _____

Standard error of estimate (R^2)   _____

Significance   _____

State the conclusions for this test using APA format. In your conclusions, describe the correlation coefficient (r) in words, and interpret and give the value of the coefficient of determination (R^2).

SPSS in Focus: Chi-Square Goodness-of-Fit Test

Exercise 14.1

An example for computing the chi-square goodness-of-fit test appears in Chapter 14, Section 14.5, of the book. Complete and submit the SPSS grading template and a printout of the output file.

Exercise 14.1: Stress Disorders Following Deployment

Many men and women in the U.S. military are required to make multiple deployments to war zones. Each deployment can last up to a year or longer and have lasting effects in terms of stress on the soldiers and their families. To better understand the extent to which multiple deployments may increase the hardships on those serving in war zones, a researcher asked a group of soldiers who had served four deployments in a war zone to indicate whether their first, second, third, or fourth military deployment was the most stressful. Frequencies were expected to be the same in each category. The frequency of soldiers choosing one of four categories is given in the table. Test whether the frequencies observed are different from frequencies expected at a .05 level of significance (assume equal frequencies for the null hypothesis).

	Number of deployments to war			
	1	2	3	4+
Frequency Observed	22	36	34	36

With regard to the SPSS exercise answer the following questions:

Based on the value of the test statistic, what is the decision for the chi-square goodness-of-fit test? (Circle one)

             Not Significant   Significant

Based on the data given in the SPSS output, state the frequency observed and frequency expected for each level of the categorical factor:

Level of Factor (k)	Frequency Observed	Frequency Expected
_____	_____	_____
_____	_____	_____
_____	_____	_____
_____	_____	_____

Based on the SPSS output, state the following values for the test statistic:

Total sample size	_____
Chi-square test statistic	_____
Degrees of freedom	_____
Significance	_____

State the conclusions for this test using APA format. Provide an interpretation for your conclusions.

SPSS in Focus: Chi-Square Test for Independence

Exercise 14.2

An example for computing the chi-square test for independence appears in Chapter 14, Section 14.5, of the book. Complete and submit the SPSS grading template and a printout of the output file.

Exercise 14.2: Making the Grade With New Textbooks

A professor noted that students who read textbooks that are used tend to complain most often that they do not understand the course material. To see if this is related to actual student outcomes, she recorded whether students in a large lecture course read textbooks that were new, used with minimal highlighting (MH), or used with substantial highlighting (SH). At the end of the semester she recorded whether or not each student passed the course. She hypothesized that the type of textbook read (new, used with MH, used with SH) would be related to student outcomes (pass, fail). Test whether these two factors were related at a .05 level of significance.

<table>
<tr><td rowspan="3">Outcome</td><td></td><td colspan="3" align="center">Type of Textbook</td></tr>
<tr><td></td><td>New</td><td>Used with MH</td><td>Used with SH</td></tr>
<tr><td>Pass</td><td>78</td><td>72</td><td>62</td></tr>
<tr><td></td><td>Fail</td><td>8</td><td>16</td><td>19</td></tr>
</table>

With regard to the SPSS exercise answer the following questions:

Based on the value of the test statistic, what is the decision for the chi-square test for independence? (Circle one)

                Not Significant   Significant

Based on the data given in the SPSS output, draw the frequency expected table and fill in the frequencies expected in each cell, row, column, and total.

Based on the SPSS output, state the following values for the test statistic:

Total sample size   _____

Chi-square test statistic   _____

Degrees of freedom   _____

Significance   _____

What is the effect size using Cramer's *V*?

State the conclusions for this test using APA format. In your conclusions, state the value of the test statistic, degrees of freedom, *p* value, and effect size. Provide an interpretation for your conclusions.

SPSS in Focus: The Wilcoxon Signed-Ranks *t* Test

Exercise 14.3

The directions for this test are not given in the book but are illustrated as an alternative to parametric tests in Figure 14.3 of the book. Specific instructions for computing this test are given in the GIG in this student workbook. Complete and submit the SPSS grading template and a printout of the output file.

Exercise 14.3: Early Childhood Traits Among Illicit Drug Users

Some research suggests that people with serious substance use disorders have delinquent traits before ever using illicit drugs. To test this, a researcher sampled pairs of siblings, such that one sibling was diagnosed as alcohol dependent and the other sibling was not substance dependent. All siblings took a retrospective survey, referred to as the self-report early delinquency (SRED) scale. This scale was used to identify differences in antisocial and delinquent behavior among siblings during their childhood (presumably before any substance abuse), with higher scores on the scale indicating greater expression of delinquent traits in childhood. The data are given in the table. Test whether alcohol-dependent siblings expressed greater delinquent traits in childhood at a .05 level of significance.

Alcohol-Dependent Sibling	Non-Substance-Dependent Sibling
12	12
38	8
23	13
27	8

Alcohol-Dependent Sibling	Non-Substance-Dependent Sibling
38	5
17	18
30	9
27	19
22	8
29	10
39	7
36	10
18	20
8	2
40	29
38	10
40	8
26	6

With regard to the SPSS exercise answer the following questions:

Based on the value of the test statistic, what is the decision for the Wilcoxon signed-ranks t test? (Circle one)

        Not Significant   Significant

Based on the data given in the SPSS output, state the following frequencies:

    Negative differences   _____
    Positive differences   _____
    Ties   _____
    Total   _____

Based on the SPSS output, state the following values for the test statistic:

    Z   _____
    Asymp. Sig. (two-tailed)   _____

State the conclusions for this test using APA format. Provide an interpretation for your conclusions.

SPSS in Focus: The Mann-Whitney *U* Test

Exercise 14.4

The directions for this test are not given in the book but are illustrated as an alternative to parametric tests in Figure 14.3 of the book. Specific instructions for computing this test are given in the GIG in this student workbook. Complete and submit the SPSS grading template and a printout of the output file

Exercise 14.4: Educating Students With Disabilities

Federal laws mandate the inclusion of students with disabilities into regular classrooms. The challenge for educators is that students with disabilities are included in classrooms with general educators (those without advanced special education training). This may lead general education teachers to have much different attitudes regarding the inclusion of students with disabilities into the regular classroom. To test this possibility, a researcher gave special education teachers (those with advanced special education training) and general education teachers (those without advanced special education training) an inclusion survey. This survey was used to determine how positively teachers viewed the inclusion of students with disabilities in regular classrooms. Scores could range from 0 to 40 with higher scores indicating more positive attitudes. The data are given in the table. Test whether these two groups of teachers significantly differed at a .05 level of significance.

General Education Teachers	Special Education Teachers
32	23
29	28
12	29
16	17
24	13

38	18
12	38
30	32
23	30
28	28
24	34
8	26
26	29
20	31

With regard to the SPSS exercise answer the following questions:

Based on the value of the test statistic, what is the decision for the Mann-Whitney U test? (Circle one)

Not Significant   Significant

Based on the data given in the SPSS output, state the following values for each sample. Make sure you label each sample in each column in the space provided:

	Sample 1:	Sample 2:
	_____	_____
Sample size	_____	_____
Mean rank	_____	_____
Sum of ranks	_____	_____

Based on the SPSS output, state the following values for the test statistic:

Mann-Whitney U _____

Z   _____

Asymp. Sig. (two-tailed) _____

State the conclusions for this test using APA format. Provide an interpretation for your conclusions.

SPSS in Focus: The Kruskal-Wallis *H* Test

Exercise 14.5

The directions for this test are not given in the book but are illustrated as an alternative to parametric tests in Figure 14.3 of the book. Specific instructions for computing this test are given in the GIG in this student workbook. Complete and submit the SPSS grading template and a printout of the output file.

Exercise 14.5: Convenience and Visibility of Vegetables

Studies show that the more convenient and visible candy is, the more people eat of it. Yet, little is known about whether or not a similar manipulation would work with vegetables. To test this, a researcher had participants sit at a desk where a bowl of carrots and celery was either placed on the desk (convenient and visible), in the desk drawer (convenient but not visible), in a cabinet 10 feet away from the desk (inconvenient, but visible), or in another section of the room separated by a partition (inconvenient and not visible). Participants were seated at the desk and told they could eat the foods available in the room while they waited to be called upon. All participants sat at the desk for 10 minutes. The number of carrots and celery consumed was recorded. Test whether differences between groups were significant at a .05 level of significance.

Convenience-Visibility			
Yes-Yes	Yes-No	No-Yes	No-No
8	0	1	2
6	4	5	5
4	2	2	6
5	3	4	3

Convenience-Visibility			
Yes-Yes	Yes-No	No-Yes	No-No
2	2	0	0
8	5	0	2
3	2	1	5
7	5	5	3
5	3	4	6
8	8	0	4
4	5	6	5
2	0	9	5
6	2	3	1
4	5	6	2
5	4	8	2
1	8	0	0

With regard to the SPSS exercise answer the following questions:

Based on the value of the test statistic, what is the decision for the Kruskal-Wallis H test? (Circle one)

Not Significant   Significant

Based on the data given in the SPSS output, state the sample size and mean rank for each sample. Make sure you label each group in the first column:

Group Name   Sample Size   Mean Rank

_____   _____   _____

_____   _____   _____

_____   _____   _____

_____   _____   _____

Based on the SPSS output, state the following values for the test statistic:

Chi-square   _____
Degrees of freedom   _____
Asymp. Sig.   _____

State the conclusions for this test using APA format. Provide an interpretation for your conclusions.

SPSS in Focus: The Friedman Test

Exercise 14.6

The directions for this test are not given in the book but are illustrated as an alternative to parametric tests in Figure 14.3 of the book. Specific instructions for computing this test are given in the GIG in this student workbook. Complete and submit the SPSS grading template and a printout of the output file.

Exercise 14.6: Canine Aggression According to Their Owners

Canine aggression can pose a serious public health and animal welfare concern. A researcher wanted to study this risk in a local community where public welfare funds had been significantly cut. The researcher wanted to know who in the community was at greatest risk of encountering canine aggression. To study this, the researcher had dog owners in the community complete a canine behavioral assessment survey. This survey consisted of three subscales (aggression toward strangers, owners, and other dogs). Each subscale was scored out of 20 points, with higher scores indicating greater aggression. In general, this scale allowed the researcher to assess the typical and recent responses of dogs in a variety of common situations. Owners of a similar number of different breeds were represented in this sample. Scores on each subscale were compared to see if there were differences in canine aggression directed toward strangers, owners, and dogs. Test whether the differences, given in the table, were significant at a .05 level of significance.

Participant	Subscale		
	Strangers	Owners	Other Dogs
A	11	10	20
B	14	14	18
C	10	12	19

Participant	Subscale		
	Strangers	Owners	Other Dogs
D	8	16	18
E	28	29	17
F	26	20	20
G	7	12	20
H	19	9	17
I	12	11	16
J	14	19	19
K	10	13	15
L	16	12	12
M	9	10	16
N	11	9	13

With regard to the SPSS exercise answer the following questions:

Based on the value of the test statistic, what is the decision for the Friedman test? (Circle one)

Not Significant   Significant

Based on the data given in the SPSS output, state the mean rank for each sample. Make sure you label each group in the first column:

Group Name	Mean Rank
_____	____
_____	____
_____	____
_____	____

Based on the SPSS output, state the following values for the test statistic:

N   ____
Chi-square   ____
Degrees of freedom   ____
Asymp. Sig.   ____

State the conclusions for this test using APA format. Provide an interpretation for your conclusions.

Statistical Package for the Social Sciences (SPSS): General Instructions Guidebook

The General Instructions Guidebook, referred to here as GIG, provides standardized instructions for using SPSS to enter and analyze data. Most instructions provided in the GIG are also given in the *Research Methods for the Behavioral Sciences* textbook. The GIG provides general instructions for using SPSS without the use of a specific example. While many more instructions for using SPSS are given in the book, the instructions in the GIG are focused on tests for significance computed with various research designs in the behavioral sciences.

Where applicable, instructions are given with reference to which SPSS in Focus section in the book illustrates the use of the directions within the context of an example. Note that the term *independent variable* is used where appropriate in the GIG. Anytime this term is used, the term *quasi-independent variable* can be used in its place. To keep the step-by-step directions as concise as possible, though, only the term *independent variable* or *factor* is used. The GIG first reviews the procedures for entering data for between-subjects and within-subjects factors and is then organized as follows:

Parametric Tests

- The *t* tests
  - One-sample *t* test
  - Two-independent-sample *t* test
  - Related-samples *t* test

- The one-way ANOVAs
  - One-way between-subjects ANOVA
  - One-way within-subjects ANOVA
- The factorial ANOVAs
  - Two-way between-subjects ANOVA
  - Two-way within-subjects ANOVA
  - Two-way mixed factorial ANOVA
- Correlation and regression
  - Pearson correlation
  - Analysis of regression

Nonparametric Tests

- Tests for nominal data
  - Chi-square goodness-of-fit test
  - Chi-square test for independence
- Tests for ordinal data
  - Wilcoxon signed-ranks t test
  - Mann-Whitney U test
  - Kruskal-Wallis H test
  - Friedman test

In Chapter 4 (Section 4.9) of the book, we introduced entering data for a within-subjects factor and a between-subjects factor. A within-subjects factor is a factor in which the same participants are observed at each level of the factor. A between-subjects factor is a factor in which different participants are observed at each level of the factor. Here, we will first review instructions for entering and defining each type of factor, which will be needed for entering data with each type of parametric and nonparametric statistical test taught in the book.

Entering data for within-subjects factors:

Enter data by column:

1. Open the **Variable View** tab. In the **Name column**, enter each variable name (one variable per row).

2. Go to the **Decimals column** and reduce that value to the degree of accuracy of the data.

3. Open the **Data View** tab. You will see that each variable is now the title for each column. Enter the data for each variable in the appropriate column.

Entering data for between-subjects factors:

Enter data by row (this requires *coding* the grouped data):

1. Open the **Variable View** tab. Enter the variable name in the first row and a name for the dependent variable in the second row.

2. Go to the **Decimals column** and reduce that value to 0 for the first row. This is because the values in this column will be coded. Reduce the Decimals column in the second row to the degree of accuracy of the data.

3. Go to the **Values column** in the first row and click on the small gray box with three dots. In the **dialog box** enter a number in the **Value cell** and the name of each level of the independent variable in the **Label cell**. After each entry select **Add**. Repeat these steps for each level of the independent variable and then select **OK**. The data are now coded as numbers.

4. Open the **Data View** tab. In the first column enter each number so that it equals the number of scores in each level. For example, if you measure five scores at each level of the independent variable, then you will enter each number (or code) five times in the first column. In the second column, enter the values for the dependent variable. These values should match up with the levels of the independent variable you coded.

PARAMETRIC TESTS

The *t* tests:

One-sample t *test*

*This exercise is illustrated in **Chapter 5, Section 5.9** (SPSS in Focus), of the book.

1. Click on the **Variable View** tab and enter the variable name in the **Name column**. In the **Decimals column,** reduce the value to the degree of accuracy of the data.

2. Click on the **Data View** tab and enter the values for the variable in the first column.

3. Go to the **menu bar** and click **Analyze, Compare Means,** and **One-Sample T Test** to bring up a dialog box.

4. In the **dialog box,** select the variable name and click the arrow in the middle to move it to the **Test Variable(s): box**.

5. State the null value in the **Test Value: box**. The value is 0 by default.

6. Select **OK**, or select **Paste** and click the **Run** command.

Two-independent-sample t *test*

*This exercise is illustrated in **Chapter 10, Section 10.7** (SPSS in Focus), of the book.

1. Click on the **Variable View** tab and enter the independent variable in the **Name column**. In the second row, enter the name of the dependent variable in the Name column. Reduce the value to 0 in the **Decimals column** in the first row and to the degree of accuracy of the data in the second row.

2. Code the levels of the independent variable listed in the first row in the **Values** column.

3. In the **Data View** tab, in the first column enter each number so that it equals the number of scores in each level. For example, if you measure five scores in each group (or level), then enter each numeric code five times in the first column. In the second column, enter the values for the dependent variable so that they correspond with the code for each group.

4. Go to the **menu bar** and click **Analyze, Compare Means,** and **Independent-Samples T Test** to bring up a dialog box.

5. Using the arrows to move the variables, select the dependent variable and place it in the **Test Variable(s):** box; select the independent variable and move it into the **Grouping Variable:** box. Two question marks will appear in the Grouping Variable box.

6. Now click **Define Groups. . .** to bring up a new dialog box. Place the numeric code for each group in the spaces provided and then click **Continue**. The numeric codes should now appear in the Grouping Variable box (instead of question marks).

7. Select **OK,** or select **Paste** and click the **Run** command.

Related-samples t *test*

*This exercise is illustrated in **Chapter 11, Section 11.6** (SPSS in Focus), of the book.

1. Click on the **Variable View** tab and enter the name of the first level of the independent variable in the Name column in the first row; enter the name of the second level of the independent variable in the second row. Reduce the **Decimals column** value in both rows to the degree of accuracy of the data.

2. Click on the **Data View** tab. List the data for each level of the independent variable. Make sure the scores for each related pair are matched in each row.

3. Go to the **menu bar** and click **Analyze, Compare Means,** and **Paired-Samples T Test** to bring up a dialog box.

4. In the **dialog box,** select each level of the independent variable in the left box and move them to the right box using the arrow in the middle. The variables should be side by side in the box to the right.

5. Select **OK,** or select **Paste** and click the **Run** command.

The One-Way ANOVAs:

One-way between-subjects ANOVA

*This exercise is illustrated in **Chapter 10, Section 10.9** (SPSS in Focus), of the book.
Compute this test using the **One-Way ANOVA** command:

1. Click on the **Variable View** tab and enter the name of the independent variable in the **Name column**. Go to the **Decimals column** for this row and reduce the value to 0 (because this variable will be coded). In the second row enter the name of the dependent variable in the Name column. Reduce the **Decimals column** value in the second row to the degree of accuracy of the data.

2. Code the levels of the independent variable listed in the first row in the **Values** column.

3. In the **Data View** tab, in the first column enter each coded value so that it equals the number of scores in each level. For example, if you measure five scores in each group (or level), then enter each numeric code five times in the first column. In the second column, enter the values for the dependent variable so that they correspond with the codes for each group.

4. Go to the **menu bar** and click **Analyze, Compare Means**, and **One-Way ANOVA** to bring up a dialog box.

5. Using the appropriate arrows, move the independent variable into the **Factor:** box. Move the dependent variable into the **Dependent List:** box.

6. Click the **Post Hoc** option to bring up a new dialog box. Select an appropriate post hoc test and click **Continue**.

7. Select **OK**, or select **Paste** and click the **Run** command.

Compute this test using the **GLM Univariate** command:

1. Follow Steps 1–3 for using the One-Way ANOVA command.

2. Go to the **menu bar** and click **Analyze, General Linear Model**, and **Univariate** to bring up a dialog box.

3. Using the appropriate arrows, move the independent variable into the **Fixed Factor(s):** box. Move the dependent variable into the **Dependent Variable:** box.

4. Select the **Post Hoc. . .** option to bring up a new dialog box, which will again give you the option to perform post hoc comparisons so long as you move the independent variable into the **Post Hoc Tests for:** box. Select an appropriate post hoc test and click **Continue**.

5. Select **OK**, or select **Paste** and click the **Run** command.

One-way within-subjects ANOVA

*This exercise is illustrated in **Chapter 11, Section 11.8** (SPSS in Focus), of the book.

1. Click on the **Variable View** tab and enter the name of each level of the independent variable in the **Name column**. One level (or group) should be listed in each row. Go to the

Decimals column and reduce the value to 0 for each row to the degree of accuracy of the data.

2. Click on the **Data View** tab. Now each column is labeled with each level of the independent variable. Enter the data for each respective column.

3. Go to the **menu bar** and click **Analyze, General Linear Model,** and **Repeated Measures** to bring up a dialog box.

4. In the **Within-Subject Factor Name** box, label or give a name for the repeated measure factor (or independent variable). Below it you will see a **Number of Levels** box. Here SPSS is asking for the number of levels for the independent variable. Enter the number and the **Add** option will illuminate. Click Add and you will see the independent variable with the number of levels in parentheses. Click **Define** to bring up a new dialog box.

5. In the **dialog box,** use the appropriate arrows to move each column into the **Within-Subjects Variables (cues)** box.

6. Then select **Options** to bring up a new dialog box. To compute effect size, use the arrow to move the independent variable into the **Display Means for:** box. Then check the **Compare main effects** option. Using the dropdown arrow under the **Confidence interval adjustment** heading select an appropriate post hoc test. Then select **Continue.**

7. Select **OK,** or select **Paste** and click the **Run** command.

The Factorial ANOVAs:

Two-way between-subjects ANOVA

*This exercise is illustrated in **Chapter 12, Section 12.10** (SPSS in Focus), of the book.

1. Click on the **Variable View** tab and enter the name of each independent variable (one in each row) in the **Name column;** in the third row, enter a name for the dependent variable in the Name column. Reduce the value to 0 in the **Decimals column** for the first two rows (for both independent variables). In the Decimals column, reduce the value to the degree of accuracy of the data for the third row.

2. Code the levels of both independent variables listed in the first two rows in the **Values** column.

3. In the **Data View** tab, in the first column enter each coded value so that it equals the number of scores in each level. Do the same in the second column (for the second independent variable). The two columns create the cells. For example, if the first two columns in the row read 1, 1, then this tells SPSS that any data entered in the third column come from a cell that combines the first level of each factor. In the second column, enter the values for the dependent variable; make sure the data correspond to each cell.

4. Go to the **menu bar** and click **Analyze, General Linear Model,** and **Univariate** to bring up a dialog box.

5. Use the appropriate arrows to move the factors (or independent variables) into the **Fixed Factor(s):** box. Move the dependent variable into the **Dependent Variable:** box.

6. Finally, click **Options** to bring up a new dialog box. In the **Factor(s) and Factor Interactions** box move the two main effects and interaction into the **Display Means for:** box by using the arrow. Click **Continue**.

7. Select **Post Hoc. . .** to bring up another dialog box. Use the arrow to bring both main effects from the **Factor(s)** box into the **Post Hoc Tests for:** box. Select an appropriate pairwise comparison for the main effects and select **Continue**. [Note: SPSS does not perform simple effect tests. If you get a significant interaction, you will have to conduct these tests separately.]

8. Select **OK**, or select **Paste** and click the **Run** command.

Two-way within-subjects ANOVA

*This exercise is illustrated in **Chapter 12, Section 12.10** (SPSS in Focus), of the book.

1. Click on the **Variable View** tab and enter the names of each group created by combining the levels of two independent variables (one group in each row) in the **Name column**. In the Decimals column, reduce the value to the degree of accuracy of the data for each row in which a group was entered.

2. Click on the **Data View** tab. In each column, enter the data that correspond to each group (in each column).

3. Go to the **menu bar** and click **Analyze, General Linear Model,** and **Repeated Measures** to display a dialog box. Enter the name of the first factor in the **Within-Subjects Factor Name** box, and enter the number of levels for that factor in the **Number of Levels** box below it. Click **Add**. Follow these same instructions for the second factor.

4. Click **Define** to display a new dialog box. Move the levels for each factor into the **Within-Subjects Variables** box.

5. To compute post hoc tests for the main effects, select **Options** and move each factor into the **Display Means for:** box. Check mark the **Compare main effects** box and select your post hoc test from the drop down menu below the **Confidence interval adjustment** heading. [Note: SPSS does not perform simple effect tests. If you get a significant interaction, you will have to conduct these tests separately.]

6. Select **OK**, or select **Paste** and click the **Run** command.

Two-way mixed factorial ANOVA

*This exercise is illustrated in **Chapter 12, Section 12.10** (SPSS in Focus), of the book.

1. Click on the **Variable View** tab and enter the name of the between-subjects factor in the first row in the **Name column** and reduce the Decimals column to 0 (because this variable will be coded). In the remaining rows, enter each level of the within-subjects factor; each level should be listed in each row in the **Name column**. In the Decimals column, reduce the value to the degree of accuracy of the data.

2. Code the levels of the between-subjects factor listed in the first row in the **Values** column.

3. In the **Data View** tab, in the first column enter each coded value for the between-subjects factor so that it equals the number of scores in each level. In each column for the within-subjects factor, enter the data that correspond to each group in each column.

4. Go to the **menu bar** and click **Analyze, General Linear Model,** and **Repeated Measures** to display a dialog box. Enter the name of the within-subjects factor in the **Within-Subjects Factor Name** box, and enter the number of levels for that factor in the **Number of Levels** box below it. Click **Add.**

5. Click **Define** to display a new dialog box. Move the levels for the within-subjects factor into the **Within-Subjects Variables** box. Move the name of the between-subjects factors into the **Between-subjects factor(s)** box.

6. To compute post hoc tests for the main effects, select **Options** and move each factor into the **Display Means for:** box. Check mark the **Compare main effects** box and select your post hoc test from the dropdown menu below the **Confidence interval adjustment** heading. [Note: SPSS does not perform simple effect tests. If you get a significant interaction, you will have to conduct these tests separately.]

7. Select **OK,** or select **Paste** and click the **Run** command.

Correlation and Regression:

Pearson correlation coefficient

*This exercise is illustrated in **Chapter 8, Section 8.11** (SPSS in Focus), of the book.

1. Click on the **Variable View** tab and enter the first variable name in the **Name column;** and enter the second variable name in the Name column below it. Go to the **Decimals column** and reduce the value to the degree of accuracy of the data for each row.

2. Click on the **Data View** tab. Enter the data for each variable in the appropriate columns.

3. Go to the **menu bar** and click **Analyze, Correlate,** and **Bivariate** to bring up a dialog box.

4. Using the arrows, move both variables into the **Variables** box.

5. Select **OK,** or select **Paste** and click the **Run** command.

Analysis of regression

*This exercise is illustrated in **Chapter 8, Section 8.11** (SPSS in Focus), of the book.

1. Click on the **Variable View** tab and enter the predictor variable name in the **Name column;** and enter the criterion variable name in the Name column below it. Go to the **Decimals column** and reduce the value in both rows to the degree of accuracy for the data.

2. Click on the **Data View** tab. Enter the data for the predictor variable (X) in the first column. Enter the data for the criterion variable (Y) in the second column.

3. Go to the **menu bar** and click **Analyze, Regression,** and **Linear** to bring up a dialog box.

4. Use the arrows to move the predictor variable into the **Independent(s)** box; move the criterion variable into the **Dependent** box.

5. Select **OK**, or select **Paste** and click the **Run** command.

NONPARAMETRIC TESTS

Tests for Nominal Data:

Chi-square goodness-of-fit test

*This exercise is illustrated in **Chapter 14, Section 14.5** (SPSS in Focus), of the book.

1. Click on the **Variable View** tab and enter the nominal variable name in the **Name column** in the first row; and enter *frequencies* in the Name column below it. Go to the **Decimals column** and reduce the value to 0 for both rows.

2. Code the levels for the nominal variable listed in the first row in the **Values** column.

3. Click on the **Data View** tab. In the first column, list each coded value one time. In the second column list the corresponding observed frequencies for each coded level of the nominal variable.

4. Go to the menu bar and click **Data** and **Weight cases** to bring up a dialog box. In the new dialog box click **Weight cases by** and move *frequencies* into the **Frequency Variable** cell. Select **OK**.

5. Go to the **menu bar** and click **Analyze, Nonparametric tests,** and **Chi-square** to bring up a new dialog box.

6. Using the arrows, move the nominal variable into the **Test Variables List** box. In the **Expected Values** box, notice that we have two options: We can assume all categories (or expected frequencies) are equal, or we can input the frequencies for each cell. If the expected frequencies are equal, then leave this alone; if they are not equal, then enter the expected frequencies one at a time and click **Add** to move them into the cell.

7. Select **OK**, or select **Paste** and click the **Run** command.

Chi-square test for independence

*This exercise is illustrated in **Chapter 14, Section 14.5** (SPSS in Focus), of the book.

1. To organize the data, write out the contingency table so that one variable is listed in the row and another in the column. Click on the **Variable View** tab and in the **Name column** enter the name of the *row* variable in the first row; and enter the name of the *column* variable in the second row. In the third row, enter *frequencies* in the Name column. Reduce the value to 0 in each row in the **Decimals column**.

2. Code the levels for both nominal variables listed in the first two rows in the **Values** column.

3. In the **Data View** tab, we need to set up the cells by row and column. For the *row* variable, enter each coded value equal to the number of levels for the *column* variable. For example, if the *row* variable has two levels and the *column* variable has three levels, then list 1, 1, 1, 2, 2, 2 in the first column of the Data View. Set up the cells in the second column by listing the levels in numeric order across from each level of the *row* variable. Using the same example, list 1, 2, 3, 1, 2, 3 in the second column. The two columns create the cells. For example, if the first two columns list 1, 1 across the row, then this tells SPSS that any data entered in the third column come from a cell that combines the first level of each factor. List the corresponding observed frequencies for each cell in the third column.

4. Go to the menu bar and click **Data** and **Weight cases** to bring up a dialog box. In the new dialog box click **Weight cases by** and move *frequencies* into the **Frequency Variable** cell. This tells SPSS that the frequencies you enter are those for each row-column combination. Select **OK**.

5. Go to the **menu bar** and click **Analyze, Descriptive statistics,** and **Crosstabs** to bring up a dialog box.

6. Using the arrows move the *row* variable into the **Row(s)** box and move the *column* variable into the **Column(s)** box. Click **Statistics. . .** to open a new dialog box.

7. Select **Chi-square** in the top left. To compute effect size select **Phi and Cramer's V** in the box labeled **Nominal**. Click **Continue**.

8. Select **OK**, or select **Paste** and click the **Run** command.

Tests for Ordinal Data:

Wilcoxon signed-ranks t *test*

*The directions for this test are not given in the book but are illustrated as an alternative to parametric tests in Figure 14.3 of the book.

1. Click on the **Variable View** tab and enter the name of the first level of the independent variable in the name column in the first row; enter the name of the second level of the independent variable in the second row. Reduce the **Decimals column** value in both rows to the degree of accuracy of the data.

2. Click on the **Data View** tab. List the data for each level of the independent variable. Make sure the scores for each related pair are matched in each row.

3. Go to the **menu bar** and click **Analyze, Nonparametric tests,** and **2 Related Samples. . .** to bring up a dialog box.

4. In the **dialog box,** select each level of the independent variable in the left box and move them to the right box using the arrow in the middle. The variables should be side by side in the box to the right. In the **Test Type** box make sure that only the box next to **Wilcoxon** is checked.

5. Select **OK**, or select **Paste** and click the **Run** command.

Mann-Whitney U test

*The directions for this test are not given in the book but are illustrated as an alternative to parametric tests in Figure 14.3 of the book.

1. Click on the **Variable View** tab and enter the independent variable in the **Name column**. In the second row, enter the name of the dependent variable in the Name column. Reduce the value to 0 in the **Decimals column** in the first row and to the degree of accuracy of the data in the second row.

2. Code the levels for the independent variable listed in the first row in the **Values** column.

3. In the **Data View** tab, in the first column enter each number so that it equals the number of scores in each level. For example, if you measure five scores in each group (or level), then enter each numeric code five times in the first column. In the second column, enter the values for the dependent variable so that they correspond with the code for each group.

4. Go to the **menu bar** and click **Analyze, Nonparametric Tests**, and **2 Independent Samples** to bring up a dialog box.

5. Notice that **Mann-Whitney U** is selected by default. Using the arrows move the dependent variable into the **Test Variable List** box and the independent variable into the **Grouping Variable** box. Click **Define Groups. . .** to open a new dialog box. Place the numeric code for each group in the spaces provided and then click **Continue**.

6. Select **OK**, or select **Paste** and click the **Run** command.

Kruskal-Wallis H test

*The directions for this test are not given in the book but are illustrated as an alternative to parametric tests in Figure 14.3 of the book.

1. Click on the **Variable View** tab and enter the name of the independent variable in the **Name column**. Go to the **Decimals column** for this row and reduce the value to 0 (since this variable will be coded). In the second row enter the name of the dependent variable in the Name column. Reduce the **Decimals column** value in the second row to the degree of accuracy of the data.

2. Code the levels for the independent variable listed in the first row in the **Values** column.

3. In the **Data View** tab, in the first column enter each coded value so that it equals the number of scores in each level. For example, if you measure five scores in each group (or level), then enter each numeric code five times in the first column. In the second column, enter the values for the dependent variable so that they correspond with the codes for each group.

4. Go to the **menu bar** and click **Analyze, Nonparametric Tests**, and **k Independent Samples** to bring up a dialog box.

5. Notice that **Kruskal-Wallis H** is selected by default. Using the arrows move the dependent variable into the **Test Variable List** box and the independent variable into the **Grouping**

Variable box. Click **Define Groups. . .** to open a new dialog box. Enter the range of codes (i.e., the smallest and largest number used to code the levels of the independent variable). Select **Continue**.

6. Select **OK**, or select **Paste** and click the **Run** command.

Friedman test

*The directions for this test are not given in the book but are illustrated as an alternative to parametric tests in Figure 14.3 of the book.

1. Click on the **Variable View** tab and enter the name of each level of the independent variable in the **Name column**. One level (or group) should be listed in each row. Go to the **Decimals column** and reduce the value to the degree of accuracy of the data.

2. Click on the **Data View** tab. Now each column is labeled with each level of the independent variable. Enter the data for each respective column.

3. Go to the **menu bar** and click **Analyze, Nonparametric Tests,** and **k Related Samples** to bring up a dialog box.

4. Notice that **Friedman** is selected by default. Use the arrows to move each column into the **Test Variables** box.

5. Select **OK**, or select **Paste** and click the **Run** command.

Grammar, Punctuation, and Spelling (GPS): A Brief Writing Guide

American Psychological Association, or APA, writing style is important to learn. In Chapter 15 of *Research Methods for the Behavioral Sciences*, the use of APA style is described, and many tips are provided to help you improve your APA writing. However, without proper grammar, punctuation, and spelling, even the best APA style can appear sloppy. For this reason, we briefly describe the following basic features of writing in this guide:

- Nouns and Pronouns
- Verbs
- Adjectives and Adverbs
- Prepositions
- Commas
- Colons and Semicolons
- Apostrophes
- Quotation Marks
- Hyphens
- Sentence Structure
- Spelling

Because this guide is written to support the use of APA style, we will focus on aspects in writing that are consistent with APA style. Hence, this writing guide is like your GPS of writing using APA style: It will get your writing where it needs to be—to a college level. This guide is thorough, yet it is also a brief overview of the essentials in writing properly. Using this guide can certainly help you improve your grades on papers, particularly those that require an APA writing style.

Nouns and Pronouns

A noun is used to name or identify a person, place, thing, quality, or action. A pronoun takes the place of a noun, noun phrase, or noun clause. A brief list of rules for using nouns and pronouns appropriately is given here.

Use of Capitalization

There are many capitalization rules. Some are straightforward, and some vary depending on how words are used in a sentence. The following is a list of fundamental capitalization rules.

Rule 1: Capitalize the first word in a sentence.

- The experiment was a success.

Rule 2: Capitalize the pronoun *I*.

- If only I had considered that alternative.

Rule 3: Capitalize family relationships only when used as proper names.

- She loves her Uncle Bob more than her other uncles.
- He came home to see Father, although his father was not home.

Rule 4: Capitalize proper nouns, such as people, places, and organizations.

- Supreme Court, Buffalo Bills, Alcoholics Anonymous, U.S. Marine Corps, Ellicottville Brewing Company, New York City.

Rule 5: Capitalize titles that precede names.

- We asked Sergeant Major Privitera for comment; however, the sergeant major was not available for comment.

Rule 6: Capitalize names of countries and nationalities, and capitalize the adjective describing a person from that country or nationality.

- She was born in Canada, which makes her a Canadian.
- There was an Austrian who found refuge in Finland.

Rule 7: Capitalize all words except for short prepositions in books, articles, and songs.

- One of his most significant books was *Beyond Freedom and Dignity*.

Rule 8: Capitalize the names of gods, deities, religious figures, and books, except for nonspecific use of the word *god*.

- His faith called for him to worship only one god, so he prayed to God daily.
- Capitalize religious books such as the Holy Bible or Koran, and deities such as Buddha or Jesus Christ.

Rule 9: Capitalize *North, South, East,* and *West* as regional directions, but not as compass directions.

- A sample was selected at a college in the <u>Northeast</u>.
- The habitat was located a few minutes <u>east</u> of the river.

Rule 10: Capitalize the days of the week, months, and holidays, and capitalize the seasons only when used in a title.

- His favorite season was <u>fall</u>, which is when he enrolled in college for the <u>Fall</u> 2013 semester.
- He did not attend class on <u>Wednesday</u>, which was <u>Halloween</u>. In <u>November</u>, he did not miss a class.

Rule 11: Capitalize historical eras, periods, and events, but not century numbers.

- The <u>Great Depression</u> occurred in the <u>twentieth</u> century and was a difficult time for many <u>Americans</u>.

Rule 12: Capitalize the first word after a colon only when the clause following the colon is a complete sentence.

- The experiment was conducted to learn about human behavior: the outcome.
- The lecturer gave an important lesson: To learn about human behavior means that we advance human understanding.

Use of Pronouns and Pronoun Case

Rule 1: Pronouns should agree in number. In other words, if the pronoun replaces a singular noun, then use a singular pronoun. Note that words such as *everybody, anybody, anyone, someone, neither, nobody,* and *each* are singular words that take singular pronouns.

- A participant was read an informed consent that <u>he or she</u> signed. (NOT: A participant was read an informed consent that <u>they</u> signed.)
- Everybody had 30 seconds to finish <u>his or her</u> test. (NOT: Everybody had 30 seconds to finish <u>their</u> test.)

Rule 2: Pronouns should agree in person. When you use first person (*I, we*), second person (*you*), or third person (*he, she, they*), be consistent. Don't switch from one person to the other.

- When <u>we</u> are working, <u>we</u> should have time to relax afterward. (NOT: When <u>we</u> are working, <u>you</u> should have time to relax afterward.)

Rule 3: Pronouns should be clearly identified.

- It is important that <u>the executive team</u> gets the decision correct. [NOT: It is important that <u>they</u> get the decision correct. (Who are "they"?)]
- Students completed a test and quiz, then placed <u>the test and quiz</u> face down when they were finished. [NOT: Students completed a test and quiz, then placed <u>it</u> face down when they were finished. (Is "it" referring to the test, the quiz, or both?)]

Here we will list some additional rules pertaining to pronoun case use. To begin, keep in mind that pronouns have three cases:

Subjective case (pronouns used as subject).

- I, you, he, she it, we, they, who

Objective case (pronouns used as objects of verbs or prepositions).

- Me, you, him, her, it, us, them, whom

Possessive case (pronouns used to express ownership).

- My (mine), your (yours), his/her (his/hers), it (its), our (ours), their (theirs), whose

Rule 4: Some pronouns do not change case or form.

- That, that, these, those, which

Rule 5: Use the subjective and objective case appropriately for formal and informal writing.

- Formal writing: In the subjective case, "It is I." In the objective case, "To whom am I speaking?"
- Informal writing: In the subjective case, "Who am I speaking with?" In the objective case, "It is me."

Rule 6: When making comparisons, use *than, as, compared to*, or *versus (vs.)*.

- The effect was larger in the experimental group <u>than</u> in the control group. [NOT: The effect was larger in the experimental group. (Larger than what?)]
- The effect was larger in the experimental group <u>compared to</u> the control group.
- Self-reports were as truthful <u>as</u> possible.
- Scores were comparable in the experimental <u>versus</u> the control group.

Verbs

A verb is used to describe an action or occurrence or identify a state of being. A brief list of rules for using verbs appropriately is given here. There are six basic tenses you should be familiar with:

Simple present: We conclude

Present perfect: We have concluded

Simple past: They concluded

Past perfect: They had concluded

Future: They will conclude

Future perfect: They will have concluded

The challenge in sequencing tenses usually occurs with the perfect tenses. Perfect tenses are formed by adding an auxiliary or auxiliaries, which most commonly take the forms of *has, have, had, be, can, do, may, must, ought, shall*, and *will*. We will use the common forms identified here.

Verb Tenses

Rule 1: Present perfect designates actions that have occurred and are ongoing and consists of a past participle with *has* or *have*.

- Simple past: We attended school for four years.
- Present perfect: We have attended school for four years.

The simple past implies that "we" are done attending school; the present perfect implies that "we" are still attending school.

Rule 2: Infinitives also have perfect tense forms when combined with auxiliaries, even when used with verbs that identify the future, such as *hope*, *intend*, *expect*, and *plan*. When the perfect tense is used with verbs that identify the future, the perfect tense sets up the sequence by identifying the action that began and was completed before the action of the main verb.

- The researcher had expected to observe the result. (In this example, the action, "had expected," began and was completed before the action of the main verb, "to observe the result.")

Rule 3: Past perfect indicates an action completed in the past before another action begins.

- Simple past: The scientist developed research protocols and later used them to conduct research.
- Past perfect: The scientist used research protocols that he had developed.

In each example, the research protocols were developed before they were used to conduct research.

- Simple past: The technician fixed the apparatus when the inspector arrived.
- Past perfect: The technician had fixed the apparatus when the inspector arrived.

The simple past indicates that the technician waited until the inspector arrived to fix the apparatus; the past perfect indicates that the technician had already fixed the apparatus by the time the inspector arrived.

Rule 3: Future perfect indicates an action that will have been completed at a specified time in the future.

- Simple future: Friday I will finish my homework.
- Future perfect: By Friday, I will have finished my homework.

The simple future indicates that the homework will be completed specifically on Friday; the future perfect indicates that the homework will be completed at any time leading up to Friday.

Irregular Verbs

Regular verbs consist of the present/root form, the simple past form, and the past participle form of the verb. Regular verbs have an ending of *-ed* added to the present/root form for both the simple past and past participle form. Irregular verbs are identified as verbs that do not follow this pattern.

To help you identify the form of irregular verbs, the list here consists of the present/root form, the simple past form, and the past participle form of 60 irregular verbs.

Present	Past	Past Participle	Present	Past	Past Participle
be	was, were	been	lay	laid	laid
become	became	become	lead	led	led
begin	began	begun	leave	left	left
bring	brought	brought	let	let	let
build	built	built	lie	lay	lain
catch	caught	caught	lose	lost	lost
choose	chose	chosen	make	made	made
come	came	come	meet	met	met
cut	cut	cut	quit	quit	quit
deal	dealt	dealt	read	read	read
do	did	done	ride	rode	ridden
drink	drank	drunk	run	ran	run
eat	ate	eaten	say	said	said
fall	fell	fallen	see	saw	seen
feed	fed	fed	seek	sought	sought
feel	felt	felt	send	sent	sent
find	found	found	sleep	slept	slept
forget	forgot	forgotten	speak	spoke	spoken
forgive	forgave	forgiven	spend	spent	spent
get	got	gotten	stand	stood	stood
give	gave	given	take	took	taken
go	went	gone	teach	taught	taught
grow	grew	grown	tell	told	told
have	had	had	think	thought	thought
hear	heard	heard	throw	threw	thrown
hide	hid	hidden	understand	understood	understood

Present	Past	Past Participle	Present	Past	Past Participle
hold	held	held	wear	wore	worn
keep	kept	kept	win	won	won
know	knew	known	write	wrote	written

Active and Passive Voice

Active verbs: Verbs in an active voice show the subject or person acting. The active voice is often a more concise writing style. For this reason, many writers feel that the active voice should be the primary voice of an author.

Passive verbs: Verbs in the passive voice show something else acting on the subject or person. This voice is often used only when needed but is usually not the primary voice of an author.

To distinguish between the active and passive voice, we will use two examples for each voice:

Example 1: The graduate student *ended* the study. (active voice)

The study *was ended* by the graduate student. (passive voice)

Example 2: The analysis *showed* significance. (active voice)

Significance *was shown* in the analysis. (passive voice)

Indicative, Imperative, and Subjective Mood

The **indicative mood** indicates a fact or opinion. Most verbs we use are in the indicative mood.

Examples: The doctor *was* here.

I *am* working late.

She *will bring* her notes.

The **imperative mood** expresses commands or requests. The subject of sentences that use the imperative mood is *you*, although it is not directly stated in the sentence.

Examples: *Be* to class on time.

Turn to page 32 in your book.

Bring your calculator to the exam.

Although not directly stated, in each example it is understood that <u>you</u> be to class on time, <u>you</u> turn to page 32 in your book, and <u>you</u> bring your calculator to the exam.

The **subjunctive mood** shows something contrary to fact. To express something that is not principally true, use the past tense or past perfect tense; when using the verb *to be* in the subjunctive mood, always use *were* rather than *was*.

Examples: If the inspector *were* here . . . (Implied: . . . but he is not)

I wish we *had tested* the sample first. (Implied: . . . but we did not)

You would have preferred *to be* in class. (Implied: . . . but you were not)

Adjectives and Adverbs

Adjectives modify nouns in some way. Adverbs modify verbs, adjectives, or other adverbs in some way. A description of each type of modifier with examples is given in this section.

Adjectives

Adjectives modify nouns in some way. For example:

- He was given a survey. (*Survey* is a noun. We know participants were given the survey; we don't know anything else about the survey.)
- He was given a *brief* survey. (*Survey* is a noun. *Brief* is an adjective. The adjective modifies the noun; we now know the kind of survey completed: a *brief* survey.)

Adjectives can answer the following questions:

- Which? (For example, "The *third* floor." Which floor? The third floor.)
- How many? (For example, "*Six* students were absent." How many students? Six students.)
- What kind? (For example, "The student took a *makeup* exam." What kind of exam? A makeup exam.)

Adverbs

Adverbs modify verbs, adjectives, or other adverbs in some way. Adverbs most often answer the question: How? For example:

- She *studied quietly*. (*Quietly* is an adverb that modifies the verb *studied*; how did she study? Quietly.)
- The professor was *very* fair. (*Fair* is an adjective that modifies the noun *professor*. *Very* is an adverb that modifies the adjective *fair*; how fair is the professor? Very fair.)

Many adverbs have an -*ly* ending. Some examples: *abruptly, absolutely, beautifully, briskly, brutally, cheerfully, delicately, endlessly, expertly, firmly, lightly, literally, quietly, quickly, randomly, really, slowly, successfully, tremendously, wholeheartedly, willfully, willingly.*

- She was a *tremendously* successful researcher. (*Successful* is an adjective that modifies the noun *researcher*. *Tremendously* is an adverb that modifies the adjective *successful*; how successful was the researcher? Tremendously successful.)

Some adverbs indicate the place or location of an action. Some examples: *everywhere, here, in, inside, out, outside, somewhere, there.*

- The class relocated *upstairs*. (*Upstairs* is an adverb that modifies the verb *relocated*; where did the class relocate? Upstairs.)

Some adverbs indicate when, how often, or what time an action occurred. Some examples: *always, daily, early, first, last, later, monthly, never, now, often, regularly, usually, weekly.*

- Participants were observed *daily*. (*Daily* is an adverb that modifies the verb *observed*; how often were participants observed? Daily.)

Some adverbs indicate to what extent an action or something was done. Some examples: *almost, also, enough, only, quite, rather, so, too, very.*

- The room was *quite* comfortable. (*Comfortable* is an adjective that modifies the noun *room*. *Quite* is an adverb that modifies the adjective *comfortable*; to what extent was the room comfortable? Quite comfortable.)

A Versus *An*

Using *a* or *an* in a sentence depends on the phonetic (sound) representation of the first letter in a word, not on the orthographic (written) representation of the letter. If the first letter makes a vowel-like sound, then use *an*; if the first letter makes a consonant-like sound, then use *a*. The following are some basic rules for using *a* or *an*:

Rule 1: *A* goes before a word that begins with a consonant. For example:

- A study
- A replication
- A limitation

Rule 2: *An* goes before a word that begins with a vowel. For example:

- An analysis
- An increase
- An effect

Exception 1: Use *an* before an unsounded *h* in which a vowel follows the first letter. The *h* has no audible sound in its phonetic representation; therefore, we use *an* because the first audible sound is a vowel (e.g., "an honest mistake" or "an honorable life").

Exception 2: Use *a* when *u* makes the same sound as *y* (e.g., "a U.S. sample" or "a united team") or *o* makes the same sound as *w* (e.g., "a one-day trial").

Prepositions

A preposition is a word or phrase typically used before a substantive that indicates the relation of the substantive to a verb, an adjective, or another substantive. A preposition functions as a modifier to a verb, noun, or adjective and generally expresses a spatial, temporal, or other type of relationship. Many forms of prepositions are discussed in this section.

Prepositions for Time and Place

Prepositions are used to identify **one point in time**.
On is used with days of the week and with a specific calendar day.

- The school week begins *on* Monday.
- My birthday is *on* March 30.

At is used with *noon, night, midnight,* and time of day.

- Class begins *at* noon.
- The stars come out *at* night.
- The deadline is *at* midnight.
- The test will be administered *at* 4:30 p.m.

In is used with *afternoon* and seasons, months, and years.

- He awoke *in* the afternoon.
- The study was conducted *in* spring.
- Snowfall was recorded *in* February.
- He earned his college degree *in* 2012.

Prepositions are used to identify an **extended period of time** using the following prepositions: *since, for, by, from, until, within,* and *during*.

- It has been two years *since* the last cohort was observed.
- Participants were observed *for* two weeks.
- The deadline has been extended *by* two hours.
- The study continued *from* morning *until* night.
- A research protocol must be completed *within* three years.
- I am always focused *during* class.

Prepositions are used to identify a **place**, or refer to a **location relative to a given point**.
To identify a **place**, use *in* to refer to the point itself, use *inside* to indicate something contained, use *on* to indicate a surface, and use *at* to indicate a specific place/location or general vicinity.

- Animal subjects were housed *in* steel cages.
- He placed his notes *inside* the folder.
- The student left his exam *on* the desk.
- Assistance was available *at* the help desk.

To identify a **location relative to a given point,** use *over* or *above* for a location higher than a point; use *under, underneath, beneath,* or *below* to identify a location lower than a point; use *near, by, next to, between, among, behind,* or *opposite* to identify a location close to a point.

- The flask is *above* the cabinet.
- The survey was *beneath* the consent form.
- The child hid *underneath* the table.
- The confederate was *behind* the participant.
- The field was located *between* two oak trees.

Prepositions for Direction or Movement

The prepositions *to, onto,* and *into* can be used to identify movement toward something. The basic preposition of a direction toward a goal is *to.* When the goal is physical, such as a destination, *to* implies movement toward the goal:

- The mouse ran *to* the cheese.
- The newlyweds flew *to* Paris.

When the goal is not physical, such as an action, *to* marks a verb and is used as an infinitive.

- The student went *to* see her teacher.
- The professor hurried *to* attend the conference.

The preposition *onto* indicates movement toward a surface, whereas the preposition *into* indicates movements toward the interior of a volume.

- The athlete jumped *onto* the platform.
- The solution was poured *into* the container.

Note that *to* can be optional for *onto* and *into* because *on* and *in* can have a directional meaning when used with verbs of motion. The compound preposition (*onto, into*) indicates the completion of an action, whereas the simple preposition (*on, in*) indicates the position of a subject as a result of that action.

- The shot went *into* the basket OR The shot went *in* the basket.
- The fossils washed up *onto* the shore OR The fossils washed up *on* the shore.

Note that some verbs that indicate direction or movement express the idea that some physical object or subject is situated in a specific place. In these cases, some verbs use only *on,* whereas others can use *on* or *onto.* The following is an example in which *on* and *onto* can be distinguished:

- The pilot landed the aircraft [*on* or *onto*] the runway. (In this case, the pilot lands the aircraft toward a surface, i.e., the runway.)
- The aircraft landed *on* [not *onto*] the runway. (In this case, the plane itself is situated on a specific surface, i.e., on the runway.)

Note also that *to* suggests movement toward a specific destination, whereas *toward* suggests movement in a general direction, without necessarily arriving at a destination.

- The student went *to* the exit during the fire drill. (The exit is the destination; note that *to* implies that the student does not actually go *through* the exit; the exit is the destination.)
- The student went *toward* the exit during the fire drill. (The student was headed in the direction of the exit, but may not have reached or gone through the exit.)

Prepositions for Introducing Objects of Verbs

Use *of* with *approve* and *consists*.

- She did not approve *of* his behavior.
- The solution consists *of* sugar water.

Use *of* or *about* with *dream* and *think*.

- I dream [*of* or *about*] making the world a better place.
- Can you think [*of* or *about*] a solution to the problem?

Use *at* with *laugh, stare, smile,* and *look*.

- I had to laugh *at* the joke.
- I tend to stare *at* the screen.
- I saw you smile *at* me.
- I look *at* a map to find directions.

Use *for* with *call, hope, look, wait,* and *watch*.

- I may need you to call *for* help.
- We will hope *for* reliable results with this new test.
- Can we look *for* a solution to the problem?
- Can you wait *for* me to return?
- He must watch *for* the signal before proceeding.

Commas

Using punctuation correctly requires that we distinguish between an independent clause and a dependent clause. An *independent clause* is a passage that is a complete sentence that has a subject and a verb. A *dependent clause* is a passage that also has a subject and a verb, but is an incomplete sentence. In this section, we will identify when it is and is not appropriate to use punctuation with independent and dependent clauses.

The following is a brief list of eight rules for **when to use commas:**

Rule 1: Use commas to separate independent clauses that are joined by coordinating conjunctions (e.g., *and*, *but*, *or*, *nor*, *so*, *yet*).

- The study was complete, *but* the data were not analyzed.
- The analysis showed significance, *yet* the results were difficult to interpret.

Note: DO NOT use a comma between the two verbs or verb phrases in a compound predicate.

- The baseball player ran on the bases *and* slid to home. (Do not use a comma because *and* separates two verbs—*running* [on bases] and *sliding* [to home].)
- The researcher explained the expectations and procedures *and* began the study. (Do not use a comma before the last *and* because it separates two verb phrases [the researcher "explaining" and the researcher "beginning"].)

Rule 2: Use commas after introductory clauses that come before the main clause. The following is a list of common words used to start an introductory clause that should be followed by a comma: *although, after, as, because, if, when, while, since, however, yes, well.*

- *After* a short break, participants had no trouble completing the task.
- *While* the student studied, his roommate was playing loud music.
- *As* stated earlier, human behavior can be understood using the scientific process.
- *Yes*, the findings do support the hypothesis.

Note: DO NOT use a comma if the introductory clause follows the main clause (except for cases of extreme contrast).

- Participants had no trouble completing the task *after* a short break. (Do not use a comma.)
- The student was in a great mood, *although* he failed out of college. (Failing out of college is an extreme contrast to being in a great mood; use a comma.)

Rule 3: Use commas to separate three or more elements or words written in a series.

- The categories of research design are experimental, nonexperimental, and quasi-experimental.
- The food environment was contrived to appear open, hidden, or clustered.
- The researcher gave a participant, who volunteered for the study, who completed all interviews, and who followed all procedures, a debriefing form.

Rule 4: Use commas to enclose clauses, phrases, and words in the middle of a sentence that are not essential to the meaning of the sentence.

- His research, *which was completed many years ago*, was published just this year.
- The verdict, *on the other hand*, did not satisfy the family.
- The patient, *however*, was not ready to be released.

Note: To identify a clause, phrase, or word that is not essential to the meaning of a sentence follow these three guidelines.

- If the clause, phrase, or word is omitted and the sentence still makes sense, then enclose the clause, phrase, or word in commas.
- If the clause, phrase, or word would otherwise interrupt the flow of words in the original sentence, then enclose the clause, phrase, or word in commas.
- If the clause, phrase, or word could be moved to a different part of the sentence, and the sentence would still make sense, then enclose the clause, phrase, or word in commas.

Rule 5: Use commas to separate two or more coordinate adjectives but not two or more noncoordinate adjectives to describe the same noun.

- Participation in the experimental group required *intense, rigorous* skills. (The sentence uses coordinate adjectives [*intense, rigorous*], so a comma is used.)
- The student wore a *green woolly* sweater. (The sentence uses noncoordinate adjectives [*green, woolly*], so no comma is used.)
- He was prepared for the *cold, chilly, snowy winter* weather. (There are three coordinate adjectives [*cold, chilly, snowy*] with a comma used to separate each, and one noncoordinate adjective [*winter*] with no comma used.)

Note: To identify coordinate adjectives used to describe the same noun follow these two guidelines.

- If the sentence still makes sense when the adjectives are written in reverse order, then the adjectives are coordinate and a comma is used.
- If the sentence still makes sense when *and* is written between the adjectives, then the adjectives are coordinate and a comma is used.

Rule 6: Use a comma near the end of a sentence to indicate a distinct pause or to separate contrasted coordinate elements.

- The study showed evidence of clinical significance, not statistical significance.
- The student seemed frustrated, even angry.
- The research findings were an important advancement, almost landmark.

Rule 7: Use commas to separate geographical names, items in dates (except month and day), titles in names, and addresses (except street number and name).

- The author was raised in East Aurora, New York.
- November 10, 2015, will be the 240th birthday of the U.S. Marine Corps.
- Ivan Pavlov, PhD, was a Noble Prize winner.
- The White House is located at 1600 Pennsylvania Avenue, Washington, DC.

Rule 8: Use a comma to shift between the main discourse and a quotation but not when the quotation is part of the main discourse.

- The parent told his child, "Every moment I am with you is the greatest moment of my life."
- Telling your child to "live every moment as if it is your last" can be inspirational. (No comma is used because the quoted material is part of the main discourse.)

Colons and Semicolons

Colons and semicolons are used to mark a major division in a sentence, typically to bring together two or more ideas into one enumeration. This section describes many rules for appropriately using colons and semicolons. The following is a list of five rules for appropriately using colons.

Colons

A colon is used to divide the main discourse of a sentence from an elaboration, summation, or general implication of the main discourse. A colon is also used to separate numbers, such as hours and minutes, and a ratio or proportion.

Rule 1: Use a colon before statements that introduce a formal passage or list.

- Three topics described in this guide: grammar, punctuation, and spelling.
- To do well in this class: Take notes! Read the book! Study often!

Note: DO NOT use a colon after a preposition or linking verb.

- Three topics described in this guide *are* grammar, punctuation, and spelling. (*Are* is a linking verb used in place of the colon.)
- You can do well in this class *by* taking notes, reading the book, and studying often. (*By* is used to link "doing well" with the three criteria listed for doing well.)

Rule 2: Use a colon (in place of a comma) before long or formal direct quotations.

- The German-born American physicist Albert Einstein once *said:* "I am neither especially clever nor especially gifted. I am only very, very curious." (A colon is used to separate the passage from the quoted material; note that a comma can also be used in place of the colon to separate the passage from the quoted material.)

Rule 3: Use a colon before formal appositives.

- Most citizens polled identified the same issue as their main concern: the economy. (A colon introduces an appositive.)
- One class was his favorite in college: psychology. (A colon introduces an appositive.)

Rule 4: Use a colon between independent clauses when the second clause restates or supports the same idea as the preceding clause.

- Scientists are not infallible: On occasion, they can, without intention, misinterpret, mislead, or misrepresent the data they publish. (The second clause expands on and supports the preceding clause.)
- Any idea you develop must be testable: An idea must lead to specific predictions that can be observed under specified conditions. (The second clause expands on and supports the preceding clause.)

Note: To be concise, DO NOT restate the same idea unless it serves to expand on or further illustrate the content in the preceding clause.

Rule 5: Use a colon to separate numbers, such as hours and minutes, and a ratio or proportion.

- The deadline was set at *9:00* p.m.
- The chances of winning the game were *4:1*. (A ratio can also be stated as *4 to 1* without the colon.)

Semicolons

A semicolon is used to divide the main discourse of a sentence and is used to balance two contrasted or related ideas. The following is a list of three rules for appropriately using semicolons.

Rule 1: Use a semicolon to separate two independent clauses not connected by a coordinating conjunction.

- Each participant chose the second option; it was the preferred option.
- She finished her exam in one hour; I completed my exam in half that time.
- The laboratory was contrived; it was designed to look like a day care center.

Note: DO NOT overuse semicolons for Rule 1. As a general rule, only apply Rule 1 when using a comma in place of a period allows for an easier transition between two complete sentences or independent clauses. As an example, for the sentences below, the transition between the sentences is not made easier by using the semicolon.

- INCORRECT: From a broad view, science is any systematic method of acquiring knowledge apart from ignorance; *from* a stricter view, science is specifically the acquisition of knowledge using the scientific method.
- CORRECT: From a broad view, science is any systematic method of acquiring knowledge apart from ignorance. *From* a stricter view, science is specifically the acquisition of knowledge using the scientific method.

Rule 2: Use a semicolon before a transitional connective or conjunctive adverb that separates two main clauses. Examples of conjunctive adverbs are *consequently, besides, instead, also, furthermore, therefore, however, likewise, hence, nevertheless, in addition,* and *moreover.*

- His hypothesis has support; *however*, his statements go beyond the data.
- It was the best product on the market; *yet*, it was overpriced.
- The student was not distracted; *instead*, she was focused.

Note: The same caution applies here regarding the use of semicolons and periods. Only use a semicolon for Rule 2 when using a comma in place of a period allows for an easier transition between two complete sentences or independent clauses.

Rule 3: Use semicolons between items that have internal punctuation in a series or sequence.

- The members of the editorial board are William James, editor-in-chief; Ivan Pavlov, associate editor; B. F. Skinner, associate editor; and Chris Thomas, editorial assistant. (A semicolon is used to "break up" the commas used to separate the names from the titles of each editor.)

- Over the next four years, our conference will be held in Buffalo, New York; Chicago, Illinois; Washington, DC; and Seattle, Washington. (A semicolon is used to "break up" the commas used to separate the names of each city and state.)

Apostrophes

An apostrophe is used to form possessives of nouns, to indicate missing letters with contractions, and to show plurals of lowercase letters. Each type of use for an apostrophe is briefly described in this section.

Forming Possessives of Nouns

An apostrophe is used for the possessive. To see if you need to form the possessive of a noun, make the phrase an "of the" phrase. If the "of the" phrase makes sense, then use an apostrophe—except if the noun after *of* is a building or room, an object, or a piece of furniture.

- The patient's file = the file *of the* patient ("of the" makes sense; apostrophe needed)
- The study's outcome = the outcome *of the* study ("of the" makes sense; apostrophe needed)
- The day's end = the end *of the* day ("of the" makes sense; apostrophe needed)
- The laboratory corridor = the corridor of the laboratory ("of the" makes sense; however, no apostrophe is needed because "the laboratory" is a building or room)

Note: DO NOT use apostrophes with possessive pronouns because possessive pronouns already show possession. For example:

- His lab (NOT: His' lab)
- The study was two hours long (NOT: The study was two hours' long.)
- The team made its quota (NOT: The team made it's quota. *Its* is a possessive pronoun meaning "belonging to it"; *it's* is a contraction meaning "it is.")

The following is a list of five rules for **when to use an apostrophe for the possessive:**

Rule 1: Add 's to the singular form of a word, even if it ends in -s.

- The researcher's conclusions
- The student's grade
- James's application

Rule 2: Add 's to words in which the plural form does not end in -s.

- The nuclei's activity
- The stimuli's presence
- The people's choice

The following is a brief list of words with a plural form that does not end in *-s*. Follow Rule 2 for the plural form of these words.

Singular	Plural
Alumna	Alumnae
Alumnus	Alumni
Child	Children
Criterion	Criteria
Curriculum	Curricula
Datum	Data
Dice	Die
Foot	Feet
Focus	Foci
Fungus	Fungi
Man	Men
Mouse	Mice
Nucleus	Nuclei
Person	People
Phenomenon	Phenomena
Stimulus	Stimuli
Woman	Women

Rule 3: Add ' to the end of plural nouns that end in *-s:*

- The countries' independence
- The universities' collaboration

Rule 4: Add 's to the singular form of compound words and hyphenated nouns.

- The scapegoat's rationale
- The rattlesnake's bite
- The editor-in-chief's decision

Rule 5: Add 's to the last noun to show joint possession of an object.

- Tom and Jerry's house
- Denver and Miami's football game

Indicating Missing Letters With Contractions

Apostrophes are used in contractions to indicate that letters are missing when two words are combined—for example, *it's* (it is), *don't* (do not), *could've* (could have). Yet, contractions are NOT used with APA style. For this reason, we will not introduce the use of apostrophes in detail greater than that identified in this paragraph.

Showing Plurals of Lowercase Letters

Rule for lowercase letters: Add 's to form the plural of lowercase letters.

- Mind your *p's* and *q's*. (Lowercase letters need apostrophe.)
- In sports, it is all about the *w's*. (Lowercase letter needs apostrophe.)

Note: Apostrophes indicating the plural form of capitalized letters, numbers, and symbols are NOT needed. For example:

- Two *MVPs* were selected.
- All students earned *As* and scored in the *90s* on the exam.
- Many *&s* were used in the reference list.

Quotation Marks

Quotation marks are most often used to set off or represent exact spoken or written language, typically from another source. For this reason, using quotation marks correctly is one practical way to avoid plagiarism. Quotations can also be used for other purposes not related to citing other sources. In this section, we will describe many of the rules for quotation mark use.

As a general rule, always open and close quoted material with quotation marks. Hence, quotation marks should always be used in pairs. Quotation marks are used for direct quotations; not indirect quotations. The APA manual provides complete instructions on how to properly cite references in text with and without quotation marks—and therefore for direct and indirect quotation use.

Keep in mind also that overuse of quotation marks can be poor practice because it gives the impression that the ideas expressed in a paper are not primarily coming from the author or writer. For this reason, make sure to use direct quotations sparingly. If you can simply summarize a work, results, or other details in the text, then paraphrase; that is, use indirect quotations. Only use direct quotations for material or language in which paraphrasing would diminish its importance (e.g., a quote from a famous author or figure such as that given in a speech, a definition for a key term, or an important work or policy).

Note for all examples below that the period or comma punctuation always comes before the final quotation mark. Follow this punctuation rule when using quotation marks.

Rule 1: Capitalize the first letter of a direct quote when the quoted material is a complete sentence.

- The author stated, "A significant outcome is not proof of an effect; a significant outcome indicates evidence of an effect."
- While he did have a viable program of research, it was another researcher who said, "High power may be the most essential factor for a program of research to be viable."

Rule 2: DO NOT capitalize the first letter of a direct quote when the quoted material is a fragment sentence or is integrated as part of an original sentence.

- The students behaved during class because the professor made clear that "self-discipline and control" were important to be successful in his class.
- These findings support the assertion that "it is not all about the calories" when it comes to understanding hunger and fullness.

Rule 3: If the quoted material is a complete sentence and is broken up, then capitalize the first part of the sentence but not the second part.

- "Isolating confounding variables," he said, "is important when conducting an experiment." (Note that two pairs of quotations are used when one quote is broken into two parts.)

Rule 4: Use single quotation marks to enclose quotes within another quotation.

- The participant replied, "He told me that 'I was being too strict' as a parent." (The single quotation marks indicate quotes from a secondary source and not those of the speaker specifically being quoted in double quotation marks.)

Rule 5: You may omit portions of a quote, typically to be more concise, by replacing the omitted words with an ellipsis.

- **Original Quote:** "An experiment with an increased sample size should be able to detect an effect, if one exists, because it is associated with greater power."
- **Revised Quote:** "An experiment with an increased sample size . . . is associated with greater power."

Rule 6: You may add words to quoted material, typically to improve clarity, by enclosing the added words in brackets.

- **Original Quote:** He explained, "At that time, I handed out the survey."
- **Revised Quote:** He explained, "At that time [when participants arrived], I handed out the survey."

Rule 7: Use quotation marks for the definition of a key term if quoted from another source. DO NOT use quotation marks for the key term; instead, use italics or boldface to identify the to-be-defined term.

- *Science* is "the acquisition of knowledge through observation, evaluation, interpretation, and theoretical explanation."

Rule 8: Quotation marks—not used for direct quotes—can indicate words used ironically or even comically.

- It was an awful game at the "Super" Bowl. ("Super" Bowl is an ironic name for the game if the game itself was awful.)
- The sprinter "ran away" from the competition. (This phrase could be construed as funny because "run away" has a double meaning in this context—it relates to winning a competition and the fact that the competition involved running.)

Hyphens

A hyphen can be used to separate words or phrases. The following six rules can be applied and are generally accepted for using hyphens correctly.

Rule 1: Use a hyphen to join two or more words serving as a single adjective that precedes a noun.

- The *well-known* study. (The adjective [*well-known*] precedes the noun [*study*]; use a hyphen to combine the words *well* and *known*.)
- The *clear-headed* researcher. (The adjective [*clear-headed*] precedes the noun [*researcher*]; use a hyphen to combine the words *clear* and *headed*.)

Rule 2: DO NOT use a hyphen to join two or more words serving as a single adjective that follow a noun.

- The study was *well known*. (The adjective [*well known*] follows the noun [*study*]; DO NOT use a hyphen.)
- The researcher was *clear headed*. (The adjective [*clear headed*] follows the noun [*researcher*]; DO NOT use a hyphen.)

Rule 3: Use a hyphen to join letters that may otherwise cause confusion.

- They were asked to *re-sign* the form. (*Re-sign* is "to sign again" whereas *resign* is "to give up" or "to accept as inevitable.")
- We had to *re-cover* the solution. (*Re-cover* is "to cover again" whereas *recover* is "to restore" or "to regain.")

Rule 4: Use a hyphen for prefixes [*ex-* (meaning "former"), *self-, all-, half-, quasi-*]; for suffixes [*-elect, -like, -typical*]; and between a prefix and a capitalized word (such as a proper noun) or number.

- Prefixes: ex-husband, self-aware, all-knowing, half-asleep, quasi-experimental.
- Suffixes: president-elect, playoff-like atmosphere, schizoid-typical behavior.
- Between a prefix and a capitalized word or number: anti-American, mid-1900s.

Rule 5: Use a hyphen to join multiword compounds (with few exceptions), usually even if the multiword compound precedes or follows the noun.

- His response was *matter-of-fact*.
- The *next-to-last* student was chosen to participate.

Rule 6: Use a hyphen to join compound numbers.

- *Thirty-six* students took the exam.
- *Twenty-two* participants were observed.

Sentence Structure

Sentence structure is the grammatical arrangement of words into sentences. In addition to words, sentences can also include numbers and individual letters or symbols. Sentence structure is important in that good structure strengthens the flow of ideas in a written work and makes it easier for the reader to correctly understand what is written. In this section, we introduce fundamental rules of sentence structure not yet discussed in this basic writing guide.

Subject-Verb Agreement

Rule 1: Use a plural verb when the subject of a sentence consists of two or more nouns or pronouns connected by *and*; use a singular verb when nouns or pronouns are linked with *or*.

- Jack *and* Jill <u>are</u> in the lab. (Plural)
- His work *or* your work <u>is</u> going to win the prize. (Singular)

Rule 2: When the subject of a sentence consists of two or more nouns or pronouns connected by *or*, the verb must agree with the part of the subject that is closer to the verb in the sentence.

- The graduate students *or* a researcher <u>runs</u> the study. (The "researcher" [singular] is the part of the subject that is closest to the verb *runs*.)
- A researcher *or* the graduate students <u>run</u> the study. (The "graduate students" [plural] are the part of the subject that is closest to the verb *run*.)

Rule 3: A verb must agree with the subject, not with the noun or pronoun in the clause.

- One of the hypotheses <u>is</u> correct. (*One* is singular and is the subject.)
- The hypotheses <u>are</u> both correct. (*The hypotheses* is plural and is the subject.)
- The book, including all appendices, <u>was</u> easy to read. (*The book* is singular and is the subject.)
- The women, even those who did not volunteer, <u>were</u> cooperative. (*The women* is plural and is the subject.)

Rule 4: The following words are singular and require a singular verb: *anybody, anyone, each, everybody, everyone, no one, nobody, somebody,* and *someone*.

- *Each* of the students <u>is</u> responsible.
- *Nobody* <u>is</u> leaving.
- *Everybody* <u>has</u> arrived.

Rule 5: Use a singular verb for nouns that imply more than one person but are considered singular, such as *class, committee, family, group,* and *team*.

- The *group* <u>is</u> ready for therapy.
- The *committee* <u>has</u> made a decision.

Rule 6: Use a singular verb when *either* or *neither* is the subject.

- *Neither* of us <u>was</u> aware of what happened.
- Either of them <u>is</u> culpable.

Rule 7: The following expressions do not change the number of the subject or the verb: *with*, *together with*, *including*, *accompanied by*, *in addition to*, *along with*, and *as well*.

- The sailor, *along with* his mates, <u>is</u> excited for the trip. (The subject is *the sailor* [singular], so the verb is also singular.)
- The cofounders, *together with* an outside supporter, <u>are</u> pleased with the outcome. (The subject is *the cofounders* [plural], so the verb is also plural.)

Rule 8: The expression *the number* is followed by a singular verb; the expression *a number* is followed by a plural verb.

- *The number* of participants required <u>is</u> substantial. (Singular)
- *A number* of attendees <u>are</u> being honored today. (Plural)

Rule 9: Use a singular verb with sums of money or periods/durations of time.

- The *$20* <u>is</u> for a parking fee.
- *Ten years* <u>is</u> a long time to continue a study.

Rule 10: The verb agrees with what follows *there is*, *there are*, *here is*, and *here are* when a sentence begins with one of these terms.

- There <u>is</u> *a question*. (Singular)
- There <u>are</u> *many participants*. (Plural)
- Here <u>is</u> *an example*. (Singular)
- Here <u>are</u> *a few examples*. (Plural)

Sentence Fragments

Sentence fragments are incomplete sentences. Fragments should always be avoided in academic writing, even if the fragment follows clearly from the preceding main clause. For example:

- The study took longer than expected. Which is why we ended it early. (The second sentence is a fragment. If read alone, we are left asking, "What was ended early?")

Possible revisions to make the fragment a complete sentence:

1. The study took longer than expected, which is why we ended it early. (*It* now clearly refers back to *the study*.)

2. We ended the study early because it took longer than expected. (*It* now clearly refers back to *the study*.)

Many fragment sentences are written as main clauses but lack a main verb or a subject. A fragment sentence with no subject often begins with a preposition. An example for each case is given here. Again, avoid fragment sentences to make only complete sentences in academic writing.

A fragment with **no main verb:**

- A study with three independent variables.

  Possible revisions to make the fragment a complete sentence by adding a main verb:

  1. A study <u>was conducted</u> with three independent variables.

  2. Participants <u>completed</u> a study with three independent variables.

A fragment with **no subject:**

- For making the most of a difficult situation got Jim promoted.

  Possible revisions to make the fragment a complete sentence:

  1. Making the most of a difficult situation got Jim promoted. (Removed *for* [the preposition].)

  2. Jim got promoted for making the most of a difficult situation. (The sentence was rearranged so that it ends with the prepositional phrase.)

Dangling Modifiers

A dangling modifier is a word or phrase that modifies a word not clearly stated in a sentence. Many strategies can be used to correct sentences with dangling modifiers. The key is to ask "who" did an action. Two examples are given here.

- Dangling modifier: Having completed all preparations, the door was opened. [Who completed all preparations? "Having completed" expresses action, but the doer is not the door (the subject of the main clause): A door does not finish preparations. The phrase before the comma, then, is a dangling modifier.]

To correct the sentence we can name the doer of the action as the subject of the main clause:

- Having completed all preparations, the researcher opened the door. [In this sentence, the doer of the action (completing all preparations) seems logically to be the researcher (identified in the main clause). The sentence is good, and it does not have a dangling modifier.]

Alternatively, we can combine the phrase and main clause into one sentence without a comma:

- The researcher opened the door after completing all preparations. [Again, the doer of the action (completing all preparations) seems logically to be the researcher in this sentence. The sentence is good, and it does not have a dangling modifier.]

Many other strategies can be used to clarify "who" is doing the action. In all, you should be able to clearly identify "who" is doing an action described in a sentence. If the doer of an action is unclear in a sentence, then revise the sentence to make this clear.

Parallel Sentence Structure

A parallel structure implies that the sentence uses consistent words and phrases. Here we give two rules to help you identify and use parallel sentence structure.

Rule 1: Do not mix forms of elements or words in a list, such as elements or words ending in *-ing, -ly,* and *-ed.*

- INCORRECT: The athletics test involved throwing, blocking, tackling, <u>and making maneuvers</u>. (Not parallel; the last word changes the *-ing* form.)
- CORRECT: The athletics test involved throwing, blocking, tackling, <u>and maneuvering</u>. (Parallel; all words in the set end in the same *-ing* form.)

Rule 2: A parallel structure that begins with clauses must keep on with clauses.

INCORRECT: Participants were told to arrive 15 minutes early for the study, to complete all forms, and <u>that they should </u>dress appropriately. (Not parallel; the last underlined clause changes pattern or form.)

CORRECT: Participants were told to arrive 15 minutes early for the study, to complete all forms, and <u>to</u> dress appropriately. (Parallel; all clauses have the same form or pattern.)

Spelling

In this final section of the guide we will review commonly misspelled words in English. Students often take spelling for granted because Microsoft® Office software includes a spell-check feature. However, many words can be improperly used in a sentence yet be spelled correctly. For example, consider "She was *hosing* around" versus "She was horsing around." In the first sentence, an *r* is missing from the word *horsing*; however, both spellings are a correct word. As another common example consider "He came *form* nowhere" versus "He came *from* nowhere." In the first sentence, the order of *o* and *r* is reversed in the word *from*; the spellings of each word, however, are correct—it is the meaning of each word that is different. Mistakes that are not caught by spell-check also often occur when we drop or forget to add letters to the beginning (e.g., *[un]necessary, [mis]used*) or ending (e.g., *common[ly], play[s], grant[ed], no[t]*) of otherwise correctly spelled words. It can be easy to miss or overlook mistakes such as those given as examples here. Make sure you carefully proofread your work before you submit it to try to catch theses types of silly and unnecessary mistakes.

Also a concern is misspellings caused by a misunderstanding of the meanings of words used in a sentence. Grammatical and spelling errors often occur because we improperly use words we think are being used correctly. Common examples include *that* versus *which, accept* versus *except,* and *then* versus *than.* Mistakes in misusing these words can be difficult to overcome because the author can often "think" the use of these words is correct when in fact the use is wrong. To help clarify some of the most common grammatical and spelling errors in English, the following table lists 26 words that are commonly misused. How each word is used in a sentence (as a noun, verb, etc.) and definitions for each word are given in the table, along with examples, if needed, to further clarify the correct meanings and uses of the words.

Words	Meaning
accept/except	*accept:* (verb) to receive something; to join, consent, or enter into agreement *except:* (verb) to exclude or leave out; (preposition) not including; other than
affect/effect	*affect:* (noun) emotion or desire; (verb) to influence or act upon *effect:* (noun) the result of a consequence, action; (verb) to bring about or implement
afterward/ afterword	*afterward:* (adverb) at a later time; subsequently *afterword:* (noun) a concluding section in a book or work
already/all ready	*already:* (adverb) by an implied or specified time; now; so soon; e.g., It is break already [by this time]. *all ready:* (adjective) completely prepared; e.g., The study was all ready [completely prepared] to begin.
alright/all right	*alright:* (adjective, adverb) to be satisfactory or acceptable; e.g., The evidence is alright [satisfactory]. *all right:* (adjective, adverb) without doubt; accurate or acceptable; e.g., The evidence is all right [accurate]. *Note: In English, alright is not widely accepted as a word; so avoid its use.
altogether/all together	*altogether:* (adverb) entirely; completely; e.g., The event was altogether [entirely] successful. *all together:* (adverb) collectively; at the same time; e.g., We completed the study all together [collectively].
among/between	*among:* (preposition) surrounded by; being a member in a larger set *between:* (adverb) at, into, or across a space separating two points in position or time
amount/number	*amount:* (noun) a quantity; (verb) a total when added to together *number:* (noun) an arithmetic or countable value; (verb) to comprise or amount to
assure/ensure/ insure	*Assure:* (verb) to make secure or certain; to put the mind at rest *Ensure:* (verb) to make secure or certain; to put the mind at rest [assure, ensure: same meanings] *Insure:* (verb) to guarantee persons or property from risk
breath/breathe	*breath:* (noun) An ability to inhale and exhale air, oxygen, etc.; exhalation that can be seen, smelled, or heard *breathe:* (verb) to take air into the lungs and exhale it; to be or seem to be alive
cite/site	*cite:* (noun) a citation; (verb) to quote

Words	Meaning
	site: (noun) a spatial location or position of interest; (verb) to fix or build [something] in a particular location
compliment/ complement	*compliment:* (noun) a polite express of praise; (verb) to praise or congratulate
	complement: (noun) something that completes or makes perfect; (verb) to enhance or improve in some way; to make perfect
counsel/council	*counsel:* (noun) advice; (verb) to give [someone] advice
	council: (noun) a body or assembly of persons convened for consultation, deliberation, or advice
everyone/every one	*everyone:* (pronoun) every person [in a group]; e.g., On this day, <u>everyone</u> [every person] agreed.
	every one: (pronoun) each one; The awardee thanked <u>every one</u> [each person] at the ceremony.
	*Note: In English, everyone and everybody can be used interchangeably and mean the same thing.
few/little	*few:* (noun) a minority of people; (adjective) a small number of
	little: (adjective) small in size, amount, or degree; (adverb) to a small extent
its/it's	*its:* (pronoun) forms the possessive case of it; belonging to it, e.g., The board had <u>its</u> meeting.
	it's: contraction of "it is"; Note: Using APA style, always write out "it is."
lose/loose	*lose:* (verb) to be deprived of; cease or fail to retain
	loose: (verb) to set free; release; (adjective) not firmly in place; able to be detached
many/much	*many:* (noun) the majority of people; (adjective) a large number of people
	much: (adverb) to a great extent; (adjective) a large amount [in quantity]
mute/moot	*mute:* (noun) a person who cannot speak; (verb) to reduce or soften sound; (adjective) temporarily speechless
	moot: (verb) to raise or suggest for discussion; (adjective) a subject of debate, dispute, or uncertainty
past/passed	*past:* (noun) a previous time; (adjective) gone by and no longer exists; (adverb) to pass from one side [of something] to another; (preposition) on a further side of [something]
	passed: (verb) move or lie in a specific direction or position
principle/principal	*principle:* (noun) a fundamental truth, rule, or belief that governs individual/group behavior
	principal: (noun) person with highest authority or importance; (adjective) most important
that/which	*that:* (pronoun, adjective, adverb, conjunction) used to identify key information about something or someone; e.g., It was in this study <u>that</u> researchers first discovered . . . [*That* allows for a clear transition and flow of key information in the sentence.]

(Continued)

(Continued)

Words	Meaning
	which: (pronoun) used to specify information related to something previously mentioned or from a definite set; e.g., The landmark study, <u>which</u> was conducted in the 1950s . . . [The information that follows which relates back to the study]; e.g., There are so many classes I like; <u>which</u> do I choose? [*Which* refers to a choice based on a definite set or availability of classes.] *Note: Which is usually preceded by a comma; that does not take a comma.
then/than	*then:* (adverb) at a given time; after that; next; soon afterward *than:* (conjunction) introduces a comparison; expresses an exception or contrast
there/they/their/ they're	*there:* (adverb) in, at, or to a place or position; e.g., <u>Go there</u> to take your turn. *they:* (pronoun) something or someone previously mentioned or easily identified; e.g., <u>They</u> get a turn. *their:* (adjective) forms the possessive case of *they*; e.g., It is <u>their</u> turn. *they're:* contraction of "they are"; Note: Using APA style, always write out "they are."
who/whose/who's	*who:* (pronoun) used to identify a person or people; introduces a clause that gives greater detail about a person or people; e.g., <u>Who</u> has the next turn?; e.g., The student <u>who</u> went out of turn. *whose:* (adjective) forms the possessive case of *who*; e.g., <u>Whose</u> turn is it? *who's:* contraction of "who is"; Note: Using APA style, always write out "who is."
you/your/you're	*you:* (pronoun) refers to the person who is being addressed; e.g., <u>You</u> have a degree. *your:* (adjective) forms the possessive case of you; e.g., It is <u>your</u> degree. *you're:* contraction of "you are"; Note: Using APA style, always write out "you are."

Answers to Key Term Word Searches and Crossword Puzzles

Chapter 1

```
Q P Z Z W E C E Y F R L G O E B U D G E N C R Q V E R
O U A V S C I E N T I F I C M E T H O D J A E Q K K I
B P A C M S J K N W M T I A A E X A B P A L K T Y C N
Q A E L K W A K E G V N H S U L F E A H U Q I X I P Y
F F S R I B Y O Q R U O O Z C B D O O Y T P Z V K R
W L E I A T Z L L U A Q V N C I W G T P H E P M U Q V
I H Q B C T A C A Z F T X N W A E U G O O I J A N R N
Z M U S X R I T P S H B I B W K K N Q T R E P N D A G
C V A O E Y E O I O I L X O T L A X C H I M V T Z J X
J X N X Y R D S N V P N N Y N H O P N E T C T I G R Y
P M T T W G G D E A E U T H T A V T H S Y Y E A Y I N
H W I E M J A A A A L R L U N D L V X I G S F R V P S
D C T N H V D T G P R D E A I O B I Z S A P C E H B B
R S A A D D W U S E P C E S T T W O S J D N P A J S I
M Z T C X G L M O M W L H F E I I C N M H E V X W J Y
U L I I R Q E A Y C P F I S I A O O S E V M D I P V X
G J V T A S Q G Q G H I O E B N R N N V V P S K K Z Y
M K E Y X A L J N K T B R L D A I C C O K I E Y W C E
O K R I I M N R Q X W E V A C R Z T H S R R J V R A
V S E J S P A P C A P S C E P J E M I E H I A D C I S
U M S R Z L F A I L Y V X R E V H S H O S C G Q Q M B
F H E Z H E C N N B R C T I Q D R T E B N I H G G U
J U A M T X C Q G W L H I N W P O H P A A S R V T H X
C X R C L U K K I B W Z P T A P U U L T R M X P K U Q
V I C I L K B M I D R D P U Y O B V A D N C O Q P G M
Q E H E P X R P B U L W H Z P A D Q F A D H W W K A
Z Z K Q I Q R U G W V B E T H P D X J C O D Z L E O V
```

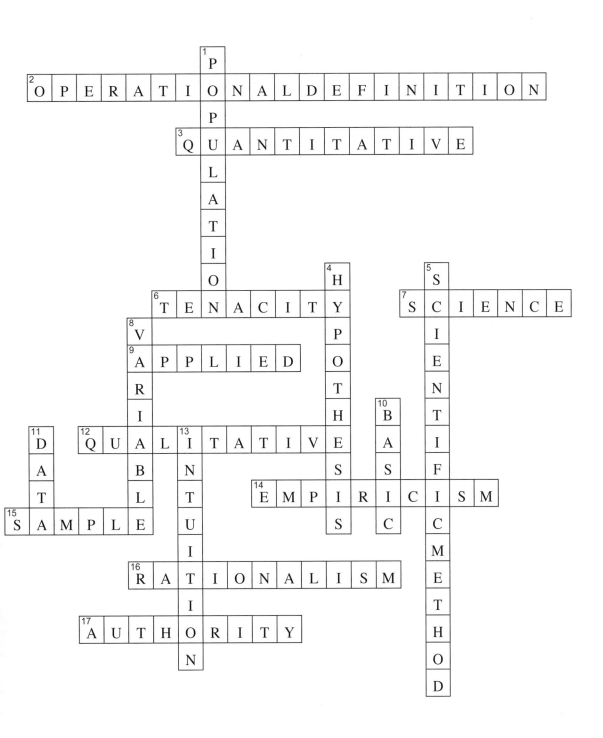

Chapter 2

```
U  P  N  E  T  C  G  L  Q  U  O  A  L  J  V  F  D  R  Q  K  M  E  B  D  M  Q  Z  C  O
U  F  M  F  V  W  A  D  L  G  L  G  R  S  E  C  O  N  D  A  R  Y  S  O  U  R  C  E  L
D  D  U  G  X  K  D  U  X  J  H  A  L  N  Y  I  W  E  I  K  E  B  G  U  L  B  O  A  R
E  Z  S  H  R  M  Z  L  L  Z  U  R  U  O  K  B  R  E  A  E  A  R  I  M  N  S  O  Y  N
D  T  V  F  B  T  G  W  F  N  A  V  M  X  N  G  E  U  P  A  V  W  P  E  X  U  G  P  F
U  C  Q  E  S  P  Q  N  R  M  L  N  L  T  B  Q  I  A  X  Q  B  N  N  E  E  E  C  O  I
C  O  N  Y  N  L  V  X  T  B  Z  F  O  Q  J  T  G  O  J  B  F  P  Y  L  T  S  J  O  L
T  N  P  E  E  R  R  E  V  I  E  W  E  D  J  O  U  R  N  A  L  A  C  A  T  N  B  J  E
I  F  W  L  K  M  Q  S  M  B  X  F  M  M  B  Z  G  M  G  Y  I  I  R  U  U  G  P  U  D
V  I  N  A  C  H  H  E  I  K  S  C  T  T  H  M  J  C  P  Y  T  T  O  E  B  D  R  J  R
E  R  N  E  I  J  P  V  C  Z  R  K  Q  B  G  X  H  B  V  R  S  I  I  S  U  R  H  H  A
R  M  W  D  O  E  R  E  Y  C  W  M  A  C  F  Y  Z  U  A  L  H  F  H  N  C  K  Q  S  W
E  A  L  Y  T  L  A  H  A  M  J  G  Y  U  F  X  K  T  A  C  W  T  J  B  Y  L  D  J  E
A  T  X  P  R  I  M  A  R  Y  S  O  U  R  C  E  X  N  A  D  C  H  Q  W  P  A  E  K  R
S  I  Q  G  F  G  P  H  C  Q  H  H  D  T  G  E  O  B  V  Y  E  E  M  S  B  H  B  A  P
O  O  F  X  W  B  A  D  G  R  Q  E  T  U  T  I  J  E  L  Q  E  O  J  G  S  M  Q  Y  R
N  N  V  N  A  O  A  X  M  P  F  A  S  L  T  S  Q  Y  D  E  A  R  J  C  B  L  R  I  O
I  A  Q  C  G  P  C  C  E  W  U  I  L  A  P  E  M  F  Q  B  K  Y  Z  Z  P  U  M  J  B
N  L  U  R  U  E  T  R  W  C  F  U  M  W  E  T  O  O  H  D  B  V  C  Y  W  G  T  J  L
G  S  J  A  G  U  L  B  N  W  F  R  P  K  W  T  C  W  P  H  U  X  H  B  L  X  L  G  E
M  T  B  B  R  W  I  Y  W  T  I  H  B  M  Z  T  E  Y  Q  D  A  G  J  V  S  W  C  D  M
G  R  J  S  H  C  D  O  Y  F  L  I  T  E  R  A  T  U  R  E  R  E  V  I  E  W  W  Z
J  A  S  T  I  A  B  W  N  P  A  B  P  U  E  F  J  I  Y  E  Q  L  L  I  W  A  G  W  B
F  T  T  R  P  U  W  O  V  O  K  V  W  R  V  L  W  C  T  L  F  B  M  R  L  U  A  F  Z
D  E  H  A  L  L  C  W  D  F  H  C  F  G  L  S  E  Z  L  D  K  J  K  W  X  L  P  J  I
R  G  C  C  N  S  J  U  C  Z  I  P  U  B  L  I  C  A  T  I  O  N  B  I  A  S  C  J  C
C  Y  Q  T  I  X  S  E  W  I  C  X  F  U  L  L  T  E  X  T  D  A  T  A  B  A  S  E  Z
W  M  Q  D  J  P  F  U  O  C  I  R  E  A  P  Q  W  N  S  E  K  H  H  Q  L  Q  H  X  W
V  I  N  D  U  C  T  I  V  E  R  E  A  S  O  N  I  N  G  O  M  D  X  T  N  D  K  X  Q
```

Chapter 3

```
R H M C A F A N Q E T S Y H P I W Q W E Q A R O E G A F
F M V Q R F J T R W M I B E H V E U K S F R Z C W K N J
B P K P I I Q E Y E V C R D R F L N J Z U X N M X R I B
C R L H J N S J S S K O L D O A T D N P E J R X N N R
N V V A K G M K N W Z E B N C F R B O X C B B K C C F Z
D Y W M G Q E O B G Q V A O F O Z I R I O W R C H H O P
Z E I D U I I Z C E Y D T R P E T M F I W Z M K F Q R J
R Z B G J T A G N D N O D E C A D E E S C I O C O D M S
F H J R P K T R L U R E R X C H N E E M L A C J M G E F
F T S E I J N I I P R T F I N E E A R E A T T A Z N D J
F A C Q N E X S H S N E L I B S S T N A K U T I E O C V
U E S I L I F C Q O M P M X T I L K H K T M T V O G O D
D C Z S T S R I M P E S V B I A A F D I K E A P N N U
N T R D E A E L N R J W G U E C N C E X C Z Y Z P K S X
Z Z Y V E N E G B G I F E W S R B A U Q E S P T K D E M
O W K S I B T B W B E T H R J R G D L C P K E D S N N V
E V E K X A R E M G V T L F W Q X C C Y A M L N W O T P
W R T Y E N L T W W T L Q N C Y C Y O H S K U B O Y U E
F P C J E Z D U P L I C A T I O N E D D F I F L H X C E
A N O N Y M I T Y C O V E R S T O R Y E E F S Q W M U R
Q X M M F J J M G R E S P E C T F O R P E R S O N S Y R
F Q T R J U S T I C E I Q J T Z R P B E A B W I P U R E
Q T X N M I T O I R B G W F P F M J F Z Z V T N D I Q V
K Q M W G D M V W E X E M U I D J H C W A Q V E Y G Q I
V E P S C I E N T I F I C I N T E G R I T Y W F L Y X E
Z Y R Y X L T W H M Z U P M O L R R K R V C Y N X F C W
D B X S E W I D A C O N F I D E N T I A L I T Y K V R U
V N R H X Y E I Y I A M E P X X V M O A F D M C X N Q F
```

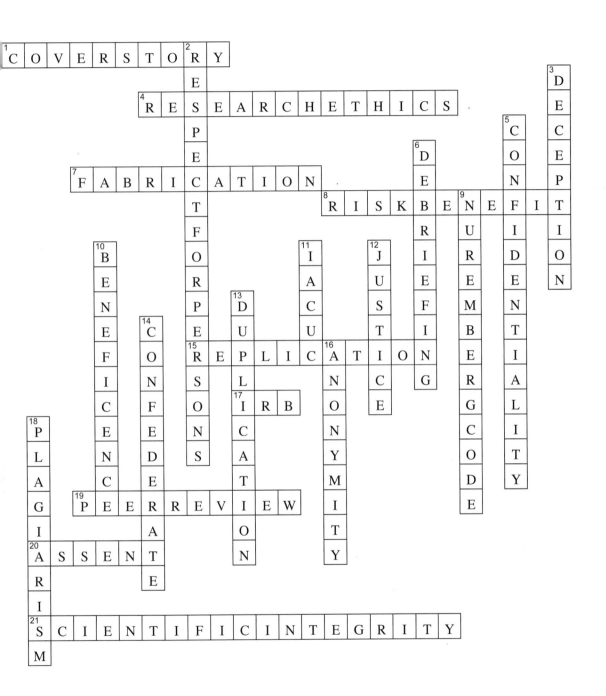

Chapter 4

```
N U C W I F H M C O I W L C R L G F U B I W C G G X C B C D S I X K Z F X L R
U B Z O G N F X K V N S B Y P N F W S I U X Y X K K E V G K M A C U F H C W W
Z O O K N L T B R P N X O C I D S T X F J T J T V A I Z G B B L T Q K T G E I
Y W O B W S A E M I P R S D M R C H E U I C U X M S L F W S F F Q G Y X L F G
Q G R A G S T P R H O O O J S E J E R V W Q H D I Y I V L P D T X Q L B O L Y
E N F V T R Z R N R W C N T F A L M I Q Z F Z V U Y N M N A I T O J A K C R A
G R R C G C A T U V A J I F E B V T A E U Y J Z K W G E J N K M Y I E V L B K
J P P F F Q D T H C F T E N A S C H O U Q A M I U O E Q J W S D R V Y N O S A
I J E Y X U R M I C T Y E I T A T X Y U Z M L Z U W F W W V O A X W Q Y D F G
B E G O D Q E C S O C V R R E E N R H N B L W I P P F N Z Z V C H C Q X T C Z
C Y O G P K W I O N S A A R R B R P E W V T Z X T G E D B E O F G K L S E Z I
T H E S M U J W A S V C T L P E X N M T D I R K Z A C V V N P W C X I J T R X
A T K E Z J P T L S C N A E I I L O A R E N V R O C T I A U K E N Y D V L E G
G S C A Q B C S U M A A B L C D Z I F L I S Z S T E T I L L H P T F Z C X L J
C C V F H E H O O P R A P L E I I J A X C O T P H A V N V C I I S X A X L I K
Z M A A P X U U I X K D P R K C L T V B J O T R T E Z K N E D D E H W Z V A O
F I H X G N X C E V C I Q H F H O G Y I I T N I E G J O B I V D I M F M I B R
X F E G I A I D V V I S S I L Y N N S I L T S L L I S L M E A P T Q J C I D
A H X T X T E E A D N C E E H T F S S O T N I Q I T I A R L E J R U Y Q I L I
E K N M R N B M L V T R T N K O L L F T A L B T A S V A B A V Z V I H J Y I N
R O Q A F H C A U S E E S S K C O Y B U R P E L Y E T A B Y K J J T A R Y T A
C O P B M W Q N A D R T C I I F O V Q Z A U U I C T I E D I Z A P A H B I Y L
S D D J O Z S D I O V E I T Y S R N V W G P C A X R V U N P L G L Z Y D L O S
D W D V G G R C I U A V H I M U E M V I I U F T A U T H A C J I T P Y S R E C
U N W X X Q W H O B L A U V P Z F B K N E J I V A S D A H M Y Q T C U Q L J A
G U M S E H S A N L S R B I R M F S A R U I W O T D Y H V T Y B V Y G L X U L
O B R G J J Q R A E C I Y T N W E M P E W L L O G V C K W X K M N U F M N X E
B A E V R Z L A P B A A L Y B R C K Z L N F L Y C C M M J C X Z O W I X I W A
P X S A T H R C P L L B M D N F T S G X B I T Q K N J Q W J X M Z K V J D
M K I P C K K T R I E L P Q O I Z L S W P A C O N T E N T V A L I D I T Y H L
D R R X I A Y E E N E E E J R E X P E R I M E N T E R B I A S P N X C E O O F
H Z C E R X M R H D A Z W G J X A X C M U L Q C H D E S I B W L A K O T V K C
J E T Y O Y Z I E S G P A R T I C I P A N T R E L U C T A N C E L H B I G E I
P H Y A J T V S N T I V W K R R R V P F B F W Y U Y K A V K K V S O R P M G C
I W O B F K L T S U C I N R O M J Q B B F F B G Q W B Q E Q T L C K H O A H D
F Z E L Q V R I I D G R A N G E E F F E C T H S G S Z B C W D U A N L W B J Y
M M U U H S F C O Y D V R B P S P F G W T D X O Z M T H X S F H L G W Z V Y C
W F X J H J V S N V A N K X J O Q Z K X B T L F C S N Y V G C X E B L E Y K Z
A E D Z E P D J B C R I T E R I O N R E L A T E D V A L I D I T Y C H P J C M
```

Chapter 5

```
F P E F L I R E L E U W F W U C M X S H G P G B B C J B A S E B F O P H
O T H C N X E D Q T A P N B L E T S S N Q T C G W G Y P A E S C W Y Q D
S U Q A E D Q W K V C B O Q Z X S B I R Z L S N O X I I F H P U Y S D Z
A I X P K S U B J E C T N Q D A G L E J T B O K A X B R C W A Y C A H V
M P O Q N O A B N J W J P A I N P B E D N I W N F G T M D M K I F M M B
P X H V P D K U G A F C X B I M D A H C T Z T F N B K P F E I A Y P Y R
L H F M G L J B M N X D E L A H U L G A X F P I Y U G R T R X S X L L P
I S D O A Z V Y K Z P S P S V G K E L W H I L W Y N Y I O N T Y K I R O
N C S W H E W H J C N M E X R Q H U I C M P C F I Q T R O T Z C C N V P
G K Q L I C D D F O A C P C V E P F I N M A Z L R X R G W Q J B L G W U
W F C W D A Z M P S N G W E H O P Z D A H F P T V E F G L O O U W Y B
I T Y G O A V S A E X Z U C P X J R S J Q M U N D R A T B Q U S S I N S
T A B M T N E T I N E V X E F V U O E L A U K R X M U J R W E T T A T
H R T B G R O N L S T A L J I J Q G P S H A A X L D X G R E K E X L E H H R
O G C S N U E I H J A B H U B H Q J Y C E D N J A J F C Y O I E R R K A
U E Y O Q V G J K K I M S K H K I T H B N N P H G L B Q V T F C S E Q T
T I N W N P M W X S Q Q P I Q H I F V A U Z T O L A F L M F V T A P O I
R P A O S B Y G S L Z J L M L H O T H D C E A M B Y F H T Q I M L S F
E O C J F Q F E G F J I X E I P H S N A X M T R T V F E Y P J O P A M I
P P Z H C V C E S I O O U B C N L S V E M N H G P I X H D K K N L C K E
L U K F L C F X B A H E A M X S G E Z Z S Z U G Q E V W N J K B I E D D
A L O B A H U T I T M B L M N A Y F R S T A T O P R R E J R B I N M M R
C A H P D P C V B C O P G K K B K Z R A Q P M O A M Y V S O T A G E G A
E T T G Y U N B E R S Z L V O T F H N A N A I P K A C Q R A Q S Y N J N
M I Y V E Z S K P E M K M I Q M W O G E M D L J L M V B I Y M C X T N D
E O L U K I B N K G K I X D N J K N U C K E O I T E X M G B O P K O O O
N N S R Q A O L T R E N A U G G K I Y E Q K I M D B T N F L B Y L T Y M
T A G D S N D Y B C N Q U H B L E C D B O U O S S M H T F A S I J E K S
M O J V O N D T E Q R D M T Y S Z R L I N Y A N O A Q F E P A R W Z B A
L D V I Y E E Q O D V J H N G I U F R Q K Q F V V Z M N R S Z N L A M
M C J B M C C G X V E Q I W H Q G J T O H B C N A J M P F G T S D J U P
W P A R T I C I P A N T I G F B J F T S R V Y W P T J Z L S N E N G P L
K I C K C H D V M M Z F M V L L J B P B P B Z Q A I Z N M I I V L G J I
L H Z U Z A N W T J C Q H J L U K Q G B Q O K S D E J H V X N Y S X O N
R C P R O B A B I L I T Y S A M P L I N G Z A P J S O Y C C V G O J G
I X W L T U U U B B D C S Y S T E M A T I C S A M P L I N G A F W U G C
```

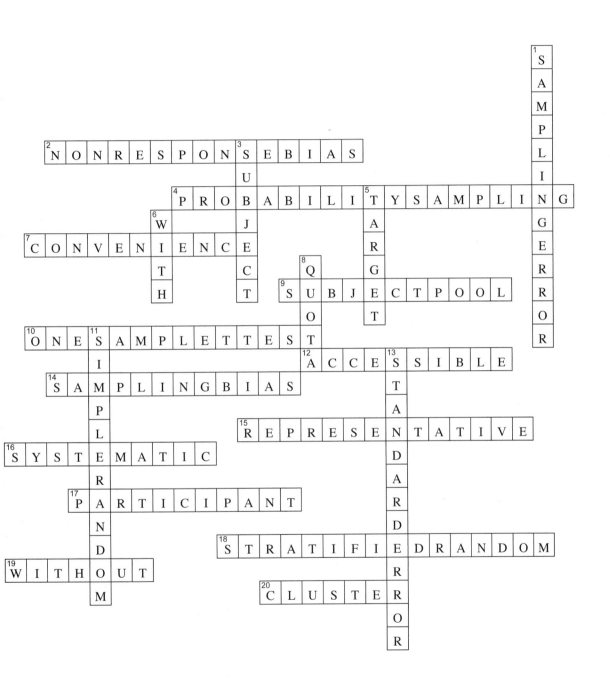

Chapter 6

T I K D M A R U R A B S J E E D D W A I S P P P C Z C T X D K C X N W Y Z Y U J C Q J U
D S V G H H S P Z C V P W C K E B B C J A Y B S V Z A F R Y I L O F O X A N V N Q X J Y
U F N P D Y R H H Z D G X R P V C I Y L J Q K N X Y J J J Q D I F Y X P Y C H N G M T H
W R O F R Q O F Q J T W A J M R P Q X F M D R K N Y C H T X T V K F Y B K U G Z S I R P
F D Q U F H O U E M J M Z G L N F Q H M N G T A C G Q A Q I P U A Y T Y T I Q I D R H Q
S I X G F I E L D E X P E R I M E N T U E U E E G X X R R Q X Q Z V A F S X L I L A I C
Q O N J Y L X Q Z Q E O J B F M N J O U R M M N M X F T Q N A K D W F E J A L F J N I O
U U F D H F G T E G C B S Q J H N F K S E N O J A P T U G G S E H B D G E A L J N D C D
A T K S E C O T C B Z I H H T T N Q D H O I B R V A O P N E A D I H M R V S L Z B O F E
S C Z G C P R L P U F U K P W O L T I T Y S K S M B R C C K F C O L N Z D J F M M M P
I O H J R X E W W M W D V P C T C D I A R F C U B E P N A N F R D A O A T Z M O O S H E
I M S N J G N N Y N K K H Q H C R I T N S C O M A I E E G L A E T I P P N D J Q T E T N
N E K S W E D Y D G Z M H Z A A R N S A B E O D V R F I O E V N T W L I N C R R A L O D
D V Q F H N K S T E J R Z Y W T E N F C N B W U E L S L S Q E A X E F J I A M N C E K E
E A E M Y S N L T K N L Y O T M M T Q E H H K F B E X E G M L E L G X C Q S R I M C V N
P L P C K U U Y E D V T T A U D J W G Y V H F R D Z R Y I U E D S I Q R E N V D D T G T
E I Q O O I R L L L H N V R D S O O O R W I Q H Z L U R P H L K O L D Z F W S S H I X V
N D W E G L P S L T O H T A D U R L C N D Z C L A W E O Q L U B O X P I H E D A R O G A
D I P P V V O G N I O S R R R E G U S L V R U T U P P Y K H S E J T H I T G X Q O N C R
E T B M Q A H G S I N M F T T I J X A V A W N P X B I H U U L B H U O L V Y Q N V B K I
N Y Z C S E G S I I Y R V E R L A U K E V E O E S V J S W L A T Z C W Z C U V T C F W A
T Y P Y W M E J X C V Q H O O R D B S U M E Q V D X E N W M L D B N A P J D H M E V D B
V E G G O R A N G F A I A S C I R E L I J K A H T K X F Z Z K V H U Y U B R W F X Y N L
A E B R G F Z T J K T L T E V Q R A R E R E H O M O G E N E O U S A T I R I T I O N E E
R F Y E L A R M U G Y C V I F L A E X X A K T Q M B E E Q Q L V I R N E B L T U B S W C
I R R N C A V B C R E J D A A N P R E X P E R I M E N T I P G K Z U O J F L Z L F A N Z
A R A D D Q B M D F A N W T L X N F Q N I S L N Q V V B R U W V S J Q X R Y R K J W F W
B T X N P H W O F E I T N N E I K P E V A W W Q F C K L P K H F V L D V V Z Y B E R Z Q
L R W F D V I E R N E E I I Y B D I N T E R N A L V A L I D I T Y I H I Q F O U Q F C E
E O O S P O G S W A M P S O T G C I H S L X A H U E X P E R I M E N T A L M O R T A L I
O C K Y W N M E T I T A R Q N T X A T F R T K K G I G Y O H X L C N W D Y E O W M G T W
B V U N I X H S R O U O R V P T Y M E Y N P N X H Z S G F S L L H O Y Z H X P S F A M Z
U T D T U K Y E A Q R D H M T I U V E B T J G M F G O Q N I Z Q L G R E U I T Z Z K Z
O Q S V Z J J P M E M X Y E Y I B X I M Q P O I Z M X N I M U N D V S O R J L G I A B S L
P E P B O X Z H R N P X E D E I N N D V H L L Q Q F D G W O I D G P R N A D M B Q W I L
T T J J E N H U J A T L I F R X G P F A G D Z A E U Q W D M J N G G N E J O G A Z H H K
Y E H N S X T L K P A L I M F I P E J D G C Q W Q U E X C E T D C Q R B D D U G F S K H
K L B I Q W Y G C N A U D N S E R E S E A R C H D E S I G N O A A E Z N H H T Y E P W F
K H C I W N B E K V I J W S G Y C T R D R M X Z Y L W F I K C T N O A U O L B P V F X Y
Z J B B I I I S L J B Y A Y W R R T A I X E J X E J N P F H Y A G R V D J J U P O H A W
H E F C R E P A D O E M U J Q H G E S L M W D H P D H U P Q D S N Q C C J P G Q X S F C
V Z K E H V N L N M O G G C O N T R O L H E K E T I A U E N K F P N I S L L J Z L M A S
R V L K I R N X L D J O O T Q U H F B U X G N K R E Q C U W K N W A W D W H F J C E W B
S D F F E N C T N F P V J B C I H Z Q H N Z L T O B W M Z I S F B L V E H L K W S X B B
S A C T F I Y A S B O J M S G H J Y H V A Y I H G L V T W Y M F I S X Z D M O K D S D R
C L X F E B R S X M U R G Y K Z D R S P A L G G K W X O C V W F T L Z I F K H T P A Y H
R E I Y N O N E X P E R I M E N T A L R E S E A R C H D E S I G N U M E H P P G G S F J
R X O C R E Z F G P C J F E J W I C B C I Z Y G L F X I S E T N D Q Y A C F L W U Z H M

Across

1. EXPERIMENTALREALISM
4. QUASIINDEPENDENTVARIABLE
5. MUNDANEREALISM
6. CONFOUND
7. NONEXPERIMENTAL
10. FIELDEXPERIMENT
11. TEMPORAL
12. ECOLOGICAL
16. EXPERIMENT
17. CONTROL
18. MATURATION
19. RANDOMIZATION
20. HISTORYEFFECT
21. DEPENDENTVARIABLE
22. RANDOMASSIGNMENT

Down

2. POPULATION
3. INDEPENDENTVARIABLE
8. EXPERIMENTAL
9. LEVELS
13. OUTCOME
14. RESEARCHDESIGN
15. TESTINGEFFECT

Chapter 7

```
Z Q T Z J S P K U L E H N G D C Y L V E I R B T X W H N J C Q B K J T C W Z V V T T Z
Y A D N Q Q T L V B R H X K Y D U E A D C A S E S T U D Y N O M J L F G W V J N F K F
T U V S O C F C B R Q K I N D I V I D U A L S A M P L I N G Y Q E E W G D G Z D H C G
E C J D L T S N A T U R A L S E T T I N G P H E N O M E N O L O G Y W J M F S M W X U
E I E G W S Y D H M S B I E K N U A R C H I V A L R E S E A R C H X F T P I U N X F W
L S Z U E C I T N K Q Q K V K Z M Y T G J A F J G F W V M W F C O L A U S G Y F I B V
Q F J L Y X E I B A T L Q R Q S F F J B Y E A N P F O E G P T W H R U Y R C C L W B U
U O I T T P A M M B S H J G A U A Z F S I Q I R O A O R T D C P H G L T T N J U L D D
A T X M S I C E P E C I N T E R V A L M E T H O D Q O I F X M E U A U G R Y S I S K O
Y B Q A B Y G S N M O U A Z X L C H Y V T F D D Z M S G L S V Q N C C S U D D C E F H
H Z U X O Z D A W Y J I F E R B C H R E W N Q M W O X V B B I A N V I Q S Z R O T W U
Q E B G A L G M W W K A B F B M P G S X L J I I P P E H J W T X I N G P T I G O V N V
N L C V P G S P J N M H B V A A R D K Y H M O E G A P W W N H Z N G T F W U M L K A N
M E T A A N A L Y S I S Y Q R F E B H G F P D Q M K P R E Y E D K Q B N O I B P P V J
K M V L S J I I B B X P O G U V R Q Y S F E T V H R Z T J Z D U Q C A V R A S K Z J I
Q S L B T U G N O P K X O P I J M E Q I V F I S Q Z N B I G V R K E E K T J G Z S R V
X T J W H K G G G N I N L R Q L R A Q I K Z X F Q O V S C R F A L I C B H U B N X T I
U R I A R R W B C E H T T G M C W N T U C B Z X C G T O B A G T R E D A I B S E H M W
N U L U O I P Q Q T G N T F N H P C N T E X E M G C M W F J P I K R U Z N U E L S F W
W C I N A G C T E O O B E N S A E P O D X N G H E S Z V A J S O M C M F E Q L Q G J S
U T W O L E L F Q C Y B T D C L T L Z P W D C F A P B V X S N N O G Z Z S J E X K I R
W U A B T J A E Q H A B F Z E J H U Y W S Y F Y C V V Q M F Z M B M T K S O C H W N U
B R Z T A M T O Z J D Z T S W D I K R U J E J Y M S I C W H F E D H C S C H T H P P Q
V E Z R V H H P R L K F N C U Z U W W A O O V T B E M O F N T T E M B N B B I N W S H
V D J U Z G W A G E P E V E N T S A M P L I N G H M T R R K X H M M E Y Q Z V Y L H H
K O Y S D W F R M B D V G G S M Q V E M H I I K M J E H M C H O Y U U H C V E I I R H
V B C I M J I T L Y O Q L P K P L S T O Z K S U G W N G O W A D K C J V J H S R X E M
H S K V L A R I E B L R O J W X V F K F D J W T O R Z Q P D Y T Q Y D V P M U A Q M Q
X E D E F Q W C A O T I Y Y B V E A W Y K Z R P I O L O B E W J E Q Z D Y A R G W R R
C R W O Q T A I G B K P F J A F G P H D S M T I L C Y N Y I K D S G R R M N V Z M M N
R V Z B O B Y P K T K D I U I M Q G M J D T J E I A O L M G D P F X O L R G I M P C B
J A M S Z M W A Z N E O T M S K F U C H N D S T C X T B G H H E Z C P R U Y V O K U K
W T B E U D N N Z K F F K Z K E Z L A S A N M B T K S E S T O A T B S X I G A Y Z Q Z
C I D R C E B T Q V X E A N O V R P S R K R I H E V P U N E P X N E P F V E L U T P M
I O J V S H F S A Y U W G T I L M S E M Q G X B P Q P J B C R R M X R L N L S Z R E S
Y N S A B J K A A W J B M W G M A A H P J B I B K U E R Y F Y V H Z S M S X I A B L Y
H O V T W F Z M A L N J A K G C X G I A K Z A L B X M P E X J M A H W N I V G C Y U I
D Z S I V Z G P R Z I L L T D V Z W S G G F O I N G F J Z P X E E T J J Y N X M G G D
V Q Z O S Y P L Q I U P Y R O W J L T A U N E P R Y V S B N H E W T I I V C I Q Q E J
H G Q N C U K I O K I N U L Q E P B O B F C M H R X O L X C L B P K H O F G O S N I Z
P I W F G B U N U I G F G C N M K F R H C E D A L S M Z M T B Z U U Y O N G B X M B N
P H L D H D W G Q H C U W G W T W R Y F Q L C X D D I N B B L Y L B M U D W H H O U F
N M T S C G B B Q M Y C G I K E C J G U U R Y C A M Q E U X O A K J T D Z K F U P A Y
```

1 P (down: PARTICIPANTOBSERVATION)

2 NATURALISTICOBSERVATION

5 ETHNOGRAPHY

7 METAANALYSIS

10 POWER

11 UNOBTRUSIVE

15 EFFECTSIZE

16 TIME

17 EVENT

19 INDIVIDUAL

20 QUALITATIVE

21 LATENCY

22 CONTENTANALYSIS

3 (down: ILLUSTRATING)

4 (down: NATURALSETTING)

6 (down: PHENOMENOLOGY)

8 (down: DETERMINISM)

9 (down: SELFREPORT)

12 (down: OBTRUSIVEWORTH)

13 (down: INTERVAL)

14 (down: EXPLORATIVE)

18 (down: DURATION)

Chapter 8

```
J D L D H B M G U N T C U Z D B R E S P O N S E R A T E V X D V Y Z Q L V S D G A R J S
Y Y A P O I F P O T A E U G J I L I R G S D P S P E Z A K T R R N R I V O V I O C V I G
V E T E V N T G U P P O S I T I V E C O R R E L A T I O N E Q O Z Q I W F E S U Y B P B
U V O J Y T P T T E Y J N G R J M Q A Q U U N T Q C M E T P I S V G G L J W Q S P W V F
N V L M L E K F L A K T F U M X T G J D Q R Y Q X N A H B T V R N J I V C S E D T B W V
G G K R E R G T I R Z T A K C W J C R O J N N C Z O F M A R E P V V T L U E C S A Z M T
W X T B A V V J E E C U Q I X F C H I L H N R Z R T I Z W F Y F N T A Y T W I E T O A C
X S I I V I R F R S E L I R Y O J M U L U T Q D Y I I T A Z Z R X P G A D Q F R B K H L
E Q D N M E O P V P L G G N H G I P F P X Y E T X L T L X T J W Q B X C E P Q M Z T V P
N W V A I W B W L O N H S O B L D E M P I R I C A L G E N E R A L I Z A T I O N O H J M
F X X F P E Q M A N C N P S B M Y X W I V L U R S S Y N R M D N I Y Y V W Z Q T V S I T
A X G E F R H Q I S R R Q V S T V N T R A K E P N P F D Z I C G N P I L V W N S T L D G
Q N H W G B Z J F E Z O G K T W S D J S E N Q D K Z R P S Z O O D V K K V E Q N K R D T
V V G N P I V H D S J D E S M O M C U G E G G Z E P D E T N I N N J H X I S I I Y H W A
W R L Y W A S S T E Q Y X J N D E A C G G H R X F X Z S D T F G V P C C V O B W E Z S K
G U K I X S L L A T I M Z F K C C E L Q H G B E J I J F A I I S Y A I H P K S M L V Z D
U X S U K A J G W Z H R R E O E O A S Y C H R Q S U V L L S C H G F R A S N M K Y O D J
M R T J X E R V K C L U Y G S H C N P L E J R O T S E H E B F T F I T I O J A K J Q P F
L I E F P E R N U S O E M R C I D N F S V S A W X R I D F Z X E O A I I A Z E T C T L B
L V D S V A M T Q E C R E S T O Z M P O P V Y Q R S H O C X O F D R T J Q B B Q N H I A
D J W G T X R U S N P V R E J N G Z O H U W K O I C Y J N C Q I V S V H F J L H O Z B N
F K L Q Q R A X A C E T R E S A T C W P K N C X R X N V N W B E E U G A V I X E G W F R
F G Z K K R I I U R A Q Y I L O M A V V F E D A W M Y O I R P U Y H N Z R S J F Y R V A
D R H R R T R C L O E L I X S A S U F V V C E V C L I G N V Q K A I Q W E I K K R B W N
S X C P Z A M V T H H V E O T X T W W I I S P R A T E A D D A W X G P L Q J A S B E T D
G Q L C V M D G T E G O J D P U J I T J E H B E A R S J E M V Z M X A S C A L B P X V O
D C Q O C F D U K D D Z P W O M D A O R N D O L R S I L U Q J L F C R J R T Z Q L A L M
H X C M H G W P O A B I B A S G G P Y N H Z E M I E E A R N F K S L F R V G J U J E A D
X C S K D B T W I E T R T O E E B E S F A R J D D R Q H B B R R W C K S H H F E R C F I
T T M N W Q K L F K L P L E N F V E E E R L A Q R I K K Q L A R P S Z E Z E J E H D P G
Z A K J C M J E S C G N W N M R P R R O Y T R A Y M U Y L L E R J S D I Y G N W I W J I
Z W A H I F I I F K S O O L U V B U C O P I B E I H H V O Z A Q S W A N C H O R S T C T
Q N L I N E A R R E G R E S S I O N V D P E E K S B M P P F P Z I I Y F S P S V V Y K D
Q H Q P O M Q R J Q U D H W B F O A D H L A K E H E I E T I D G R S S T L C H R D A Q I
M F D M P Z F G Z T T Y B R K S B Y D B T R Q X D B A B C I N W K H U D E E O L Z S P A
U S P X E L C Q K B W B W T R L X V U H E B W F L J P R O K D Z H G K R L P A R U T G L
N R J T C A S H B A C M P A L R L O D P H O I T C B W V C G M T R T V O V W P Q X I Z I
S X M H N D X M M T N J E Y C H D C O Q N C C U F G X G Z H G E P Z D N I E X E J N P N
V P C M I H H D I O K P R C X O P E N E N D E D I T E M D I D N X M R W M K Y K S U I G
O L I R K K K G J I C Z I M B D W S C A T T E R P L O T B S X E J J Q Y N I M Z H O W H
P A R T I A L L Y O P E N E N D E D I T E M W W U R J R D M N B S N B C Z C I E N Z I N
V D O S R O J F E Y C O R R E L A T I O N C O E F F I C I E N T I I J A S J Q E U R P
F T E Y W B Z W G C L O S E D E N D E D I T E M O R W Y J R L Z Q L G P H C P F F A P F
W F D G A G Q A R R H R G C M X F R E S T R I C T I O N O F R A N G E N U Z B G R V S I
D B U Y N P V I F U S I X Y C E K V W G G H S V X X A I R E V E R S E C O D E D I T E M
```

Across

- 3. NEGATIVE CORRELATION
- 6. RESPONSE RATE
- 8. OUTLIER
- 10. COVARIANCE
- 11. REVERSE CODED ITEM
- 13. EMPIRICAL
- 14. RESPONSE SET
- 16. PEARSON
- 17. LIKERT SCALE
- 18. OPEN ENDED
- 20. LINEAR REGRESSION
- 21. PREDICTOR VARIABLE
- 23. REGRESSION LINE
- 24. CORRELATION COEFFICIENT

Down

- 1. DOUBLE BARRELED
- 2. INTERVIEWER BIAS
- 4. THEORETICAL
- 5. ANCHORS
- 7. CONFOUND
- 9. RANDOM DIGIT DIALING
- 12. REVERSE CAUSALITY
- 15. SCATTERPLOT
- 19. RESTRICTED
- 22. SURVEY

Chapter 9

```
C R O S S S E C T I O N A L D E S I G N Y I M L P K L T K Y M A D P I F Y C J N
U Y S X I F S K M M J M I R A W L V H Q M I W D T E C L U Y P K T N P T V L L M
M Q O H W N L W X Q Q P B Y B T Z Q C G L M F Q N E C L Q F E G P O C V N X N G
Z U F C R B G L P R I K X M R X P S Z O I K P Y O P L W M Z F T X N Z V F G O G
N A H I P M T T J G E Z E Q J B D E P Q N G S R P D C N C U X M G P C N I K M K
W S O B F E L X D D V O M T J R Q Q N P F R I M U U D B D W A I V Z T S X P T G
J I P I F M F K F Q I J L R Y I O Z O O E T Z V C R T Q Z F S S F A E E M K F Z
Y I Q Q S U F P W D C O H O R T E F F E C T S Y F O J J K E T M L D X Z J W F N
C N V U F H H Z R T I M E S E R I E S D E S I G N L N M D K T D L Z K P X Y F Y
B D Y T A J P J I J I W C O O E Z W S Y W Q U A G P T Y F A P A D N W F N G V D
M E E X M S I V C B O R D I F F S C T T J E D B U D L I O F S C G O J G M I F K
V P R S S J I J X R X C E I O Z S I E R N W T O Q N B Q I R C I L G I Q Y Z I E
U E D O T Z S E G X T C A H N V L U G Y R E R E O E T X E N S U D S S A V X X G
I N B V C L X X X I F O H J L I K W K I V G O T G L T V O E H M E W T N I H E A
H D O N N M V K Q P Q H Q A B N S T I D L F S L S L E W D H E D G H G P A W O G
Q E K W U I O N P C E F F A N B E S Q O L E X U K R Q E R H T Q J I B B T X V Q
V N H N W W D T U N H R T V V G J S R D T P Y F J N N M S S V L S V Z R L B Z S
J T B Y D Z U X H X T S I K V J I T C T K A W G R I G E E J G E V K O A S D V P
F V G O N N Q M O Z X A A M O P N N S G K B P T L H C T P D D P G H V D W E Q M
N A X V C P J I B C A Z P Q E O T O G X I H C E W N T B X L T J O U W J I G F W
P R E M U W I S U G Q W V R C N P C K C K M S M E S G U A L Q C H S X T A V S A
H I V E M F Z M B Z S K O T H P T I Z J R A O R O S Y N V F C U I V W D R I W J
V A V R J P W O T H P P N M U H E A N S B I E P Y A I X O F Z C P L S L I A W D
H B X B T A P X O I L E U O Z X L C L E J F T C I D I T I J J M K T G M A W S R
Y L I M L W O H D K L R R N T I M Y L R F S L E U S D Z D X L T B A T O C F D G
I E J V Q V C K J A T G G M Y V U P B I E J T T R Q O L F A B G Z B W M N P Z
G K N F W D Z C V Y E M G L Q C I M D T P S I R K I B Q M C S D S E A H J V R S
O O U E R E D I E N R R N W H T M N E H J G E B X Q O Y B M X H B J O I X V R Q
T Q R X E H U O Y V R Z C L A O R O K N W A X J T N Y C A Q H T E K Z B S C
C S C C U Q C B V E T Q S U U I P R P O X P W B R D E P D A D G Z N Y Z Z Q P L
R V Z O E N A L A O X S M R T P F X L H E J N Y S C T P H E S X N C P P P N S S
H A O N S X N G H S H Y R C U S H C V D F V F E N A H Q W A S N E I B I F S Q J
I P O H G B G R B T E L E O G A P Q Z W W O W X S A Z D I C S I T E T G E N U M
U N Z Z L M O Z T H P L R G Y J K Y T R Z L E B V F L O E B M E G K V U V C M S
Z W Q S F G P A W N E G I S B Y W E G T Q X Q H B Z U J E S R N F N A B D H C T
M V L B U Z T P X S E A E N A X C X P L F G B M K K L E A C I R C O C F P E D K
R F F G R Q E V G N K A B E V Q S M H Z U C J N P E I D T D G L K U I Q H J T
A G W L R V I X O D C N D Y L E Q B L K W K Q A G Z U S V N B S N A I D A Y P
B T J Q C O Z P M U K N O N E Q U I V A L E N T C O N T R O L G R O U P I N Y Z
I A C T X G W Q K D S I N G L E C A S E E X P E R I M E N T A L D E S I G N T I
```

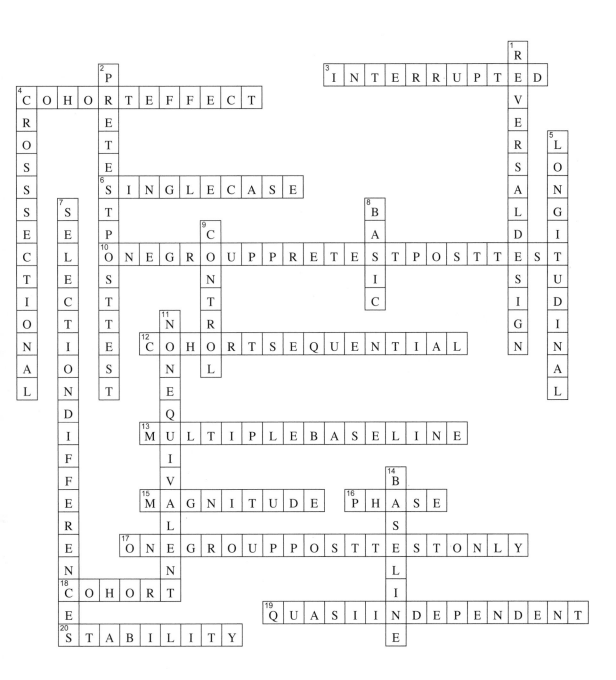

Chapter 10

```
O W I C H B L F P Z E S X E S G L V D M F B T V G Z F K E B C I B D U Z I X
N R S S W O T D J T Q Q O V X Q U G I R X D W A A L N U T Z P U D X J F B V
Z N Q W M C O W N J B U R R E C C L M M C O N T R O L G R O U P I T W P R W
C A U P C H O Z Q V H Z V P F H G G Y V E P C C D Q Z Z V A O O I N P N K O
S S Q R O V H N W I X B E H A V I O R A L M E A S U R E G Y N C F L O B E N
K T A M N S M N T B N N J T B K O Y H N V E M H E Z I J S C S L I I F Y R E
V A R Z T T T R A R K D W G F E R T T S Q S H M F O T D T H R K T T P D R W
M C Y O R Z E H X T O G E Z V J T M W G O H V O T S X E A O R A X A O R O A
I Z L H O C N S O Y F L T P K P U W X O E U L O E C J U I K L Q R I M G R Y
N A Z I L B J E T C S K B K E Y H C E K V P J T I X B F I U F H B J W N V B
D A N H B S S R H S T E H Y G N D Y E E F I T T K L E H P Y V L N A M H A E
T L Y U Y T O Y L R T E L D M D D F S O N S P R I T H I J C U C D T G O R T
T J G M H A G S Z K N A S F G A D E B I E S Z S R T N O O B B L B W M Q I W
R P A G O G F V E E R U T T R J T J N L O W U H C A N P O S J W N J Q F A E
G U X L L E D U I I V L Y I S E Y C P T C L J B M U Q M Q P D B G C Q Y N E
I S R N D D Z C Y T X O A F S M P M H Z S R O L J C B F H L N L Q P C V C N
O G Z Z I M I H A E J F L P Y T A O M I L A A G E X P F D R I G V Q X E S
Y F W S N A X H I E A E N V I S I X R P N R M N I Y C Z E I C B J M U A D U
U Y T Z G N D C Z D O Y W P T D Z C E T U G E P Y C C T V Z H S V P S E G B
C E I G C I S I I R S M U N R G S U F T M Q T L L S A X S N R E B W Q Z H J
M N A P O P V X V M O Y E N V R D J A Q E E U M T E M L P D E C C Z P H O E
X H R H N U O N A I U D X B X J N N Y B C I A U W U S V M K E G G B H R X C
Y C C L S L Z A R Z N E S Q X N V N N J O I W S W A Q T H E D S C N O Q Y T
P G N L T A E F J E R U M S K J H X K V N W M B U V C Z T V A O I P V O H S
K L B N A T T B P W N M E C K O Y L F E T W C U E R G E C E E S Y G C M B A
B I S M N I F E O G N H Q V H U G X P W R O V H P K E I V O S P U U N V A N
S E N O T O D F V C V N G W L G F B N U O D R U O R B X R K X T Z R S T M O
X E N S W N K F L V A V B N J M Y B U R L U I O U M W Y Y U I Z I L E R Q V
G T R N I B L L B E C E B S I I Y U E X P E R I M E N T A L G R O U P R N A
I M R L E O K A P A I R W I S E C O M P A R I S O N S A J F Q F V N W L A P
H S T Z L C W B E T W E E N S U B J E C T S F A C T O R I B C L S H I O W U
B O H F U O T E X P E R I M E N T A L M A N I P U L A T I O N V K F B P D X
E E N E Z L A A A K P E Z R A H T R X K I Y X P C S F D Q K R J E Y Y X N
K E J P I Y A F E Z Y R E S V Q U H I O L S R H B V E J K Z D E C I S L U R
F S Q O F Q K U X C M R A D P P J Q V J C G S H Q O L C R Z F A T L L Q Z Q
V Z D Q Z V I N D E P E N D E N T S A M P L E D K A N K I C L D F D T K H P
J O F A S Z A P B N R Q O K I R N U P P O A X Z T H W A Q P M E Q F Z E C C
R J L J R E S T R I C T E D R A N D O M A S S I G N M E N T V G H I W C M F
```

1. ERRORVARIANCE
2. CONNORRO (down: CONNOR...) — C O N N O R R O
3. SELFREPORT (down)
4. ONEWAY
5. TESTSTATISTIC
6. PAIRWISECOMPARISON (down)
7. RESTRICT (down)
8. INDEPENDENTSAMPLE
9. CONTROLBYMATCHING (down)
10. BEHAVIORAL (down)
11. PLACEBO (down)
12. POSTHOCTEST
13. TAGE / STAGE (down)
14. BETWEENSUBJECT (down)
15. EXPERIMENTAL
16. INDEPENDENT (down)
17. NATURAL
18. PHYSIOLOGICAL

Chapter 11

```
T I P Q P R N X W E S E U I G S G Q P R Y E C S A A R H E L K E T F
O I Z X Q A C L Q I Q S V H Y Y B W L Y S A T M C W U V G V T S H H
P R S V L O R A B D T C O F K W K K D J P C P Z S Y V U S D U B I Q
C K W F A V Y T E E B H X K P M H X I N E D A Y T J T X F O G V R E
O J I I R R V F I D T P I Y Q F S W M F X T R I K S O T J V G M Z V
M I T O E K A Y E A M W P N U H Z S F H S N L J E B B A N S N C U O
P T H Q L S H U F Q L U E W G W C E A E G I T T A V L G N O W Z S R
L N I H M L X W D L F C X E J R R O T Y B F T P E U I E R W O M H I
E C N U E K N K I L O P O D N E O T U A B S R S A S I W I C A B I E
T M S F R Q C F Z T W J G U D P S U I N E W F K E I M T R V F V P I
E E U L X Y I G A O H O F R N E E R P L T B O D L S T H Z F C B N W
C X B W X G L B I K A I O U L T A R P S S E S B E N K U L D C Y P N
O G J P L I S P Z D D R N P P V E M S Q V E R L Y M E R B J E C F Q
U W E C X X X H L A B O M S S V A R H O L A P B J J Z A U P Y I E L
N P C Z O K Q H X Y C A U P U S M Q B P N M R V A C Y X J Z X X I T
T A T P Q B F W J P S H U K D B Z W M A A S I I V L K D D V B N J Q
E R S T N D L C I D C O V E O S J A J S L N V M A T A N I H H D J U
R T D A X R C R E F R A R S C H S E D R P A H A I B Z N W Y O Z G V
B I E W N U B T O G L I F W X D W E C R J B N L R S I V C L P Z F F
A C S W U X A V N C A E D Z E T T U B T N K H C H I L L Y I D A F I
L I I P V L E E S P D P R H I A W T B S S P X K I T A F I L N N Y R
A P G J E C E C B R A A C K L P P X E K X F A F Z N G B W T G G S O
N A N R A W R B S Y G T P E Z L G U Q A V V A Q I L G L I L Y D H J
C N Y Y T G S V V S A T R T Y D H O Z X U B C C E F P W H L N N O G
I T F E X R G F Q M A Y I L A T I N S Q U A R E T X S E H A I W Z G
N F B L U Z M X Z D I V C J V V D V C M C O D D A Q D G O J G T P W
G A Z M C Q I S T T P K C U R L H I E R T Y L A Q P R B M U H V Y N
I T I Y R W Z X O N E W A Y W I T H I N S U B J E C T S A N O V A J
C I P E C A R R Y O V E R E F F E C T S U O J Q B E N E W Y L J D M
F G Z C M F D D F K T O L X Y S R O S Q W R P F R M A N V E D X U I
F U I O Z U O K I T V V R H H U J U T T P J X B L C W G T P M X T V
V E M K Q N Y H X K I O F B U B A J C G A L H D T L O Q T K O D W J
D U Y M S E P Y J O V X I N A U K S E P T O Z J C W M O D S W P M A
K G C X G J X Y R I J B F G Q I E R D P S L Q K L V U C Y R J U P Z
```

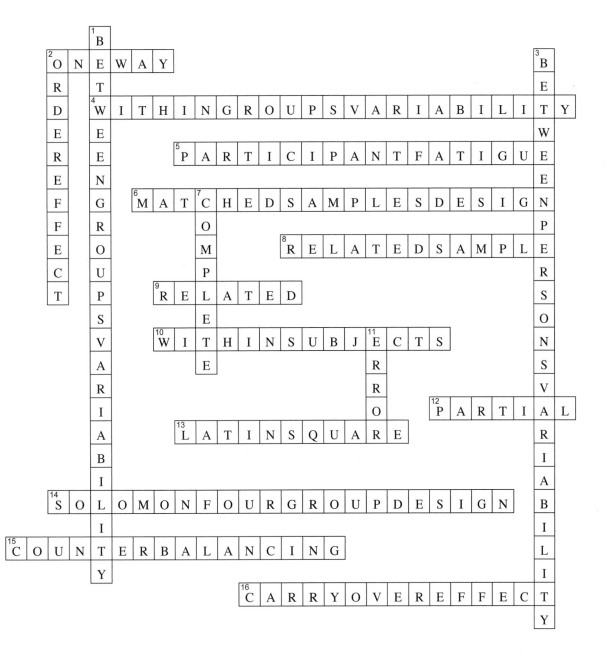

Chapter 12

```
Y Z D X E Q I C M I X E D F A C T O R I A L D E S I G N I V N A M R I G
E Z F U S Z M I P P A R T I C I P A N T V A R I A B L E S G S M S C B Z
I H G M Y D Y Z U L L T Q X O Z C H L S Z D S D C U F K I N S L E O O O
Q H Q B I F J G W D V J Q W Q C I P Y J T Q L U K X H S G E P R U F P Y
I M P I W R D B J S S D H Z O V A L P V Q H E K G P E H C B K T Z K Z J
Q Z G D M Z M D P X C Q B A S G X M M X D I N U C D R M O T Z W F O N B
T H I B H R B R K G L X G R N M E Z X U R O N T L R I X I P A O F U M R
W E H O X L H Q O G I E S X N C T M Y B D Y G A I U O F U E O W A G U U
I O M I C Z L Y P P F U Z R I G O M D F B V I R W T V Y O P R A F C R J
S W F E B D G R Q G Z O L J A S K T O V N R F B P B N S X N J Y A O J T
P C L C M U X K W G J L C M C H B O P X Q O W D Q Z N B I A M A C M W W
M V P X P J L I A M T W O W A Y F A C T O R I A L D E S I G N N T P M N
L T D X C G Y T V K O C T X S V C K C V N J O V N X N K X P U A O L N N
T V Q Z E J N O E L P F I Z E I B A X F K A J S E O T W S O E L R E O J
S E G L M D N D F Q B A W Y G K F N E V Q F M T I H Q U M O Y Y I T F D
A K K O G W B P U D A T K J W S L J G J L L A T T I L S P Q V S A E N N
D U H B X R E W N W K T P F T U L P M A W A C C I C D T S L H I L F O D
N G V R E F X I G L H T L C D B O D W B W A F W C E W S Y A U S D A W G
L H E G G H C G H I N T E R A C T I O N R L A V L R U B Y T V O E C V U
R V N A P A T V P L B J A N T A V J S E Z Y N I U C V W O B R F S T T E
M P I U M L C Y B S B Y Z M V R U S T O Y A A Q I K M P N R M V I O D L
I X Z Z M Y H I D U T J O P A I N N T K E I S Y E T I O W B U A G R X H
G R I A B F X U S T U I N J Z I I V R C T G F R I D K E Q J N R N I T O
Z D H I E H I N B W V Z U L G R N L P H W W X O P T B J G Q D I C A Z X
G C U H W D E S A V Z E A L E G Z E Y Y Y D S P Y O A D F B H A Z L R A
F Z X G L E V F N W G Q P D S P C A F M F U X G A G J W Y S O N P D U D
B P T E W O Y V R W S R R H F T F L W F F N O N P H U R I A N C Q E J D
S I I T Y Q A G Q K H O S U L W H N V D E M S B I F L O U W M E O S Y R
Q C E M A P N P R N R I R I E R D N N Y I C M I F V M K T R C G D I H K
G B O X H R Q W N E R B Z H U I H Y A A I G T L T B A W Y H P M L G F A
Y S F W J E A U H J J U P R P Z I W F O C F S M M J S F O O U P L N G R
M I V C Q Y N G H Y K E X F E M Y C T J Y E Z W D C H N B F Z S M A H T
Q T V P A J I V J F A Q L X D Q Q I H M B O K G U E G C B Q L W Y Z T Z
R H X J W H I G H E R O R D E R F A C T O R I A L D E S I G N I V L A M
R S W I T H I N S U B J E C T S F A C T O R I A L D E S I G N Y H Q Y G
E P J O E V C D S B Y J G Z J N E L M W G X R G L P D F R I Z Y W X C W
```

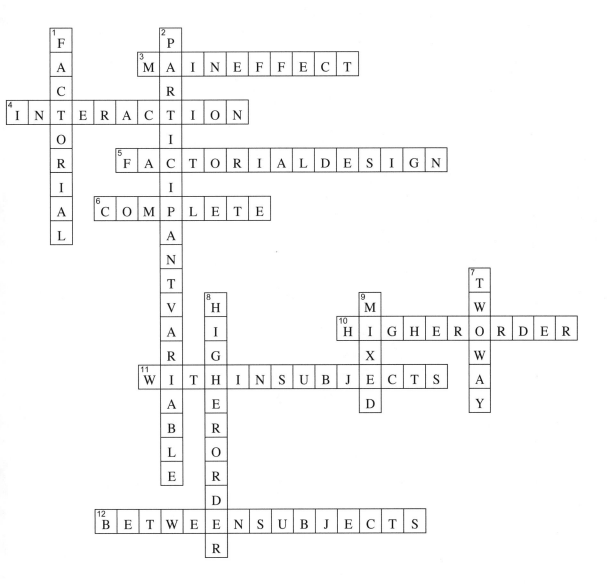

Across:
3. MAIN EFFECT
4. INTERACTION
5. FACTORIAL DESIGN
6. COMPLETE
10. HIGHER ORDER
11. WITHIN SUBJECTS
12. BETWEEN SUBJECTS

Down:
1. FACTORIAL
2. PARTITION
5. FACTOR
6. COMPLETE ANT VARIABLE
7. TWO WAY
8. HIGHER ORDER
9. MIXED

Chapter 13

```
Y J Y M O D E H Q U B V H M E D I A N V V A R V Z F Y X
K F C O H E N S K A P P A T U E F N V M R B B G K U M Z
G W G Y L I I I G R O A K A J S B K K Z Z O T I Z B J N
B D J V F R E Q U E N C Y D I S T R I B U T I O N S E X
A E S D N S N Y Z S B D X R W V D A Y G E C K D J I J V
R S X A W I U O J R P M D Q S G S H S U S I X Z F L C P
G C B C M S S J R F N H L C A E X M M Y X Z U I D W S D
R R O E M P R K J M R A M M D P A R N G N X F I E D U E
A I O N C K L T E L A C L H J R I C Z O B L S H G Y M P
P P A T U E T W W P L K P G P M E G C C I V D R G O V
H T Q R C G W J S F E B D O P R B Y C M M T G G E F F Y
O I X A B R E W T C D T I X F L A V H P X B C E R S V
R V Q L H M O Q S Q A S D L S O N T R Z A T Y G S E Q C
A E E T P I G N H S I N G I P T S B S C C R P J O Q U S
Q S M E B Y J Y B H T D D Y S H R F Z L H D T M F U A C
T T P N Z V K G E A S H C A B T G I W P U A Z O F E R A
L A I D Y C E N H J C N B G R R R M B U S N R I R N E T
I T R E M P I F C U E H W V S D J I E U N C C T E C S T
Q I I N H R Q I H U N B S K R A D N B Q T L Y N E Y W E
O S C C W C G E Q N C W R A B M M E K U M I Y R D F Y R
U T A Y Q R C E Q U O B N P L G O P V T T R O H Q B P
O I L H C F R X J U V F C X U P N F L I F I U N M K T L
M C R T C F F J S J U A U X W F H O Y E A P O J O U S O
C S U V V D H W D O I H D Q W P A U U M T O N O N Z T
G S L N C S A M P L E V A R I A N C E U X E I W V M A W
I C E Y Q G Z V N V C V A R I A B I L I T Y A O D V X I
Z Z H P M O W L P U I H D V R C X X F M M W F N N H Y A
C R G X O T U R I N N U C P Y P M W T Z M K X L T H Y
```

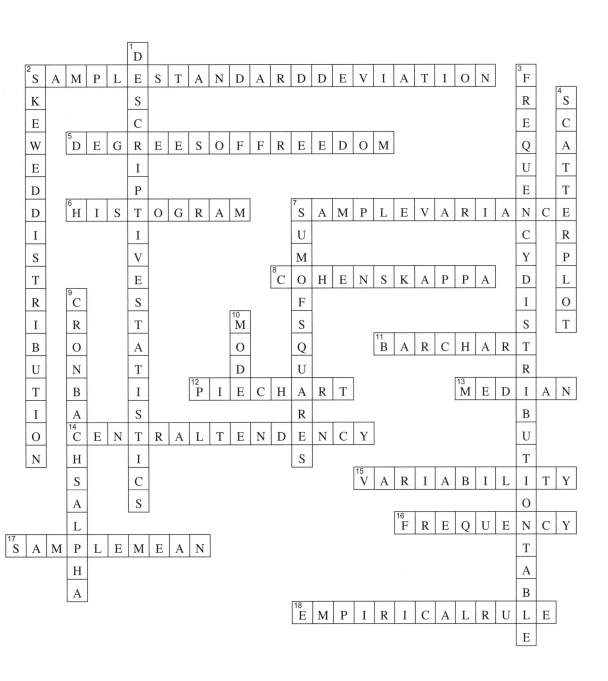

Chapter 14

```
N W D Z E I C Z C Q J I Z W E T A S Q U A R E D S P K R C D F Z D E S T V
U Q R N W F P I L J P R O P O R T I O N O F V A R I A N C E C P O T Z N W
L S C K W U A H G K A U L S B A X D U B N C R A M E R S V T Q B S X M K G
L Z N W S E R N F P D X E J D C K K J L K W U D W K N G M O U E B X U Z W
H N V B O W A G M A N L R F N P B Q P Y V Y Y G C S A Y L P T G K B V L Q
Y I T N V P M C O P I N F E R E N T I A L S T A T I S T I C S Y W F R I S
P Z M E Z L E U K S A W L X M F Z H E N P M I H U B R F I A E R Q T P N L
O L X F A B T U Z D C S B N I J N C P B D A G S D B P R S W T F G K K O M
T F X U X O R T H C E O W I C O N C V I S H F P M S T I P Y W X F C O N V
H D B B P G I K N A O J N R D A S Y K D B Y V K O E Q C X N U X A E N D
E U J F F F C R E P S E Y F C E Y I E B Z T A A M I E P Z N C K F C C W T
S Z I A L Z T C X H I S F I I D A T H C L Y M A X E N J L Q A R V L S T E
I G V A Z J E I N U F T F N D A G T H W H R O L X X T J T O X A D V E S
S V G W F P S W P R M I H B I M E L C F S A L D Z B N B E V E V T J T T T
S R V R M Z T P C R N V S V I C R N Y A P A Q T N O R T M S R K K F X M F
T K J B B Q S T G G J I T T H O I A C N E A S H D G V N F E T A S J Z M O
H U D H M Q R C I O C N S X F I C E O E P O X M R Y T H T D W I O X V M R
M H U L J W G S I J O E J W G B E N N I L D P X G F W N I Z F P M K B H I
Y B Z I C L F J Z M L D E T I G U L F T K I G J S X I H Z Y I V H A Y W N
Y M I V G O J R E A T M N A I M A E C J O F M T X E U O I G S Z P H T I D
C V H L L T A J V S I Z V E S R C I Z P W F A I C E Q J A V E N Y R E E E
G Q L E J A N R S P G P F C S N T E P L I Y D N T R A P H X Q W Z Z U G P
J R V C T J E M N Y S O T W E S K V C K C V E E X S L Q J Z C H I C Y G E
M E U Q J T Y X U E N W K D I C O H E N S D Y F T P I C D F O S I N Y W N
L J C G N O S H A I J V I T J B D F P I I V Z H J E X C E Z T J H S J E D
G P Z I I U D N L S P F A X Z C R G F F Q L S T N W R X T C M T S L R R E
Z W G W Y Q F V J H N T C A H L Y V N I V N K N P Q E M E R P W M I S Q I N
T A L L G V B R D O S L U F B J U O J A T D N U T T V F I G E V C S A Q C
M E L N X H W F C T D L C E T S C O V U Y T J T I N F I U N H J S C S O E
J J Q J E S F S W R R P G M P V A L U E E E I L E C K U G A U Q O S R D
Q N N K T G O E T E L Z Y P A N S U A W Q O R S Z G L S C O Z T C Q T T L
R S O F L L T Q W J N I R A X O D C Q O I L I Y T L Z E A D A U I D N S V
G S B L E B B O K W G C J P S I G N I F I C A N C E L E V E L B Y O Z B J
S R W V H X P Y I M A W S S B P L Q A W Q L E A G D X T E T X V I T N X Q
D B E A T C M E V Z N Q Y T L G E U M O L U H K Q M O X Q F R P R U N Z M
V L W I X G M R P R E S T I M A T I O N F C Q V M H Q O E B F Z I Y A R B
B S I E F K B R X X S Y T S K V L G J U Y V S I G N I F I C A N C E R E S
```

Across / Down answers:

1. LEVELOFCONFIDENCE
2. SIGNIFICANCE
3. PARAMETER
4. TESTSTATISTIC
5. NULLHYPOTHESIS
6. INTERVAL
7. EFFECTSIZE
8. GOODNESSOFFIT
9. POWER
10. PROPORTIONALREDUCTIONVARIANCE
11. TESTFORINDEPENDENCE
12. PVALUE
13. EFFECT
14. COHENSD
15. NONPARAMETRICTESTS
16. LEVELOFCONFIDENCE
17. ETASQUARED
18. INFERENTIALSTATISTICS
19. CONFIDENCELIMITS
20. CRAMERSV
21. POINTESTIMATE

Chapter 15

```
T  S  R  E  A  X  X  B  U  B  Q  X  L  T  O  B  J  Z  H
L  K  P  P  H  O  S  G  A  O  H  T  Z  Q  K  P  X  O  L
E  F  H  Y  S  N  K  P  T  A  A  C  N  P  I  R  N  Z  I
G  K  Z  O  T  W  A  P  H  G  Y  O  A  M  V  U  S  H  T
P  T  X  K  Z  S  Z  I  X  H  I  C  C  Q  Y  S  V  Y  E
R  B  K  W  Y  J  I  D  U  S  O  J  T  H  Q  M  F  O  R
Z  O  R  E  L  N  D  H  S  V  M  M  Y  G  R  M  M  J  A
A  P  A  S  T  Y  L  E  M  A  N  U  S  C  R  I  P  T  T
S  C  Z  K  H  A  S  F  Z  R  Q  U  X  Q  W  O  W  L  U
H  O  N  N  S  R  I  E  X  F  G  P  F  S  F  E  D  U  R
O  P  J  Q  E  F  M  J  J  S  L  H  U  C  I  F  M  N  E
P  D  V  T  I  G  C  U  Q  H  V  V  Y  V  B  J  L  O  R
H  D  S  C  M  W  T  O  S  L  I  F  E  I  S  X  K  T  E
S  O  W  S  N  X  O  F  V  M  R  R  W  J  Z  U  H  I  V
P  S  I  S  P  O  S  T  E  R  R  N  O  P  U  U  D  D  I
T  R  T  W  R  D  P  O  V  E  W  A  K  G  R  E  N  O  E
L  E  V  Y  I  A  A  J  E  Q  T  E  V  Z  T  P  B  W  W
E  R  I  V  B  T  N  P  P  B  R  A  N  S  X  N  N  H  M
O  V  X  L  A  T  A  F  I  H  U  X  A  B  C  B  Y  K  U
```

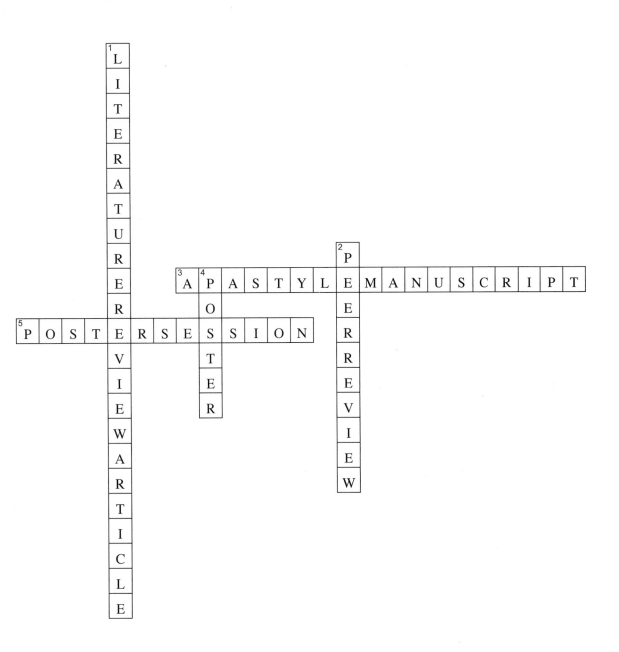

Answers to Practice Quizzes

Chapter 1:

1. A	7. A	13. B	19. B
2. B	8. B	14. A	20. B
3. D	9. A	15. D	
4. D	10. D	16. C	
5. C	11. C	17. A	
6. C	12. D	18. A	

Chapter 2:

1. A	7. C	13. D	19. B
2. C	8. D	14. C	20. D
3. B	9. A	15. C	
4. D	10. B	16. A	
5. A	11. B	17. A	
6. A	12. A	18. B	

Chapter 3:

1. B	7. B	13. C	19. A
2. D	8. A	14. B	20. C
3. A	9. D	15. D	
4. C	10. D	16. A	
5. A	11. C	17. C	
6. B	12. A	18. A	

Chapter 4:

1. B	7. B	13. D	19. B	25. C
2. C	8. D	14. B	20. A	26. A
3. A	9. D	15. C	21. B	
4. B	10. B	16. A	22. C	
5. D	11. A	17. D	23. D	
6. A	12. C	18. B	24. C	

Chapter 5:

1. C	7. B	13. D	19. C
2. A	8. D	14. C	20. A
3. B	9. C	15. B	
4. D	10. A	16. A	
5. C	11. B	17. D	
6. A	12. B	18. C	

Chapter 6:

1. D	7. A	13. A	19. A
2. A	8. A	14. C	20. B
3. B	9. D	15. B	21. C
4. B	10. C	16. D	22. D
5. B	11. B	17. D	
6. C	12. D	18. C	

Chapter 7:

1. B	7. A	13. A	19. A
2. C	8. D	14. B	20. C
3. A	9. B	15. C	
4. D	10. C	16. D	
5. A	11. A	17. D	
6. C	12. B	18. B	

Chapter 8:

1. D	7. A	13. D	19. A
2. A	8. D	14. B	20. D
3. C	9. D	15. A	
4. B	10. B	16. C	
5. C	11. A	17. C	
6. B	12. C	18. B	

Chapter 9:

1. D	7. D	13. B	19. D
2. B	8. B	14. A	20. C
3. A	9. A	15. B	
4. C	10. C	16. C	
5. D	11. A	17. D	
6. C	12. D	18. A	

Chapter 10:

1. A	7. C	13. A	19. B
2. B	8. A	14. B	20. C
3. B	9. D	15. B	
4. A	10. B	16. C	
5. C	11. C	17. D	
6. D	12. D	18. A	

Chapter 11:

1. B	7. B	13. C	19. A
2. A	8. A	14. C	20. B
3. D	9. C	15. D	
4. C	10. D	16. B	
5. A	11. A	17. C	
6. C	12. B	18. A	

Chapter 12:

1. C	7. B	13. A	19. B
2. C	8. C	14. C	20. C
3. B	9. D	15. A	
4. A	10. C	16. A	
5. D	11. A	17. D	
6. D	12. D	18. B	

Chapter 13:

1. B	7. C	13. A	19. A
2. D	8. D	14. C	20. A
3. A	9. C	15. B	
4. C	10. C	16. D	
5. D	11. D	17. B	
6. B	12. A	18. C	

Chapter 14:

1. B	7. D	13. C	19. B	25. A
2. C	8. B	14. A	20. C	26. A
3. A	9. A	15. A	21. D	
4. C	10. B	16. C	22. B	
5. D	11. C	17. D	23. C	
6. A	12. D	18. B	24. B	

Chapter 15:

1. D	7. B	13. A	19. B
2. D	8. C	14. D	20. D
3. C	9. A	15. C	
4. B	10. B	16. B	
5. A	11. D	17. A	
6. D	12. C	18. A	

References

American Psychological Association. (2009). *Publication manual of the American Psychological Association* (6th ed.). Washington, DC: Author.

American Psychological Association. (2010). *Ethical principles of psychologists and code of conduct.* Washington, DC: Author.

American Psychological Association. (2012). *Guidelines for ethical conduct in the care and use of nonhuman animals in research.* Washington, DC: Author. Retrieved from http://www.apa.org/science/leadership/care/guidelines.aspx

American Society for the Prevention of Cruelty to Animals. (1996). *"Regarding Henry": A "Bergh's-eye" view of 140 years at the ASPCA.* Retrieved from http://www.aspca.org/about-us/history.html

Block, S. M. (1996). Do's and don'ts of poster presentation. *Biophysical Journal, 71*(6), 3527–3529.

Centers for Disease Control and Prevention. (2011). *U.S. Public Health Service Syphilis Study at Tuskegee: The Tuskegee timeline.* Atlanta: Author. Retrieved fromhttp://www.cdc.gov/tuskegee/timeline.htm

Cohen, J. (1961). A coefficient of agreement for nominal scales. *Educational and Psychological Measurement, 20,* 37–46. doi:10.1177/001316446002000104

Cohen, J. (1988). *Statistical power analysis for the behavioral sciences.* Hillsdale, NJ: Erlbaum.

Cronbach, L. J. (1951). Coefficient alpha and the internal structure of tests. *Psychometrika, 16,* 297–334.

Fisher, R. A. (1925). *Statistical methods for research workers.* Edinburgh, Scotland: Oliver & Boyd.

Fisher, R. A. (1935). *The design of experiments.* Edinburgh, Scotland: Oliver & Boyd.

Milgram S. (1963). Behavioral study of obedience. *Journal of Abnormal Social Psychology, 67,* 371–378. doi:10.1037/ h0040525

National Commission for the Protection of Human Subjects of Biomedical and Behavioral Research. (1979, April 18). *The Belmont Report: Ethical principles and guidelines for the protection of human subjects of research.* Retrieved from http://www.hhs.gov/ohrp/humansubjects/guidance/belmont.html

National Research Council. (2011). *Guide for the care and use of laboratory animals* (8th ed.). Washington, DC: National Academies Press.

Office of Research Integrity. (2011a). *Avoiding plagiarism, self-plagiarism, and other questionable writing practices: A guide to ethical writing.* Retrieved from http://ori.dhhs.gov/education/products/plagiarism/plagiarism.pdf

Parker, I. (2005).*Qualitative psychology: Introducing radical research.* New York: Open University Press.

Privitera, G. J. (2012). *Statistics for the behavioral sciences.* Thousand Oaks, CA: Sage.

Sherif, M., Harvey, O. J., White, B. J., Hood, W. R., & Sherif, C. W. (1988). *The Robber's Cave experiment: Intergroup conflict and cooperation.* Middletown, CT: Wesleyan University Press. (Original work published 1961)

Trials of War Criminals before the Nuremberg Military Tribunals under Control Council Law No. 10, Vol. 2, pp. 181–182. Washington, DC: U.S. Government Printing Office, 1949.

Zimbardo, P. G. (1975). On transforming experimental research into advocacy for social change. In M. Deutsch & H. Hornstein (Eds.), *Applying social psychology: Implications for research, practice, and training* (pp. 33–66). Hillsdale, NJ: Erlbaum.

⊛SAGE researchmethods

The essential online tool for researchers from the world's leading methods publisher

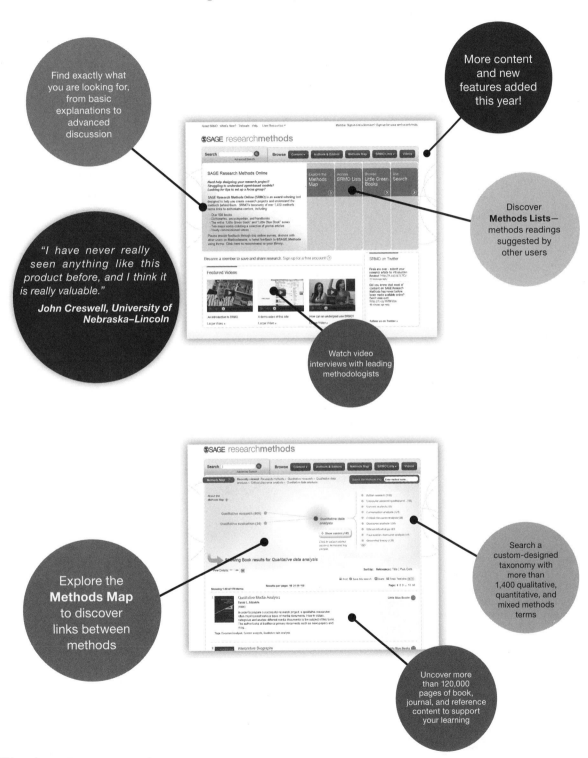

More content and new features added this year!

Find exactly what you are looking for, from basic explanations to advanced discussion

Discover **Methods Lists**— methods readings suggested by other users

"I have never really seen anything like this product before, and I think it is really valuable."

John Creswell, University of Nebraska–Lincoln

Watch video interviews with leading methodologists

Explore the **Methods Map** to discover links between methods

Search a custom-designed taxonomy with more than 1,400 qualitative, quantitative, and mixed methods terms

Uncover more than 120,000 pages of book, journal, and reference content to support your learning

Find out more at
www.sageresearchmethods.com